I: Hope you enjo...

LIFE'S A PITCH

THE GROUNDSMAN'S TALE

BY IAN DARLER

Best Wishes

Ian Darler

G2 entertainment

First edition

Published by
G2 Entertainment
www.g2books.co.uk

Author: Ian Darler
Editor: Pat Morgan
Designer: Jon Appleton
Cover photo: Alan Burge

The author wishes to thank Cambridgeshire Constabulary,
The Institute of Groundsmanship, Simon Lankester,
Jacqui Matthews Photography, Kensington Palace, Ben Phillips,
Reach Group PLC (publisher of the Cambridge News)
and Turf Business for permission to use photographs

ISBN: 978-1-78281-384-2

Printed and bound in the UK

ACKNOWLEDGEMENTS

I would like to thank Jules Gammond and G2 Entertainment for offering me the opportunity to write this book. I also have to thank Pat Morgan for his help in putting the book together.

Thanks also to all the contributors who spent hours reliving the events that I've written about. Some of these people are among those who have helped this publication to see the light of day, a number of whom are listed on the 'Friends, family and supporters' page at the back of the book.

Thanks to my wife Lisa, son Liam and daughter Ruby for their support over the years. I apologise wholeheartedly for not always putting you before my work, my beloved pitch and stadium.

Thanks to my parents, Keith and Jill Darler, and my brothers Richard and John, who put in countless hours of unpaid work in my early years at Cambridge United and have contributed massively to the success of my career. My father's health means he is now unable to assist at the ground but his brother Brian spends hours helping out.

I could not omit to mention the man who gave me a chance to become a groundsman: Bill Scott, the head groundsman at Pye's sports ground. Without his guidance, knowledge and friendship – all freely given – I would not have had the chance to have forty amazing years in professional football at Cambridge United.

Never forgotten: my grandparents James and Rosie Legge and Mary and Alfred Darler, who kept me on the straight and narrow and had a huge influence on my early life.

There are two other individuals I couldn't leave out of this list of thank-yous: Percy Anderson, who taught me so much about angling over fifty years, and Chris Turner, a true friend who was a kid at heart but was also an outstanding player and manager. Their deaths were sad losses to the world.

Finally, all my friends and workmates over the years; there are too many to thank individually but I would like you to know that I'll be eternally grateful to you all for being there for me by offering hours of free labour; thousands of pounds' worth of free materials in many cases; and so much support when I was really poorly.

IAN DARLER 2019

CONTENTS

FOREWORD

BY ROY MCFARLAND

I hadn't been at Cambridge United long enough to get to know Ian Darler well when the time came for the players to train on the Abbey Stadium pitch – we had a couple of new lads and I wanted them to get a feel for the surface.

It was my first real chat with Ian but I needn't have worried that he would draw any battle lines. He bought a hundred per cent into my thinking that our team should play football and said: 'That's fine, not a problem. All I would ask is that you limit yourselves to an hour.'

From that moment on I knew we would have a great relationship and work well together.

It doesn't matter if you're a player or a manager, you have to realise how deeply a groundsman loves his pitch – it's his baby. He wants it to look its best on a Saturday, and you have to take that into account in your working relationship with him.

It's important that all the staff at a football club feel they're driving towards the same aims – they're part of the team. Ian exemplified that philosophy.

I remember the time when, after the season had ended, I asked Reg Smart if we could get rid of the players' bath and install some showers in the home changing room. Reg recognised that football had moved on and by the 1990s players didn't follow the age-old routine of the post-match bath, but there was no money available and he said no.

I couldn't believe what I was seeing when, on the first day of pre-season, I found Reg and Ian in a huge cloud of dust, knocking seven bells out of the bath with sledgehammer and pickaxe. Within a week they'd cleared everything out, retiled the bathroom and installed six or eight showers.

The money wasn't available, so they did the job themselves.

To my mind that was the spirit of the club: everyone, even the chairman and groundsman, in it together for the love of the club. I'm a Liverpool man through and through, and that sort of feeling reminds me of the afternoons I spent on the Kop as a supporter: you're all pulling together out of sheer love for your football club.

Ian respected the fact that Reg had to run a tight ship, with budgets cut back to the bone. There was never enough money in the pot for everything that was needed, but Ian didn't hesitate to put his hand in his own pocket to pay for fertiliser or whatever else was required. Which other groundsman would pay for equipment or materials out of his own wages?

Ian's love of the job and the club was all-consuming and he wanted his pitch to be the best in the country. The lack of money made that a massively difficult task, but he managed it.

Without supporters, football doesn't have a heartbeat, so I will end with this message: keep your love of the football club alive, just as Ian does, and you will keep Cambridge United on the right path.

ROY MCFARLAND
MANAGER, CAMBRIDGE UNITED, 1996-2001

CHAPTER 1

—

LIFE'S NOT ALL BLACK AND WHITE

With the perfect timing and attention to detail for which I was later to become known, I made my debut in this world on an August night in 1959, at the RAF Ely military hospital in the fenlands of Cambridgeshire. My mum Jill was not accustomed to military surroundings but dad Keith, an air traffic controller at RAF Oakington, probably greeted the news of my arrival with a smart salute and a few bars of the Dam Busters theme.

Dad had had his first taste of military life during national service and had then trained to make it his career at West Kirby on the Wirral. He served in the RAF until a diabetes diagnosis brought an end to his rise to the rank of corporal. Like him, the hospital didn't stay in the RAF for ever – it became a district general hospital, was renamed the Princess of Wales and various people are now arguing about how the site should be redeveloped. Mum was working in the Unilever office in Milton, a village just to the north of Cambridge. She had met Dad at the old Central School in Cambridge (later a girls' grammar school and now Parkside Community College) and married him in 1957.

The infant Darler evidently didn't think much of the cold, draughty mobile home in Longstanton, to the north-west of the city, in which Mum and Dad made their first home. Mum recalls with a shudder the sleepless nights my relentless bawling gave her and Dad, and it must have come as a blessed relief to them – doubtless the neighbours too – when we moved into a bricks-and-mortar house in the Chesterton district of Cambridge.

Dad had begun an accountancy career with the Pye electronics company, a major employer in the city, and the group's Telecom works in St Andrew's Road was at the other end of Chesterton High Street from our new house in Lents Way. A stone's throw from the river Cam, the street was named after the 'bumps' rowing races that take place on the Cam's narrow waters during the university's Lent term, and the influence of the river is shown in the names of other nearby thoroughfares: Mays Way (bumps also take place in the May term),

Anglers Way and Izaak Walton Way (named after the seventeenth century author of The Compleat Angler). It was undoubtedly in those early days that my love of the river was born; I can't count the many thousands of days and nights I've spent, rod in hand, on its banks.

Another of my lifelong passions first blossomed in the small garden behind our Lents Way house: from the time I took my first steps, a football was never far from my feet. My first memory is of the giddy excitement I felt when Keith Barker, who would later play 120 games in goal for Cambridge United, kindly gave me my first leather ball when I was around four. Keith lived two doors away and his parents helped to fan the flames of my football fanaticism by taking me to my first games soon after.

The Darler family was growing, with football playmates arriving regularly – brother Richard came along in 1963 and John joined us in 1965 – and in 1966 we moved to a detached house, which my parents later extended, in Roseford Road on the fringes of the Arbury housing estate.

Mum and Dad had promised us boys that we would have a large garden to play in, but when we stepped out of the back door on moving-in day, we could only see a few overgrown trees and shrubs. I remember feeling massively let down – until Dad pushed the shrubs out of the way to reveal a huge expanse of open ground. It was horrendously overgrown but, once the garden had been cleared of rubbish, my father laid the entire area to lawn. Over the following ten years it took a severe hammering. My brothers and I played football from dawn to dusk, destroying Dad's lovingly created lawn and also smashing countless windows. It was a miracle that no one got hurt.

The first year we were at Roseford Road was a special one for any English football fan. My parents lashed out on a colour television for the 1966 World Cup, an amazing experience made even more fantastic by England's victory in the final. Visions of Geoff Hurst's hat-trick and an ecstatic, toothless Nobby Stiles dancing around the Wembley pitch after the 4-2 win over West Germany live with me to this day.

It was around this time that Jack Galer came into my life. Jack, who owned a big scrapyard off Coldhams Lane, on the other side of the river, had daughters but no sons, and he treated my brothers and me as if we were his own. Mum kept the books for Jack's business, and he would pop around to Roseford Road three or four times a week to cast an eye over the accounts. Happy days for us lads – Jack couldn't get out in the garden for a kickabout fast enough.

He always wore expensive pinstriped suits, made to measure by his tailor in London, and completed the look with suede shoes. Kicking a ball about in this get-up during the summer was not a problem, but in the winter months he would traipse back into the house looking like he had walked through a cattle trough, his trousers and shoes plastered with mud.

Jack bought a 36-foot cabin cruiser called the Amethyst from the long-established Banham's boatyard in Cambridge, and we would spend days as a family travelling up and down the rivers of Cambridgeshire: the Cam, the Ouse, the Old West River. Encouraged by my maternal grandad James Legge, I had been fishing from the age of four, but the hobby leapt into a new league aboard the Amethyst. I was in paradise.

Jack acquired a fifty per cent shareholding in Cambridge City football club and became vice-chairman. I remember him asking my father to hold a small share percentage for him, to ensure that if a vote was required it would go in his favour. Dad insists to this day that his vote was never used, but I think he enjoyed being involved. He was a very decent footballer himself, a right winger who came up through the City youth set-up to play half a dozen times for the first team. He also played for Pye for sixteen years before becoming a referee, and played county-level badminton for Cambridgeshire.

The family's links with Cambridge City – the biggest club in the city for many decades before United came to the fore in the 1960s – ran deep. Grandfather Alfred Darler, a mechanic in the police force before working as a maintenance engineer for the Cam river authority, was a great supporter and was heavily involved at the Milton Road ground, pitching in for the social club and raising funds by selling lottery tickets, memberships and so on. Mum worked in the programme kiosk on match days. Ours was very much a Lilywhites household.

Even at a very early age I seldom missed a trick. A few weeks after Jack became City's vice-chairman, I asked if he could get me a ballboy's job at Milton Road. To my amazement, he turned up at our house a week later with a blue cotton drill tracksuit, then picked me up the following Saturday and took me to the ground. I was introduced to the other ballboys, although any glamorous notions I might have been entertaining were soon dispelled when I saw the meeting place: we would hang about in the boiler room, waiting for the players to run out on to the pitch before making our own entrance.

This part of my story may not go down too well with Cambridge United fans who remember the rivalry and the bitterly fought local derbies of the Fifties and Sixties – we lived in a divided city. But I had been a City fan for a couple of years and this was an exciting time to be pitchside with Scottish manager Tommy Bickerstaff, watching players like granite-hard defender Gerry Baker, goalscorer extraordinary Phil Hayes and my favourite, Welsh international winger Cliff Jones. I didn't think life could get any better.

How wrong I was. I arrived at the ground one Saturday to be met by a bloke selling lucky number draw tickets at 6d a pop – that's six 'old' pence; there were forty of them in a pound. Mum always gave me sixpence to buy a drink and something to eat, but on this occasion the money went on a ticket. I'm not sure what gambling laws were in place in those days, but the bloke selling the tickets didn't seem too bothered. At half-time, when the winning number was announced, I was in position behind the goal that backed on to Chesterton School, and nearly fainted when I realised I was the winner.

I made my way into the old wooden main stand to find Grandad, who collected my winnings – an absolute fortune at £17. Naturally, some of the money went on new football boots and better fishing tackle; the rest went straight into the bank.

By now I was attending Arbury junior school, and most mornings I would be one of the first kids in the playground, fitting in a hotly contested game of football on the netball court before registration. Schooling at Arbury was OK, I suppose: I was lucky in that all the sport in the garden with my brothers, Dad, Grandad and Jack paid off as I was selected as captain of the football and cricket teams.

Most of the kids were bigger and stronger than me – some were nearly a year older and one of them was Roger Avery, who became one of the first local lads to sign for Cambridge United in the club's Football League era – but that didn't stop me dribbling round them and scoring a shedload of goals. To this day I believe it was sport that got me through school.

The weekly football lesson was presided over by the headmaster, resplendent in a tracksuit that had once been dark red but had faded over the years to a fetching shade of pink. Mr Bagnall was always enthusiastic, and these games were so important to me that I would always give it my all. But one day during a game, when I was a mere seven years old, my world came crashing down.

The game was poised at 1-1 when we won a penalty and I stepped forward to take it. My reaction to blasting the ball wide was a foul-mouthed oath – possibly the first that had ever escaped my young lips – and Mr Bagnall was appalled. 'What did you say?' he asked, open-mouthed. Like a fool, I repeated the mouthful. 'Get off,' he instructed calmly. 'Don't ever use that word again. Come and see me this afternoon.'

In his office Mr Bagnall told me that I, the first person he had ever sent off, was suspended for two weeks. Further punishment followed: I was given the job of cleaning and applying dubbin to every single football the school possessed.

He might have been unused to dealing with potty-mouthed seven-year-old footballers, but Mr Bagnall was always very supportive of me and put me forward to play for Cambridge Schoolboys, of which I became a squad member. I earned a pat on the back from him when, during the course of a routine 28-1 win over Mayfield School, I claimed a personal goal tally of twenty-one. I'd learned my lesson and never swore again – at least not on the football field.

Football was never far from the Darler family's thoughts, as we demonstrated very early on Christmas Day, 1967. My two-year-old brother John, having got his first pair of football boots, thought he would get in some practice with a ball on the landing at three o'clock in the morning. The training session ended abruptly with Dad confiscating the ball and showing John the red card – back to bed for the youngest Darler.

––––––––––––

Fishing was fast becoming another passion. Grandad had shown me the basics and I was taking part in junior matches but becoming frustrated at my lack of success. I wanted desperately to improve my techniques and ability and at the age of nine, after yet another poor result in a junior angling competition, I arrived home despondent.

'Whatever's the matter with you?' wondered Mum. 'I'm fed up with all the other kids beating me,' I blurted out. 'They have lessons with a bloke called Percy Anderson.'

Without a word to me, Mum phoned Percy, who ran an angling shop not far from United's Abbey Stadium on Newmarket Road, to ask how much he charged for lessons. 'I don't charge,' declared Percy. 'Bring your lad to my shop next Saturday morning and I'll go through his tackle. We'll see how it goes from there.'

When Mum told me what Percy had said, I wished I had kept quiet. No wonder I was nervous: the man was a legend not only in local fishing circles but much further afield. In 1974, just a few years after that fateful phone call, he was crowned UK national angling champion and he became Europe's top angler three years later. He knew every inch of the rivers of East Anglia and was probably on first-name terms with most of the fish. He loved passing on his skills and knowledge, taking local kids under his wing and running his legendary summer teach-ins for forty years until shortly before his death in 2006. Little did I know as I approached his shop that the great man would be a huge part of my life for the next fifty years.

I was proud and protective of the tackle I had assembled, although to be fair it would have fitted into a washing-up bowl. I walked through the shop door to be met by Percy asking: 'Yes, son, what do you want?' I replied apprehensively that I was there for lessons.

Percy towered above me as he set about examining my tackle and, to my horror, snapping just about every bit of it in half and hurling it away as if it offended him. 'OK, son,' he announced after a while, 'all these floats are shit.'

I couldn't help wondering what was going on as he nipped across the shop and brought back a handful of Benny Ashurst and Ivan Marks floats. These were holy names in the canon of angling saints. He picked out a reel, put some line on it and said: 'There you go son, that'll get you started.' I gulped – this tackle would surely make me skint for many months to come. 'How much will that cost?' I stammered. 'Go on, get out of here,' growled Percy.

My lessons started on Stourbridge Common, one of many areas of common land in Cambridge and the former site of medieval Europe's largest annual fair. The common was also where Abbey United – the precursor club of today's Cambridge United – had played their home games in the early 1920s.

'You can't fish until you can cast accurately,' pronounced Percy, and lesson one consisted of me casting an Arlesey bomb (a kind of weight) forty yards towards a polystyrene tile pegged to the ground with a six-inch nail. After a few evenings I had mastered the art and could land the bomb on a sixpence.

My first unforgettable day with Percy came soon after. He had a big match coming up on the Cam at Clayhithe north of Cambridge, he said, and I could go along and sit behind him to see how he fished. This was a really big deal, for at the time Percy was to the fishing world what David Beckham was to become to football. But it quickly turned into a culture shock for this impressionable young boy as my hero scattered the f-word around like groundbait – f this, f that, f everything else for that matter.

To his dying day, he never let me forget the events that unfolded. The match started and Percy was off to a flyer, catching good-sized bream from the off. I quickly learned that he didn't take food or drink with him to a match. Why would he, when he could rely on other poor suckers to feed him? 'What have we got to eat then, son?' he enquired innocently. My sandwiches and cake disappeared down the Anderson gullet, quickly followed by half of my flask of tea.

A couple of hours into the match I started to feel poorly and passed out briefly, probably through a combination of the bitterly cold weather and lack of food. 'Are you OK, son?' Percy asked as I came round. 'No, I feel ill,' I groaned. There was another volley of f-words as Percy packed up his kit and threw what by then was a large netful of bream back into the Cam.

'You little sod,' he fumed. 'I was winning that match by a street.' That really made me feel better. 'Next time you go out in the cold, put a pair of your mum's tights on. They'll keep you warm.' As poorly as I felt, I couldn't help thinking: 'Tights? You've got to be joking, mate.' No nine-year-old Cambridge boy would be seen dead in tights.

Being taken back to Percy's car was not a great experience. To every query about why he had packed up he replied: 'This little bastard passed out.' He topped it all when we arrived at the car by instructing: 'Next time, bring more food and drink.' What, I thought, so you can scoff it all yourself?

At this time I was finding that school, apart from sport, could be torture at times. I just longed to be outside.

Every Monday morning, the teacher would ask the kids what they'd done over the weekend – had we had any new experiences or learned any new words? And every week, my answer was unfailing and predictable: I'd played football or gone fishing. I was still having lessons with Percy and would join in when a group of the national junior angling squad met in the Five Bells pub opposite his house on Newmarket Road – ideal territory for a nine-year-old, I think you'll agree.

One evening we were taught the art of float-making with peacock quills and balsa wood. Some had really neat paint jobs but many landed on the pub floor, deemed not fit for purpose and snapped in half. The lesson was about float sensitivity, inertia and what happens to a float in water when you get a bite – all very technical, but I lapped it up.

Along came Monday and the teacher's question: what had we done at the weekend? Her face was a picture when she came to me expecting the words 'football and fishing' and instead I chirped up: 'Making fishing floats and learning about inertia. Mr Anderson taught me.' She suggested I see more of Mr Anderson if I was learning subjects and words like that, and awarded me the one and only gold star I ever earned at school.

The following week I was off with Percy again, this time to a match on the river Welland, where we were to meet the legendary Ivan Marks. If Percy was angling's David Beckham, then Ivan was its Pelé. He was angling's first superstar and the pearls of wisdom he dropped in his Angling Times column were awaited eagerly every week.

I'll never forget sitting at Ivan's table in a greasy spoon café, eating breakfast, listening to his fishing tales and taking in the smutty banter dealt out around the table. But that half-hour wasn't the only unforgettable happening that day.

As soon as we arrived at the Welland, I felt an urgent call of nature – that grease-laden breakfast had not been suited to a nine-year-old's stomach. Percy had drawn his peg and was tackling up when I announced that I needed the loo. 'Go and have a pee then, son,' said Percy, busy with his tackle. 'No, Percy,' I said, hopping from one foot to the other. 'I need the *loo*.'

Percy sighed. 'Well, go over there by the fence,' he said. 'But I don't have anything to wipe my bum with,' I pointed out. Percy was getting exasperated. 'You've got a crisp packet,' he humphed. 'Use that.' He then went one better by leaning over the water and pulling out three or four lily pads. 'Here you are, son,' he declared triumphantly, proffering the dripping leaves, 'sit on the fence and wipe your arse with these.'

Feeling very uncomfortable in more ways than one – the fence was of the barbed wire variety – I dropped my trousers and perched. I hadn't noticed the road behind the fence, or the cars that were passing on a regular basis. My bare-arsed performance, complete with lily pads, drew a number of admiring blasts from car horns.

Monday came around and back at school my teacher seemed eager to find out if Mr Anderson had taught me anything new. 'Yes, miss,' I replied. 'He taught me how to have a shit in the countryside.' The other lads in the class were creasing up but the teacher failed to see the funny side and sent me outside to think about what I'd said.

When I was allowed back in, she advised me not to see Mr Anderson again. Fat chance of that: as I mentioned earlier, our friendship lasted fifty years.

Mum's parents, James and Rosie Legge, lived nearby in Stretten Avenue and I spent a great deal of time with them, fishing and getting a grounding in a few trades from a very early age. Grandad was a carpenter, signwriter and small works builder, and from the age of six onwards a piece of wood or a tool were seldom far from my hands. My grandfather was one of the very best friends of my life and I owe him so much.

After junior school I moved on to Chesterton senior school and the first morning of my first term found me sitting outside the headmaster's office. I'd managed to put a football through the hall window and I was shaking in my shoes. My apprehension was growing as I stood in front of the stern-looking Mr Brown. 'Name?' he demanded. I told him I was Ian Darler. 'No, you're not,' he replied, 'you're Darler. Well, Darler, not a good start to your school career, is it, Darler?' After the stiffest bollocking of my young life, I was sent on my way and told not to end up outside his office again.

Strange how, once again, being OK at sport helped me at school. At the first sports lesson the teacher asked: 'Which one of you is Darler?' I put my hand up. 'You played for the City Schoolboys, didn't you? Right, you're football captain.' Blimey, I thought, I haven't even kicked a ball yet.

The first three years at Chesterton were great fun but I have regrets now. I was an absolute shit to Mr Bradbury, a lovely fella, always kind but an easy target for our schoolboy pranks. If we weren't taking a bolt and wing nut out of his desk so that it collapsed when he leant on it, it would be his chair that fell apart, but the chap seldom let rip at us. He sent an amazing email following one of my awards in later life and I tried to make contact to apologise for my juvenile behaviour, but the message board it appeared on didn't give me the option of replying.

If my first three years at Chesterton were great, the last two were disastrous. I was pretty good at carpentry (thanks to Grandad) and metalwork, and was interested in art, so I opted for all three subjects, only to be told there were too many pupils applying for them and I'd been placed in chemistry, physics and biology. I regarded this as a very poor joke.

The sport side of things, however, continued to be brilliant. My form and games teacher Peter Joyce was fantastic, making me both football and cricket captain, and I played for the school at basketball and at scrum half in rugby, although I soon found a way of getting dropped from the latter team. The rugby coach wanted to play a running game but every time I got the ball I leathered it forward, not being keen on having my head kicked in. In fairness, at fourteen I was still small because I was one of the youngest kids in the year. I blame my dad: if he'd held off a couple of months before dipping his wick, I would have been in the year below.

When I was fifteen, Peter Joyce asked if I would consider playing cricket for his adult team, which I did on a few occasions. Sport went a long way to getting me through my final years at school. I'm not proud to say I bunked off more lessons than I attended – I just couldn't stand the physics, chemistry and biology. The detentions came thick and fast but I didn't mind too much – I enjoyed them more than those bloody lessons.

At this time, Dad's days playing for the Pye club in the Cambs League were coming to an end, although he was still working for the parent company. On Saturdays, if Pye were playing at their lovely St Andrew's Road ground, I would go along with brothers Richard and John and Mum – she was Pye FC's match secretary. During the first half

I would either go fishing in the Cam, which passed the bottom of the football pitches, or watch the match, waiting for the half-time whistle to blow so we kids could play our own game on the pitch.

We were larking about in a goalmouth one Saturday when some bloke, wearing the kind of hat I'd only ever seen on Sherlock Holmes's head, yelled: 'Get out of that bloody goal!' (This turned out to be traditional groundsman language, and I now understand why we were pissing him off so much.) 'If you want to make yourself useful, why don't you replace some divots?' In your dreams, Sherlock, I thought.

At home that evening a kangaroo court convened: why had we been shouted at? Fully expecting a parental bollocking, we three brothers got in first – we didn't know we weren't allowed to play in the goalmouths. 'Don't do it again,' was as bad as it got from Dad.

A fortnight later, there we were again at the Pye ground. It was too cold for fishing and we weren't allowed to play in the goalmouths, so at half-time I walked out on to the pitch and started putting divots back. Out came ruddy Sherlock in his deerstalker. Before I could speak he said: 'Thank you very much for doing that. It's very helpful.' And I'd thought he'd been going to tell me to sod off.

'I'm Bill Scott,' he said. 'I'm head groundsman here. If you'd like to help at the end of the game, you could give me a hand taking the goal nets down.' I'd rather be kicking the shit out of them with a ball, I mused, but I went with the suggestion and helped him out.

It's strange how Bill took to me so quickly after the unpromising start of a fortnight before. He seemed a caring sort of fella. After we'd put the nets and steps away, he thanked me and asked my name. Then, to my surprise, he said: 'If you'd like to help next time your dad's playing, you'll be welcome.' Helping Bill soon became a regular Saturday afternoon activity.

One day he asked what I was going to do for a job when I left school and, on hearing that I hadn't a clue, asked how I was getting on at Chesterton. 'Hate it,' I replied. 'Not interested in half the lessons.' Bill thought for a moment and said: 'It's a shame the school won't let you have a few hours here with me.'

The following week I had a meeting with the school's careers teacher. Not over-impressed by my attendance record, she started preaching about how important it was to attend school and get good grades. I wasn't going to stand for that and told her in no uncertain terms that had I been put in the subjects I had opted for instead of being bombed out into physics, chemistry and biology, I would have been in school every day and working to a high standard. 'Hm,' she said. 'So what are we going to do about this?'

I seized my chance. 'Well, the groundsman at Pye's says it's a shame I can't help him during the week.' The teacher's face lit up. 'Would you like that?' she asked. 'And would you be sure to turn up?' I nodded. She shuffled the papers on her desk and told me to leave it with her.

A few days later I was called back to her office to be told we would be going to Pye to talk to Bill and a chap called John Newman, the maintenance department manager. The upshot of the meeting was that I was allowed to go on what they called work experience, which was pretty much unheard of in those days.

My first day at work certainly was an experience. Bill greeted me with open arms – he was just grateful for a pair of helping hands. The first job he gave me was cutting a full-size football pitch with a 21-inch Flymo as Pye's gang mowers would cut the grass but not the bents (long stalks). Well, I thought, it may not be the best job in the world but it's better than being stuck in school for those crap lessons. In fact I loved every minute, and two and half hours and a very sweaty T-shirt later I was finished.

I took the Flymo back to the machine shed happy with my day's work. 'Well done, good job,' said Bill. 'Now you can cut pitch two.' Flipping heck, I thought, but I got on with the job and finished it by lunchtime.

As I was tucking into my sandwiches, a rep called Robert Chesham, from machinery company SISIS, turned up. After learning what I was doing, he gave me a piece of advice I've never forgotten. 'Son,' he said, 'you need to stick with this. There are so few youngsters taking on the role of groundsman as a career, you'll never be out of work.'

Bill chirped up. 'I didn't think you would stick with it today,' he said, 'but you've done a really good job.' I was chuffed to pieces until Bill lobbed a bombshell: 'Pitch three needs cutting – how do you feel about that?' I was keen to impress, had appreciated Robert's comments and had only to think about those detested school lessons to agree to the job. Knowing I had only until four o'clock to get it done, I asked Bill if I could start before the lunch hour was up. 'Just do what you can, mate,' he said. I cracked on and by four had finished cutting three pitches with a two-stroke Flymo in seven hours.

The next meeting with the careers teacher was rewarding. Expecting me to say that I wasn't doing work experience again under any circumstances, she grinned as she asked: 'How did it go?' The shocked look on her face when I replied 'Brilliant!' was worth a million pounds.

The work experience continued for a few months and I really enjoyed being outside, away from the dreaded lessons. One afternoon Mum and Dad said we should have a chat. Bill and John Newman had been so pleased with the standard of my work that they had offered me a groundsman apprenticeship, they said. Was I interested? I'd recently failed a couple of football trials due to my lack of height and skinny physique, and this seemed a good offer – I really, really wanted to work outside. A few days later, on 7 August 1975, I signed a contract promising a weekly wage of £17. I was an apprentice groundsman at the age of sixteen.

CHAPTER 2

—

KIPPER ON THE CATWALK

Dear Ian,

When I was playing at the Abbey in the 1960s, there would be no grass on the surface after December. In later years I would often pop over to the ground for a cup of coffee, and I could see the amazing difference.

I would have loved to play on one of your surfaces.

After football I worked in the fire service. I remember one occasion when you were worried about the pitch – it was bone dry and you didn't have the equipment to irrigate it. I persuaded my guvnor, who was a football fan, to let us do a practice water relay from the lake on Coldham Common. That's a good idea, he said.

'See that football ground over there,' I said to the lads, 'it's a big house, it's on fire and we're going to do a water relay and put it out.' Dry pitch problem solved.

I've heard supporters say they can't wait to see if what the players are saying about the pitch is true. You only get out of a job what you put in, and with the countless hours you put in, you certainly get out what you put in.

Rodney Slack

Cambridge United player 1962-70

My parents thought I should take at least a couple of weeks off before starting the apprenticeship, but at the end of the school term I had a three-day break and plunged head first into working at the Pye sports ground. I had no idea what was just around the corner.

On my first day the rain was sheeting down. Bill took me on my first visit to the greenhouse area, where there had been a big delivery of potting compost and bales of Irish moss peat. Our task was to move the wet, heavy bags into the greenhouse and then repot some plants in bigger pots.

We had moved a few bags and I was getting used to the task when, as I was passing through the greenhouse door, the slippery bag I was carrying slithered out of my hands. My left hand flew off the bag and smashed through a pane of glass. There was blood everywhere and, as I stared horror-struck, I could see the bone on the top of a knuckle sticking out. I remember thinking: this can't happen, that's one of my favourite hands.

'Off to the medical room!' roared Bill. I was scared and learning lessons fast; if I'd known then what I know now, I would never have run to the medical room with a laceration that was bleeding like crazy. But the nurse patched me up, told me to go home and added that I shouldn't think about coming back for a week. As I walked back to the field to tell Bill he was brilliant ('These things happen,' he observed philosophically), I was wondering how my working life could possibly have got off to a worse start.

It didn't take me long, on my return to work a week later, to realise what a great bloke Bill was. His attention to detail was simply staggering. The Pye sports field enjoyed a reputation as one of the best in Cambridge, despite competition from all the lavishly funded college grounds, and already I could see why Bill's stock was sky-high in groundsmanship circles.

Short in stature but well built after decades of working on the turf, Bill possessed a head of snow-white hair that made an occasional appearance from beneath the Sherlock Holmes. A slight Suffolk accent betrayed his youthful origins but he'd lived on Cambridge's Hills Road, almost opposite the Eastern Counties bus depot, for donkey's years. Over the years I got to know his wife Elsie well; I also got to know the cakes she packed up for Bill's lunch every day. The old boy seldom managed to eat them, and I felt obliged to help him out.

My official working hours were from 8am to 5pm but I started clocking in at the maintenance department by seven o'clock, after a ten-minute bike ride from home. Bill wanted to know what on earth I was doing there so early, and my reply – I just thought I would get in early to see if I could help out – went down well. The two other members of the ground staff came in on staff buses (in those days the company ran around ten or twelve coaches every day) and arrived around 7.45am.

At this time I was still using the dreaded Flymo and a rotary cutter to cut the banks along the Cam which, being a keen angler, I enjoyed. Cutting along the ditches and paddocks also became my jobs; they were basic but I understood that I was the apprentice and that sort of labour was expected of me.

My first big day came after a few months. Bill took me round to the front of the offices and told me that, as I was doing so well, I could cut the prestigious lawns there with the Ransomes Marquis walk-behind mower. Dozens of offices overlooked these immaculately tended lawns and I immediately felt uncomfortable under the gaze of all the people looking out. I went back with Bill to collect the mower and grass cart and started work, providing some first-class entertainment for the girls in the post room.

This room, which was glazed from floor to ceiling, was staffed by a number of girls in their late teens. One in particular, a strawberry blonde, was delighted to have a beetroot-red audience for her lewd gestures, which consisted of putting her hands under her tits and lifting them at me every time I walked past, just like Les Dawson playing his Ada role. It was my first really embarrassing moment in life, never mind at work, and I did my best to ignore the giggling gallery.

Bill reappeared. By now I knew when something was bothering him: he would push his Sherlock hat back and scratch his head. He broke the bad news: 'I know this is the first time you've used this mower but there are a lot of misses in the lawns. We can't leave it looking like this – you'd better let me tidy it up.' As I passed the post room window I felt like a batsman trudging back to the pavilion having been bowled for a first-ball duck. The girls, in fits of laughter, were ripping it out of me.

The following day Bill took me across to the bowls green, and there I got my hands on another new bit of machinery: a Ransomes Certes mower. I was required to cut the green in two directions, and this time I made sure that both my diagonal cuts were spot on. 'That's better,' grinned Bill.

I may have been a skinny little kid but I was proud of my crowning glory: a head of hair that sprouted so thickly it had to be thinned out before my hairdresser could style it. Stop laughing at the back: OK, there's not much left nowadays but I think you'll find it's all about quality, not quantity.

I'd been using one of the best-known Cambridge hairdressing salons, called Scruffs, which was owned and run by Jon Chapman. It's still going, although it moved into the city centre from its original site on Victoria Road some time ago.

Jon was renowned as one of the country's top hairdressers and he and his stylist, Andy Pethick, often entered styling competitions. I was more than a little suspicious when Andy, a brilliant stylist, asked if I would be interested in being his model. You're on a wind-up, I thought, but Andy assured me he was serious. He explained what would be involved and won me round: why not give it a go, I decided – it sounded like a good laugh. Fashion shows were often associated with the hair-styling competitions, and on several occasions we travelled with outfitters like Austin Reed and Top Man to seaside resorts and London.

Andy may have been serious about making a model of me, but he stitched me up like a kipper at one of the competitions. Saturday Night Fever, the disco musical that made John Travolta a superstar and his white suit an icon, was a massive hit in cinemas at the time, and I was flattered when it turned out that I was to have a Travolta-style cut for the contest. Bless his cotton socks, Andy somehow forgot to tell me that Austin Reed were going to put me in the Travolta trademark suit.

The evening came along. Once Andy had configured the Darler barnet in the styling part of the show, I went to the dressing area to see what clothes I was going to wear on stage – and stared open-mouthed as the Travolta suit loomed into my vision. They had to be kidding me – I would never regain my Cambridge street cred if I strutted my stuff in that get-up. Suppressing a feeling of panic, I agreed to wear the suit and, as I did my teapot walk on stage, I looked out to the audience. There was Andy, laughing like a maniac.

I saw the funny side eventually – it was an amazing experience and great fun. But, resplendent in my new hairstyle, I was back out in front of the office buildings, cutting the main lawns, the following week. I really copped it from the post girls, who were making the familiar bawdy gestures and blowing kisses as I walked past their window, but this time I just smiled and carried on. The performance carried on for months – unless Shirley, the post room manageress, happened to be in the room. I found it amusing that the girls ignored me when she was around, and would delight in turning the tables and taking the piss out of my female tormentors.

The other two chaps on the ground staff were Albert, an old country boy in his sixties from the Fenland village of Coveney, and Donald, who was in his fifties. I spent many an hour with Albert, who was also one of the company coach wardens, and I soon found that he enacted a funny little ritual at the end of each day. Unwisely, he put his trust in me when he was getting ready to head for the bus, asking: 'Is my tie straight? Is my collar down?'

For a few months I made sure that his tie was perfectly straight but on one occasion I winked at Bill and adjusted it so it was completely off centre. Bill was laughing fit to bust. Over the next few weeks, poor Albert headed off to the coach park with his tie all over the shop and a number of other changes made to his dress code. One day Bill gave me some daffodils to take home for my mum. I kept a few back and Albert went through his routine unaware of the four blooms I had tucked into the back of his coat collar.

But there were times when it was best not to take liberties with Albert. I noticed that he sometimes acted strangely, becoming aggressive and snappy when challenged about the slightest thing, and generally being less helpful than normal. When I mentioned this observation to Bill, he said he'd noticed the odd behaviour too – and it only happened at certain times of the month. It appeared the old chap's actions were affected by the phases of the moon and the weird stuff happened when the lunar disc was fully illuminated. Blimey, I thought, I'm working with a werewolf called Albert. Silver bullets were in short supply in Chesterton at the time, so I made sure not to take the piss when there was a full moon.

My next challenge at work came while I was being taught to drive an old Fordson Dexta. I found the tractor quite easy to handle, but driving it with a seven tonne trailer on the back was a different matter. Bill, using two traffic cones, spent hours teaching me how to reverse tractor and trailer; there's a real knack to this manoeuvre. But once I'd mastered it I was sent off on the road. Happy days; this was so much better than school.

I was in the second year of my apprenticeship when Bill set about showing me how to use the Allett mower, with a view to me progressing to cutting the three football pitches and the one used for hockey. The Allett had a trailing seat and when you fired this baby up its Robin Reliant engine made it sound like a real mean machine. Bill explained how to use the mower, how to set the cylinder up and how to set out the pitch to ensure the shades were accurate.

The pitches were enclosed by wooden two-by-two-inch posts, about a metre high, with blue rope around them. No matter what job he was on, Bill was always well dressed, and on this day he wore his customary Sherlock hat, a tweed jacket and dress trousers. The mower's throttle was in the central position on the handlebar as he set off up the outside of one pitch, turned at the far end and returned to where I was standing. But as he leant forward to turn again, his jacket buttonhole caught on the throttle lever and, when he leant back, the mower shot off at top speed, careering through the ropes and yanking the posts out of the ground.

This was easily the funniest thing I'd ever seen, but I knew when to keep a straight face. I asked Bill if he was OK, to which he replied: 'Fine. I just wanted to show what can happen if you have loose clothing and don't concentrate at all times.' Yeah, right, I thought. He was lucky he hadn't throttled himself; excuse the pun.

I took to the Allett like a duck to water. I was given the responsibility of cutting football pitches two and three, while Bill cut pitch one and the hockey pitch. I remember standing at the top of the pavilion, surveying my work and getting a real buzz from what I'd achieved. What I didn't bargain for was the shit I got from one of the other members of staff who thought he, rather than the new boy, should be cutting the pitches.

I continued to get into work early, beating Bill in on a few occasions. I couldn't get enough of the job. I loved everything about it – the smell of the soil, the glorious dawn chorus, learning the trade and all the tricks you could use to enhance the way the pitches, the cricket square and the bowls green looked. Being a little sod at school appeared to have had its benefits after all.

I was growing in confidence and the job started to become a little easier. I now understood the process for looking after the machinery and hand tools. Each and every day all tools like spades, shovels and forks had to be washed down in a bucket with a small hand brush and then wiped with an oily cloth. Each and every day the machines were washed down in the washing bay and re-greased before being put away.

It was May and after work I was due to play for Pye's first team in an away football fixture. Work had over-run a little so I skipped washing down the equipment I'd been using and stood outside the machine shed with my jacket and football bag, ready to head off once Bill said I could go. He came round the corner saying: 'All done? Everything washed and put away?' I hesitated. 'Look Ian, I know you put the tools away dirty,' he said, 'now you can get every piece of machinery out of the shed, wipe it down, clean the kit you used and then put it away again.'

I was horrified. 'But I've got football this evening,' I protested. 'Not tonight you ain't,' was the reply. 'You'll never forget this lesson – in future you will always wash your tools after use, and that goes for your sex life as well.' A mischievous grin came over his face. 'Make sure you wash your tool after use.'

Lesson learned. I apologised, got cracking on my punishment and eventually got away at seven o'clock. And, true enough, I've never forgotten the lesson of that evening. As I roll off and lie back on the pillow, I just can't get the vision of a grinning Bill and his flipping deerstalker out of my head.

I felt things had gone really well for me at Pye but one day, out of the blue, came a sickening shock. The ground staff were called to a meeting with the senior maintenance manager, to be told there were going to be redundancies. I was devastated: I was the new kid and the axe would inevitably fall on my neck.

Several weeks passed before I was called into the office. I was feeling physically sick as I sat down, with John Newman and Bill on either side of a desk, both looking as uncomfortable as I felt. 'We've made a decision about the redundancies,' said John, 'and we're pleased to confirm you will retain your job.' A wave of relief washed over me as I left that office ... but the guilt was also welling up: I knew one of the other poor fellas was likely to lose his job.

When Bill came back I asked to see him. 'I think I should have been the person to leave,' I admitted. Bill stopped me in my tracks: 'Listen here you, I fought your corner because since you joined you've been in early every day, worked hard every day and stayed on after work if something had to be finished, when the other two jumped on the company bus and went home. You use your initiative when I'm not about and, most importantly, I think you'll make a good head groundsman.'

His words were slow to sink in but Bill was still talking: 'I'm going away on holiday in ten days' time and I need to ask you something. I'd like to leave you in charge.'

I couldn't believe what I was hearing. 'In charge of what?' I asked. 'Everything,' he said, 'the sports field and Albert. Now go home, think about what I've asked you and let me know what you think tomorrow.'

I must have cycled home that evening but I don't recall any of the journey. All the positives of saying yes to Bill's proposition and the responsibilities it would entail raced through my mind, fighting it out with the negatives – what if I got it wrong? But deep down I knew this was a terrific chance to impress and my parents were supportive – it was entirely my decision, they said. I passed a sleepless night, tingling with excitement and trepidation, but my decision was made.

The following morning I was in work early, sitting on a chair outside the pavilion when Bill arrived. 'Couldn't you sleep?' he asked. 'Funny you should say that,' I replied. 'In answer to your question – yes, I'll give it a go.' Bill grinned. 'That's great,' he said. 'You'll be fine.'

Surprisingly, Albert seemed relieved by the decision to put me in charge. I made the most of it during the lead-up to Bill's holiday by firing dozens of questions at him. 'Bloody hell,' he said, 'I need a holiday after all that.'

The day before Bill went away he produced a list of all the work to be carried out and what cricket and bowls fixtures we had to cover. With my nerves bubbling over, my first day in charge came round and I asked Albert to do certain jobs, which he did with good grace. He was a great help.

The cricket outfield was normally cut with the gang mowers but I'd been thinking about what Bill always said about standards and the appearance of the pitches and outfields. For the forthcoming match I decided to cut the outfield with the Allett.

Albert was cutting out the cricket wicket while I started on the outfield. I could see the old fella scratching his head, so I stopped to ask what was wrong. He was mystified. 'What the hell are you doing?' he asked. 'Cutting the outfield in circles,' I replied.

It was something I'd not seen in my time at Pye. To tell the truth, it took an hour longer than cutting it with the gang mowers, but when it was done it looked the dog's bollocks. I was gratified when the following lunchtime the cricket captain came over to thank me, saying the set-up was the best he'd seen since he started playing for the Pye team.

The week flew past. I reckoned Bill would pop in as soon as he got back from holiday at the weekend, so I stayed on a couple of hours after work on Friday to repeat the circle-cut for Saturday's cricket match. The shades had more depth to them this time, and the square and outfield looked amazing.

Monday came, and when I went into work Bill was already in the office, checking the weekly fixtures. Alarm bells rang when he performed the routine that signified something was bothering him, lifting the deerstalker and scratching his head. 'Are you after my job?' he demanded. I really didn't know what he meant, but he quickly went on to explain: he had popped in on Saturday, as I had expected him to, and he hadn't been able to believe his eyes. The compliments were music to my ears.

All my football mates were pairing off with girlfriends around this time. To be honest, I was more interested in fishing and football, but one of the plant department boys said a girl who was an assistant in the catering department was on the look-out. I agreed to see her, we went out for a few drinks and things developed. I was chuffed to have a girlfriend and, more importantly, I started to get free food and bigger portions from the staff canteen.

I was smitten. We would see each other most evenings and lunchtimes and life felt pretty good. Work was amazing and I was enjoying the experience of learning greenkeeping, with the touch of romance helping it all along.

One morning in April 1979 I was at the sports ground – just another day at work, or so I thought. From where I was cutting football pitch two, I could see Bill in the car park, talking to an elderly gentleman who was puffing away on a cigarette. From his nervous twitches I could see Bill was a little agitated, but the conversation ended with him and the other fella shaking hands. At lunchtime he came up with a concerned look on his face. Could he have a private word, he asked, adding that it was nothing for me to worry about. We found a fairly private spot on the first-team pitch that I had cut that morning.

Bill coughed nervously. 'You remember me saying you'd make a good head groundsman one day?' I nodded and Bill went on: the gentleman he had been talking to was Jack Cooke, a director from Cambridge United Football Club and a well-known Football League referee. He knew my dad, who was by then a referee himself, and was asking if I would be interested in attending an interview for the vacant position of head groundsman at United. Mr Cooke had been told I delivered a high standard of work, Bill said, adding that he had had to correct that impression: I delivered a very high standard of work.

I experienced conflicting emotions as the words sank in. This was an amazing opportunity, but I was in a position of comfort with my work and personal life at Pye. I fretted for the rest of the day but Bill was very supportive – it was up to me what I wanted to do, and he promised that, whatever I decided, he would help me.

There was another obstacle standing in the way of this incredible opportunity. Nine years previously I had been among the 14,000 spectators crammed into the Abbey Stadium to watch United play Chelsea, FA Cup winners a couple of days previously, in a game arranged as part of the deal that saw Ian Hutchinson transfer from the U's to the Pensioners. But that was the only time I had ever set foot in the Abbey. Along with Grandad, Dad and the rest of the family, I had been a City supporter through thick and thin. To be honest, even considering the job felt like an act of treachery.

I took advice from my parents and from my girlfriend Sharon. It seemed the sensible thing to do would be to attend the interview. It was just an interview after all, and it would be a new experience that might help me in the future.

I contacted Mr Cooke and the date was set. In the meantime, Bill had told sports and social club chairman Peter MacCorkindale (father of the actor Simon MacCorkindale) about United's approach, and Peter promptly offered a wage increase if I stayed at Pye. That's nice, I thought. I've worked my balls off and at the first sniff of leaving he waves a pay rise under my nose. Nice gesture, but why wasn't it made earlier?

The day of the interview arrived and Bill, as ever, was there to offer support. I had planned to walk from Pye's ground across Stourbridge Common to the Abbey but Bill said he would drive me and be available to answer questions should the directors want confirmation of the quality of my work.

When we got to the stadium there was a reserve game in progress, but it wasn't the match that gripped my attention, it was the pitch. I couldn't believe my eyes. The playing surface was in a truly awful state: full of holes, it had hardly any grass and resembled a dust bath more than the home pitch of a professional football club. I watched, horrified, as one of the goalkeepers drop-kicked the ball out of his hands; when it landed I could have been watching a safari programme on telly, with herds of wildebeest and zebras kicking up the dust.

I met United vice-chairman Tony Douglas and club secretary Les Holloway, and was invited to watch the last fifteen minutes of the first half before sitting down for the interview. As soon as the half-time whistle blew I asked if I could have a walk on the playing surface, and I was able to have a close look.

We were joined in the guest lounge by Jack Cooke and team manager John Docherty but the interview was conducted by Tony Douglas, who posed a number of questions about the playing surface. To this day I remain surprised that I was offered the job – I didn't hold back in my criticism of the way the pitch had been maintained.

Tony's first question appeared simple: why is the playing surface in such a poor condition? It's entirely due to compaction and lack of maintenance, I replied. He then wanted to know why compaction was an issue and I explained that it increased the risk of waterlogging, shallow rotting which in turn could create an anaerobic layer that leads to root break, which could then cause instability in the top surface.

Tony, perhaps blinded by science, asked if I could put that in simple terms. 'Yes, Mr Douglas,' I answered. 'If I were to shut you in an airtight cupboard for forty-eight hours, how would you feel?'

Tony took that point on board and produced a report from the Sports Turf Research Institute. 'Ian could have saved us some money,' he said jokingly to Les Holloway. 'He's just told us exactly what's in the report.'

He and John Docherty then asked Bill a couple of questions about my age and ability to work at a professional level, and I squirmed with embarrassment as Bill gave his impressions of me and my positive work ethic. Tony finished up by asking me if I thought I could improve the pitch if I were offered the job. 'Stevie Wonder could improve it,' I replied, which brought out a snigger from Les.

After a few days during which other applicants were interviewed, I was gobsmacked when Les phoned to confirm that United's board of directors were offering me the position of head groundsman. The following day he arrived at Pye with my proposed contract of employment. The season had finished at United and I had to give a month's notice to Pye, but I was aware that I had to get cracking with the Abbey pitch, and we agreed that the club would pay me an hourly rate if I worked evenings.

My first return to the stadium, to assess the pitch and quantify what materials I needed to renovate it, turned into a horrifying wake-up call. Where I was used to working, the tools and equipment were well maintained and in tiptop order. The toolshed at the Abbey Stadium was a doorless pre-cast garage. All the equipment was open to the elements and consequently fit only for the scrapyard. Reality hit home hard and fast – to put it in football pundit parlance, I had a mountain to climb.

I asked for a meeting with Jack Cooke and Tony Douglas and showed them that we simply didn't have the kit to do the job once the pitch had been renovated. They appreciated the problem, and the Mastiff mower and SISIS outfield spiker were taken away for service and repair. My dad helped me to carry out the pitch renovation over ten evenings but, coming after a full day's shift at Pye, it was still bloody hard work.

The playing surface was scarified back to the dirt, which caused a bit of a stir – Les was worried we wouldn't have a pitch for the new season – and the pitch was over-seeded and top-dressed. The very poor standard of surface and the depth of the divot holes meant we had to use a dumper to tip and push the root zone all over the surface, and this instantly improved the levels.

The next problem I faced was that of irrigation. There were no automatic pop-up sprinklers in those days, but sometimes you get lucky. The day we finished the renovation it started to piss down and for the next few days there were heavy showers alternating with nice warm sun. I felt my excitement growing as the seed germinated and I could see that we had a hundred per cent coverage three weeks after germination. On went the summer fertiliser, which really pushed the new grass on.

It was at this time that I met Rodney Slack. A true legend at the Abbey, Rodney had played almost 350 games in goal for United between 1962 and 1970, as the U's prepared for life in the Football League. Often called England's best non-League goalkeeper, he had starred in many of the Cambridge derbies I'd watched as a kid at Milton Road, and it was sad that his brilliance was never seen at a higher level.

Rodney, who lived almost opposite the ground on Newmarket Road, had by now retired from football and was working as a firefighter. He commented on the excellent state of the pitch, at which I explained my concerns about irrigation. 'Leave it with me, Ian,' he said after a moment's thought. 'I've got an idea.' A few days later he reappeared, grinning all over his face. 'Here's my number,' he said. 'If you need water on the pitch, give me twenty-four hours' notice and I should be able to help.' I was puzzled until Rodney explained: 'My station officer says we can carry out drills when you need water.'

It was a win-win proposal for me and the fire service and, after just a month in the job, it was my first contra deal. The fire crews would arrive on Coldham Common in a tender, roll out the hoses and flood the pitch inside an hour. This happened regularly, but I lost count of how many times the lads got a shout, had to pack everything away in haste and blue-light off to a job.

It didn't take me long to realise that the club could call on the services of a brilliant group of volunteer painters – between ten and twelve people who would turn up after they'd finished their day's work and paint barriers, turnstiles, seats, whatever needed their attention. And it was all done in the best possible humour. Their banter flew about the Abbey for the best part of a decade, until other commitments arose and the group's numbers started to drop off. I'll always be grateful for the amazing job those guys did.

There were other people keeping me and my dad company during the evenings – the staff and agents of the club's lottery department. At the time United had one of the country's largest lotteries, masterminded by a commercial genius by the name of Dudley Arliss, and it raised huge amounts of money for the club at a time when every penny was vitally important. The lottery office opened at eight in the morning and closed at ten at night, and there was a constant stream of agents paying their money in and collecting their next batch of tickets – but the office staff still found time to keep Dad and me supplied with tea and coffee.

I was very sad to leave Pye. A lot of my good friends were there as well as my girlfriend, and I appreciated the fact that without Bill Scott's help and guidance I wouldn't have had such an amazing job working in professional football.

CHAPTER 3

—

HANGING AROUND

Dear Ian,

When you started work at the Abbey in 1979, the pitch was in very poor condition. The change you were able to make was immense, and what we didn't know at the time was that you were making it with a tiny budget. What you achieved was something that other groundsmen were spending thousands of pounds on.

You probably looked at us, the late-Seventies United team, as a side that set out to entertain – and we were able to entertain because of the pitches you prepared.

It's all about getting a true bounce. I was the kind of player who often didn't want to have a second touch of the ball, so I had to trust the pitch.

I would never say that one pitch is better than another, but by the time I left United, yours matched the very best, and that's the best accolade I can pay.

You're also a really nice bloke. You may not remember, but when I was going through a difficult time off the pitch, you often pulled me aside for a little chat. Just coming in to work with you helped me a lot.

Alan Biley

Cambridge United player 1975-80 & 1986-87

Full-time employment at United during the close season was strange compared to life at Pye – there were so few people around. Les Holloway was always on hand, as were his secretary Amanda Clowes, head scout Ron Howard, physio Peter Melville (who was busy painting the dressing rooms, officials' room and bathrooms) and John Docherty. That was about it apart from two retired volunteers: Tom Tingey and his mate Sid. I also had an occasional visit from the previous groundsman, who was still living in a club-owned house backing on to the ground and kindly offered his help if I needed it.

The close season flashed by, and I was grateful for the support I received from Les and John Doc, who was an absolute diamond. He was complimentary about the pitch as it all started to come together and Pete Melville would pop out to have a chat and escape the eggshell paint fumes. My first impressions of Pete were that he was a bit of a perfectionist, liked a good moan and was very hard-working. I didn't know it at the time, but he would become my partner in crime in later years. Les was forever popping across from the office to check on me, although he always seemed to be in a hurry to get somewhere. To this day I don't know where he was speeding off to.

The pitch was marked out and, as I prepared to put the goals back up, I saw that the goalpost boxes were not concreted in. The sockets had to be dug out and put in place with enough concrete to prevent them moving, on the very day a Cambridge Evening News photographer arrived to take photos of me at work. What an experience that was … he had me posing with a shovel on my shoulder and my shirt off – not a good look as I was still a skinny little sod who had to run about in the shower to get wet. But the photographer cheered me up when he told me that the paper believed that at nineteen I was the youngest ever Football League head groundsman.

A couple of days later, when the concrete had set, the posts went up and they were followed by a new set of white nets. The pitch looked pretty damn good. This was the first day of pre-season for the players and they were making some pleasing comments about how good the pitch was compared to when they had left for their summer break.

I was working around the eighteen-yard box at the Allotments End – in those days the 'away end' was just a shallow bank of terracing and a wall, behind which were acres of, you guessed it, allotments – when goalkeeper Malcolm Webster and two other players came over to comment on my work.

One of them put out a congratulatory hand but the handshake turned into a push and in a flash I was on my arse – one of the other lads had been on his knees behind me and I'd tumbled over his crouching form. Amid much hilarity at this playground prank, I was helped up, only to be hoisted and hung, arms outstretched, from the crossbar – my chunky jumper turned out to be perfect for attaching innocent young groundsmen to net hooks. Struggling to believe what was happening to me, I was left dangling helplessly as the players, the chortling hangmen among them, left for a light jog around Coldham Common.

I'm not sure how long I was hanging there, trying to wriggle out of my jumper; suffice it to say that the Common measures up at forty hectares, it's a fair old distance round its perimeter and these were late-Seventies footballers out for a loosener, not Mo Farah at his peak. I was still dangling and contemplating murder when they finally staggered back into the ground, but my ordeal wasn't over.

Malcolm emerged from the tunnel with a couple of balls and proceeded to chip them gently towards me, before arranging to have me taken down (I now know Malcolm had missed me intentionally: I found out later just how accurate his kicking was). Bloody hell, I thought, hung up to dry and then used for target practice. For a moment I wished I'd never left Pye.

Meanwhile, the pensioner volunteers Tom and Sid had turned up for work and, taking pity on me, asked if I would like a drink in our rest room. To describe this facility as squalid would do it an injustice – it was far worse than that. The mice that had a free run of the place didn't seem to mind it, but they were the only ones. As I sat down cautiously, Tom started to lay down the ground rules.

'Tea, coffee and sugar are mine,' he announced. 'You can use them, but that other bastard groundsman comes in here at night and pinches them when he's locked out of his house. So I hide my tea and coffee but leave this sugar bowl out for him. Whatever you do, don't use that sugar!'

I was already having a nightmare of a day; now I thought I must be hallucinating. 'Why?' I asked hesitantly.

'I put granulated sodium chlorate in it,' explained Tom cheerfully. 'I nearly killed a delivery driver once. He made himself a coffee but used the wrong sugar.'

I sat silently, contemplating the lethal toxic nature of sodium chlorate weedkiller, sipping my tea and wondering what the hell I had let myself in for at this place. It appeared to be full of homicidal maniacs including crucifixion enthusiasts and poisoners.

After a few weeks I managed to talk Tom round and was allowed to remove his hazardous sugar substitute. I probably stopped him killing someone. And over the months that followed I grew to enjoy the company of the two lads.

Sid was a gentle, kind man; Tom, who had a wonky hip and heavy limp and walked with a stick, was not very tall but built like a brick shithouse, with hands like dinner plates. They stayed with me for several years until Sid, despite several operations, succumbed to cancer. Tom then called time, but on his last day he left me with an unforgettable parting shot. 'I'll be back to haunt you!' he threatened. 'It's going in my will that when I die my ashes will be buried by the tunnel where the players run out.' I couldn't resist asking why. 'So I can trip up the opposition players,' he chuckled. And that was the last time I saw Tom ... or at least I thought it would be.

Some areas of the stadium were unkempt: dozens of old advertising boards were dumped behind the east stand (what supporters call the main stand) and the grass behind the Habbin stand was a metre high. Dad spent weeks helping me clear these areas, arriving after a day at the office and working until it was dark. We would often have a visit from the chairman David Ruston, who had a yellow, nicotine-stained quiff resulting from the fag constantly stuck to his lip. He was a sincere gentleman who was full of praise for what I and Dad had done in a short time. Tony Douglas and Jack Cooke were also frequent visitors in the evenings and always had time to chat.

When the pitch was ready for the opening home game of the season, John Doc was once again full of compliments about the quality of the playing surface. A few days after he'd hung me from the crossbar, Malcolm Webster came over for a chat. This time I was on my guard, a lot more aware of what could happen with these buggers, but all Malcolm said was: 'Ian, when we get wet weather later in the year, can you not put Pete in the penalty box?'

I was mystified. Why would I even think of putting the physio in the penalty box? Suspecting this was another of Webster's tricks, I asked cautiously: 'Who's Pete?'

I watched even more puzzled as Webby bent double, helpless with laughter. 'Not Pete, peat!' he spluttered.

The previous groundsman, he eventually managed to explain, had covered the six-yard box with peat, leaving Malcolm unable to push off the unstable surface to dive and having to deal with unpredictable bounces from back passes. I assured him that I would never use peat anywhere – I would be laying sand in those areas. Malcolm was happy with that; he might have hung me from a crossbar, but he seemed a really genuine fella.

The pitch was now ready for the first game and John Docherty was very complimentary about the quality of the playing surface. The Doc was always there for me; always supportive.

The day finally arrived. The referee for the pre-season friendly was Dave Hutchinson, a friend of Dad's from his reffing days. I walked the pitch with him and asked what he thought. 'The grass is magnificent,' he said, 'but if you want my advice, try to make your lines a little sharper on the junctions of the boxes.' All advice gratefully received.

Cut Throat Lane is an unmade byway that connects Newmarket Road to Elfleda Road, forking off halfway down to lead to the Abbey Stadium's main car park. Sorry to disappoint: the fellas at 100 Years of Coconuts, who have helped out with this book, have searched in vain for stories of dark deeds that might have led to the lane getting its name. It appears that 'Cut Throat' might instead be a corruption of the words 'cut through'.

At that time, match days saw the players arrive via Cut Throat Lane, drive through the safety gates next to the turnstiles and then along the edge-of-pitch running track in front of the east stand – inches from my precious pitch – to find a parking space at the rear. No one appeared to have thought about the safety of supporters entering the ground at the same time. Winger Derrick Christie, driving his orange and black VW Beetle, was slow, sedate and sensible but full back Jamie Murray drove his Mini as if he was competing in the Barnwell Grand Prix.

The playing surface survived – we've only ever had one car career all over the pitch doing handbrake turns. But the vehicular traffic on the running track did have a downside: puddles would form when we had heavy rain, and each car would send a wave of water on to the playing surface. The problem dogged us for a few seasons, until the club bought a plot of land behind the stand, allowing direct access to the car park from Cut Throat Lane. We then encountered another problem: the lane had a tight dogleg and it was not uncommon for a car to crunch into a neighbour's wall.

The first League game of the 1979/80 season, against Leicester City, was upon us. On Tuesday, August 21 I was in work very early to prepare the pitch, cutting it both ways in single mower widths to achieve a chess board effect. It looked top notch. I then marked out the pitch with one hundred per cent concentration, remembering what Dave Hutchinson had said about making the lines sharp.

After putting the corner flags out I made my way up into the east stand to have a look at what the supporters would see as they entered the stadium. I knew the playing surface had improved dramatically but I wasn't prepared for what I was looking at. The pitch looked outstanding – a perfect emerald green all over, the mower shades crisp and accurate and the lines so bright they were almost dazzling. The players walked out for a look and Malcolm Webster came over to say the pitch was like a carpet. All my misgivings over my ability to do the job vanished that day.

After the match (a 1-1 draw) I was replacing divots and repairing scuffs when a group of men appeared on the pitch with chairman David Ruston. David called me over. 'My boy,' he said, 'these are the directors from Leicester. They would like to congratulate you on the quality of the pitch.' He chuckled and added: 'They thought the grass was artificial.'

I was chatting with the visitors when Leicester chairman Dennis Sharp asked if I would be interested in working at Filbert Street. I was flattered but passed it off. 'No thanks,' I said. 'I'm a Cambridge lad just starting out on my professional career, and United gave me my break.' Thinking that was the end of the accolades, I then had the Cambridge Evening News chasing me for comments about the transformation, using the headline 'Wonderful pitch impresses visitors' and quoting the Leicester directors.

I had to pinch myself to make sure all this acclaim was really happening, but Dad and my old boss Bill Scott had helped me at the

Leicester game, and at the end Bill patted me on the back and said how proud of me he was. He reminded me of the time when the redundancies were flying about at Pye and I thought I was for the chop; he had kept me on, saying I would make a good head groundsman. The compliment, one of the most gratifying I've ever had, remains with me to this day.

Later that evening I was invited into the players' bar, a very small area under the main stand used only by the players and their wives and girlfriends. I was drinking a Coke when Les Holloway came in and started laying into me. 'Get out of here,' he snapped. 'What do you think you're doing? Go home and think about it.'

Not having a clue what Les was on about, I hardly slept that night. Next day I went to see him to be met with: 'Have you learned your lesson?' Lesson? What lesson? Les finally explained: 'The last groundsman had a problem with alcohol, and I won't let that happen to you.' I explained that I was only drinking Coke but Les was firm: the players' bar was off limits. Another lesson had been learned.

The games came thick and fast with clubs like Watford, Chelsea, QPR, Newcastle, West Ham, Burnley and Birmingham playing at the Abbey Stadium every fortnight – teams I'd watched for years on Match of the Day. The quality of the footballers playing on my pitch was scary. This really was my dream job.

The playing surface continued to receive praise, from both our club management and visiting managers. I'd been carrying out some very fancy designs with my cutting – something that had not really been seen in football before. I had also grown in the letters CUFC across the pitch, using a liquid feed laced with iron that enhanced the colour of the treated area. It was such a simple idea, but it seemed to mesmerise the public.

Getting to the stadium around seven o'clock every morning, I was normally the first person to arrive. On one occasion, however, I was beaten to it by our young star striker Alan Biley, whom I discovered fast asleep in his Cortina outside the front gate. It didn't seem right to wake him, but I managed it with the noise of unlocking and opening the gate.

Poor Alan, looking a little lost and anxious, raised his hand to acknowledge me and I went over to check he was OK. Not really, he said – he was struggling with injury and a few other things going on in his life. I tried to reassure him by saying I wished I was in his shoes: to be a top-rated, in-demand Division Two player was something to be proud of, injured or not. I went on to say what a great player he was – every time the ball was at his feet, I expected something special to happen, and very often it did. Alan smiled and said: 'Thanks, mate.'

He wasn't the only one struggling with his private life. Sharon had dumped me and I had no idea why. I was gutted – I lost a deposit I'd put down on a place where we'd planned to live together and had, I thought, treated her well. Fishing mates and my new workmates supported me through the next few weeks, taking me out and about.

One morning I was cutting the pitch when I saw a giant of a man standing on the running track at the north end, which was known as the Corona End at the time. He beckoned and, feeling uneasy – the bloke was huge, his beard and moustache were scruffy and he had a large gash, with several stitches, above one eye – I walked over.

'Where are the dressing rooms, son?' he asked. I was directing him towards the players' tunnel when he put his hand out and, expecting a handshake, I stretched out mine. As with Webby at the start of the season, no handshake was forthcoming. The mystery giant snatched my arm, wrestled me to the ground and started dragging me along the cinder track towards the tunnel. I was scared but also indignant: I took a dim view of being hauled along the ground for eighty yards by a monster who looked and behaved like an unhinged pirate, and of the gaping hole ripped out of my corduroy trouser arse by the cinders.

We came to a halt and the lump let go. 'I'm Chris Turner,' he announced. 'Nice to meet you, son.' He extracted a massive roll of cash from a pocket and peeled off a fiver. 'There you go,' he said, 'that should pay for some new trousers.' It was not the last time I would be left wondering 'what the hell was all that about?' in my dealings with Mr Turner.

Comments about my pitch were not always positive. When United drew 1-1 with Aston Villa in the FA Cup in January 1980, with Chris scoring his first goal for the club, the headline in the evening paper was 'Saunders fumes at bumpy pitch'. The News went on to say that Ron Saunders had angered United staff and players by blaming a bumpy pitch for upsetting his team's play. The pitch looked great from the side but it was actually very bumpy, he had grumbled. The bounce was uneven and had affected Villa's game; there was only a handful of one- and two-touch passes in the game.

John Doc stood up for me, saying the pitch had been praised by Sunderland, Leicester and Chelsea that season, it was 'magic' and the groundsman worked very hard. Player Peter Graham said my pitch was as good as any in the country and fellow midfielder Steve Spriggs added there was no way Villa's was better – he had played there several times and it was always heavy. And it was interesting that the Midlands press men who watched the action at Villa Park week in, week out found Saunders' comments hard to swallow; at least two of them described the playing surface as terrible. Ron's comments showed the pressure managers are under when they don't get the result they expect – but that's the joy of the FA Cup.

I travelled to the replay at Villa a week later, and what I saw put a smile on my face. I had to wonder what planet Saunders was on. The pitch was flat but grassless, a rolled mess that resembled a beach. After twenty minutes the ball was bobbling all over the shop – a bit rich after the previous week's comments.

A few weeks later, Sharon phoned out of the blue, saying she was sorry for the break-up and asking if we could get back together. It was a difficult decision – I'd really missed her but had started to get my life back together – but after a few days I agreed to start seeing her again.

Working with John Doc and the staff continued to be exciting and enjoyable. I felt like one of the team and JD really looked after me. I was starting to add bits and pieces to my game and understand the importance of having a pitch that works for your team and disrupts the visitors' game.

We were due to play Sunderland when the Doc asked to see me in the medical room, where Pete Melville was treating the walking wounded. Sunderland had a good passing game, he said, and he thought our pitch would benefit them. Could I do anything to make the ball hold up?

I got on the phone to Rodney Slack at the fire station and arranged a heavy watering session. Timing was going to be critical, and Rodney arranged for a crew to roll up at the stadium at 11.45am, just over three hours before kick-off. Barnwell Lake gave up much of its water – not enough to waterlog the surface but certainly enough to blunt Sunderland's style. We drew 3-3 and John thanked me after the game.

But before that game there had been another incident that convinced me I needed to grow a pair of eyes in my arse.

I was getting ready to mark out the lines with my usual two twenty-litre buckets of marking material. As I stood filling the pitch marker from one of the buckets, centre forward Joe Mayo crept up behind me and emptied the other over my head. This triggered a panic in Pete Melville who, knowing the previous groundsman had used lime to mark the pitch and fearing the caustic stuff would ruin my good looks, raced to my aid. In fact I wasn't harmed physically – I'd swapped from

53

lime to ground chalk and a product called Indiline, a form of emulsion – but my dignity was irreparably damaged. White from head to toe, I looked as if I'd been battered and was ready for frying.

The chairman, vice-chairman and directors would always stop to speak when they visited the ground. When David Ruston came on to the pitch one afternoon, he looked like a man with more than his fair share of worries. I asked him if he was OK, to which he replied: 'Well, we've got some very difficult times ahead.' He went on to explain: the rules for away fixture gate receipts were about to change.

At that time, United would play in front of huge crowds at clubs like Chelsea, Newcastle and Sunderland, and benefit from a high percentage of the gate receipts. This was going to stop. In future, visiting clubs would get none of the gate, and this would have a dramatic effect on our club's income.

Despite the worries, Christmas turned out to be an entertaining time at the club. All the non-playing staff and directors were invited to lunch at the Royal Cambridge Hotel on Trumpington Road and, when the meal was over and John Docherty had had a few drinks, the stories started to flow. They were followed by a few of Pete Melville's tales from the medical room. Sadly, most of these are unsuitable for repetition in a family publication like this one. On the outside, chairman David Ruston appeared to be a quiet, mellow sort of chap – everyone's idea of the stereotypical accountant, perhaps – but I can tell you he had a wicked sense of humour and more than his share of hilarious anecdotes to relate.

I was still living at my parents' house in Cambridge at this time, and it was just as well. I joined in with the festivities wholeheartedly, toasted the board's generosity with a few glasses of wine and then followed up with a beer or several, and there was little chance of me going back to the stadium after lunch to mark out the pitch. If I had, we would have ended up with the waviest touchlines in the League.

Les Holloway kindly took me home, and I was expecting another bollocking after the telling-off earlier in the year for being in the players' bar. To my surprise and relief, Les's only words were: 'Don't be late in the morning.'

The following morning Les called me to his office. I stood outside expecting the worst but, when he called me in, he merely muttered: 'B for Turkey.' Was this some kind of coded telling off, I wondered, or was our secretary speaking in tongues? My mystified expression brought an explanation: 'Everyone gets a joint of beef or a turkey at Christmas, as a thank you from the club. So which do you want?' It was a lovely gesture from the directors, and it continued for a number of years.

Christmas Eve was upon us and, as we all left the stadium around three o'clock with the usual festive greetings, I had to admit to myself the pitch looked in great nick for the time of year. Nevertheless, I felt I had to pop in on Christmas Day to check everything was as it should be. I was walking the pitch when Jack Cooke, the director who had headhunted me earlier in the year, wandered over for a chat.

'What on earth are you doing here today?' he asked. Just checking everything was OK for the Boxing Day game against Oldham, I explained. Jack took a pull on his cigarette and urged: 'Well, don't hang about too long.' With that we left the ground, more than happy with the state of the pitch.

Boxing Day dawned bright, sunny and cold. At the stadium by eight o'clock, I was crossing the pitch to put the corner flags out when I spied something not quite right out of the corner of one eye. I whirled round to face the centre circle, fighting to keep my heart from bursting out of my chest: some kind person, armed with a spade, had crept into the stadium overnight and dug up an area of turf. Of the perpetrator of this foul deed, spade or turf there was no sign. All that was left was a bloody great hole in my lovingly tended centre circle.

Les Holloway arrived about half an hour later. 'What are we going to do?' he wailed, appalled. 'We've got to play the game. It's Boxing Day – there's going to be a big crowd.'

All the turf suppliers had shut up shop for Christmas, but I'd been thinking. 'I could ask Dad if we could take up some of his lawn,' I suggested. Using Les's phone, I explained the situation to Mum and listened, relieved, as she and Dad agreed we could use some of their turf. I drove home and measured out an area of turf matching the size that had been nicked, and in no time five square yards of the stuff was speeding to the Abbey Stadium.

Unless you had noticed that one part of the centre circle was a slightly different colour to the rest, you wouldn't have been any the wiser about the morning's drama. The game was a thrilling 3-3 draw, the pitch played really well and my fears that the replacement turf would roll up proved unfounded.

Big games against Newcastle, West Ham, Burnley and Preston came and went with United claiming a draw and three wins and, still pinching myself to make sure I wasn't dreaming, I approached the end-of-season renovation. Using a pedestrian machine, the playing surface was scarified in three directions to remove loose divots and thatch and reduce the meadow grass that had infiltrated the turf. The surface was then aerated, which was followed by overseeding and then a hundred tonnes of 80/20 sterilised top dressing. A drag mat was run over the surface to work the dressing in. The seed germinated just eight days later, and within three weeks the pitch looked better than ever.

———————————

The 1980-81 season will stay in my memory for the wrong reasons. Everything was hunky-dory for the first few fixtures, but then, in September, United played Chelsea.

This was a huge match and there was a very big crowd. The areas behind the goals had eight-foot high metal mesh fences designed to prevent fans getting on to the pitch. But a group of forty or fifty Chelsea supporters, gathered in the middle pen of the away terrace at the Allotments End, had other ideas.

For starters they set to work on some crush barriers. Held together by Allen keys, they would have failed present-day load-testing requirements and didn't stand a chance when the fans worked them backwards and forwards until they snapped. To emphasise their superiority, the gang then hurled the broken barriers over the fence on to the running track. This show of strength was followed by a number of fans removing some of their clothing and weaving the garments into the welded security fence at the front of the terrace. They then set their handiwork on fire and set about pulling at the fence, backwards and forwards, until the welds failed and it peeled open like a can of baked beans.

Out they poured, on to the pitch where the players of both teams were warming up, provoking fan-player confrontations. And on they ran, the full length of the pitch towards the U's supporters, at which point a massive fight broke out on the home terrace – other Chelsea fans had somehow foiled the segregation measures and infiltrated the Corona End. Outnumbered but determined and disciplined, the police managed to restore control – but the peace was short-lived.

Two Chelsea fans broke through the security fence and barbed wire protecting one of the floodlight pylons and clambered to the very top – at more than 120ft this was quite a feat, but also highly dangerous and very stupid. While this was going on, another group climbed on to a tea bar roof and then on to the roof of the Habbin Stand, in the middle of which sat a cameraman from Anglia TV. Two Blues invaders inched along the roof until they reached the camera position – the TV man had had the sense to scarper – and one of them sat in his seat and started to swing the camera around.

By this time the police had used the scaffold staircase at the rear of the Habbin to get on to the roof. The freelance cameraman bolted, but it didn't end well for him or his mate: both were arrested, but not before one had slipped off the roof and landed astride a scaffold pole, making a sorry mess of his wedding tackle.

Meanwhile, the game had kicked off and more drama was unfolding on the pitch. A United free kick at the Allotments End was blasted into the back of the goal with such force that it rebounded out after hitting the stanchion. Chelsea keeper Petar Borota, knowing he had conceded a goal, kicked the ball away but, to the entire ground's amazement, referee Keith Hackett waved 'play on'.

Towards half-time, a number of Chelsea supporters who had been refused entry to the stadium found their way to the allotments that gave that end of the ground its nickname. Having failed to get into the Abbey by clambering over the wall, they resorted to uprooting handfuls of fruit and veg and lobbing them over the wall on to the pitch. At one point it looked as if Barnwell Baptist Church's harvest festival had changed venue.

By now I'd received reports via the police radio that the south terrace toilet was flooded. With two officers for company, I made my way to the public convenience in question, to be faced by water pouring out of the door. Wading through the flood waters, we found that the WC had been ripped out, leaving a four-inch hole in the ground, and excrement had been smeared all over the walls. Armoured electric cables had been pulled off the ceiling and pipes were hanging in mid-air with water hosing out of them.

Something has mystified me from that day to this: how do you hide a WC in a small-ish stadium like ours, or smuggle it out? We never found it, it's not something you could hide in the pocket of your Levi's 501s and no one reported seeing a Chelsea supporter sauntering over Coldham Common with an Armitage Shanks on his shoulder.

Even with the coppers flanking me, I was finding this situation intimidating. The lads were receiving barrages of abuse from skinheads clad according to the original bovver boy dress code: Doc Martens AirWairs with rolled-up jeans showing the boots off to best advantage, braces, the lot.

I've never been so delighted to vacate an area of the Abbey, but the ordeal wasn't over and a new experience awaited me at the final whistle. As I ventured hesitantly on to the pitch, the air was suddenly thick with coins aimed in my direction. I exited stage left, quick-sharp, and didn't go back until the stadium was empty.

I took several United directors over to survey the damage in the toilet and other areas of the ground. Luckily for us, there was plenty of building trade knowhow in the club, and Tony Douglas, the vice-chairman, got some of his Mills & Douglas labourers to help repair the damage and clean up the mess.

I was still a youngster and keen to kick a ball about, and I grabbed every chance that came along. One such occasion was when BBC Radio Cambridgeshire put on a charity match at the Abbey and, luckily for me, several participants cried off, leaving them short of players. The Beeb's Julian Dunne asked if I would like to play and I didn't need asking twice – out came the boots, on went the kit and out on to the pitch we went.

United manager John Docherty, a tricky winger with the likes of Brentford and Reading in his time, was playing wide right for the opposition. He was on the ball by the corner flag at the north end and, as I lunged into the tackle, the cheeky bugger nutmegged me. I turned and chased after him, only for JD to stop in order to nutmeg me again, putting himself back by the corner flag in the process. John still had quick feet and a few tricks with the ball, and he showed just how easy it was to make me look a complete plum.

Later in the game I showed I was better in front of goal than with my back to it, smacking a half-volley from outside the box past Richard Key, United's reserve keeper and a relative of mine.

Big games against the likes of West Ham, Newcastle, QPR and Blackburn came and went, and soon they felt like the new normal. But then, on the 31 January 1981, we played Sheffield Wednesday.

There had been a few crowd disturbances in the first half and, as I set about the half-time replacement of divots, I discovered that some supporters didn't believe in taking a break. As I made my way towards the Wednesday fans they bombarded me with coins, which sent me scampering in the opposite direction. Goalkeeper Malcolm Webster must have wished he'd worn a tin hat in the second half – his penalty box was shiny with coin of the realm.

We lost the game 0-2 – that pissed me off for starters; I've never been a good loser – and my resumption of divoting duties brought another coin-storm down on my head. The police lads were picking up the coinage and I followed suit, which provoked a nasty, racist chant of 'Jew boy!' Sod you, I thought, these coins will bugger up my mower. I carried on divoting and trousering coins until all my pockets were bulging, while the Owls fans changed their chant to 'We hope you get cancer.'

Counting my takings later that evening, I was delighted to find that I'd picked up just over £50. That paid for a week's holiday on the Norfolk Broads. Thanks, lads.

The United coaching staff faced challenges when it came to finding training facilities during the winter months, and the players often found themselves running on the track around the Abbey pitch. It was hard work – I often stood in the tunnel watching them complete full laps, half laps, then racing against each other, sprint after sprint. On one occasion Chris Turner came over to John Docherty, who was with me and injured winger Graham Daniels in the tunnel, and said: 'Doc, you know this is no good for me. I just can't do it on the hard surface.' His plea fell on deaf ears. 'Get out there,' growled Doc.

It was around this time that I found out just how accurate Malcolm Webster's drop-ball half-volley kicking was. I was on the pitch using the SISIS Auto-Trac – like a mini-tractor – with a brush on the back while Webby and Richard Key were practising their kicking on one side of the pitch. As I drove past Malcolm, some twenty-five yards away, he fired off a ferocious half-volley that smacked into my shoulder and knocked me clean off the machine.

As I picked myself up, to a chorus of delighted laughter, I realised that when Malcolm had aimed a few chips at me while I was hanging, helpless, from the cross bar, he had been missing intentionally. In fairness to Malcolm, he managed to control his mirth sufficiently to be able to run over and see if I was OK.

Soon after, he picked up a serious knee injury that entailed surgery and months of rehab work. When he was on the point of resuming training and wanting to practise fielding crosses, Peter Melville would cross balls from one wing while I did likewise from the other. This became a regular thing, and Malcolm asked me several times if I could cross a few balls for him after the other players had left the ground. Here I was, helping a Division Two goalkeeper out with his game – I was living the dream.

Malcolm knew a trick or two when it came to training sessions, in particular the common run from the stadium around Coldham Common and back. He had become a regular visitor to my office at the end of a corridor under the main stand, and 'Get the kettle on!' was his favourite phrase. The players would pass the corridor as they embarked on the common run and Malcolm was always the last to leave and the last to get back.

On one occasion, as his teammates jogged grimly away, he ducked into my room for a leisurely cup of tea or two in the dark with me. Realising he needed to look as if he'd just completed the dreaded run, he drained his mug, poured water over his head and shirt and waited for midfielder Willie Watson to run past before rejoining the procession in his customary last place.

Did John Docherty ever twig that the wet-look Webster had not actually shed a drop of sweat? I don't think so.

At the end of that season Willie stood back from playing and took over as the bar manager in the Harris Suite lounge, as it was known then – nowadays it's the site of one of the club's hospitality areas. No man was ever better suited to the job of managing licensed premises than the gregarious Willie, and he proved it later when he managed pubs in the villages of Wilburton and Comberton. The Friday evening club he set up for punters wanting to play darts and pool proved so popular that the lounge was rammed every week. Willie lived in the old groundsman's house at the back of the stadium and was often in and around the ground, popping in regularly for a mug of tea.

My groundsman apprentice Trevor Ball, volunteer Wally Rookes and I were in my office one day when an excited Willie burst in, yelling: 'You'd better come and help!' We took a sip of tea and enquired what was up. 'It's Catweazle,' gasped Willie, stifling a laugh. 'Quick!'

Almost from my first day at the club, volunteer painter Bruce Agarstrath has been part of the furniture. Rejoicing in the nickname of Catweazle after the eccentric wizard in the 1970s TV series, he's a hesitant sort of fella but always willing to try to help, bless him. His downside is a distressing lack of co-ordination – it didn't take me long to realise that for every ten litres of paint he took from the store, five would shortly be kicked over.

We raced outside, to be confronted by a sight none of us will ever forget: Cat, apparently wearing a top hat at a jaunty angle, was covered from head to toe in gloopy red oxide paint. His eyeballs and teeth were the only body parts showing through.

He'd been painting the handrail on the main stand's rear staircase and his ladder had slipped. While the unfortunate Cat was plummeting to earth, the paint tin had flipped over and landed smack-bang on his head. It was a cosy fit.

Still doubled over with laughter, we started cleaning the poor bloke up, looking for signs of blood. He appeared to have had a lucky escape and was uninjured, but the paint-stripping job was a tricky one. Willie and I used a whole bottle of white spirit to remove the worst of it and Cat then padded off for a shower in the away dressing room. I rooted out an old boiler suit for his journey home and he cut a miserable figure as he trudged away. This was far from the last of a catalogue of disasters involving Bruce the Catman.

CHAPTER 4

—

LEFT IN THE DARK

Dear Ian,

When I first came to Cambridge United, I thought you were a player. I was on trial and you were taking part in a practice match. 'Who's this fellow Darler?' I asked the manager. 'He's the groundsman and if we need him he'll have to play,' said the Doc. It took me about a week to work out he wasn't joking.

If you say to me 'Ian Darler', I think of conviction and a character that still burns with zeal after forty years. You can't buy conviction for a million pounds. Your passion is unbelievable and your willingness is as hot as ever.

You must have had cause to be cynical at times, about football and the club, and you've not been well, but your energy in showing me what needs to be done on the pitch really impresses me.

You're more concerned about the cause of Cambridge United than about your own welfare. You can never have enough of those people.

You're like all groundsmen – your worst quality is your grumpiness. But you can't have your level of commitment without being grumpy at times.

It really matters to fans that they know your heart is in the job. Your contribution has been gold dust.

Graham Daniels

Cambridge United player 1983-85, director 2013-present

Wally Rookes, who was the spitting image of the seedy landlord Rigsby out of Rising Damp, and Catweazle, more of a Stig of the Dump lookalike, were involved in an endless piss-taking saga, with the argument focusing on which of the two was better preserved and fitter. My assistant Trevor hit on the ideal way to settle the matter – they should race each other round the pitch perimeter track – and to my surprise they agreed.

As they took their places on the starting line, it was decided that they would race in opposite directions, thus eliminating the undignified sight of two elderly plonkers jostling and shoving. The race got under way, and I recalled with a sense of dread that Wally had undergone major heart surgery. I didn't fancy administering CPR to either Rigsby or Stig, but my fears were unfounded – both competitors came through the ordeal unscathed and Wally won by several yards. Not that the result changed anything – they continued to rip the piss out of each other with great enthusiasm.

Wally was a popular choice of victim for the many wind-ups that enliven life at any football club. On one occasion the club arranged to produce a Christmas card featuring a photograph of the club mascot, Marvin the Moose, adorned by a few Christmas decorations. Wally happily volunteered to wear the moose suit and stand in the middle of the pitch while the photographer did his bit. It was all over inside two minutes, but Wally, with limited vision inside the mascot get-up, was not aware that the snapper had been and gone.

How long could we persuade Wally to stand motionless in the uncomfortable, hot and heavy moose suit, arms in the air as if celebrating a goal? Shouted encouragements and commands from delighted bystanders took us past thirty minutes with ease, but when just under an hour had passed Wally/Marvin evidently began to suspect something wasn't quite right and started to take the moose head off. We scattered to various hiding places and watched as Wally peered around him, a big grin on his cheery chops. He'd known it was a wind-up all along.

I've always found that something that will bring you down to earth is just around the corner. It was just another day at work when I was approached by a bloke who said a relative of his, after a terrible road accident, had been fighting for his life in Addenbrooke's Hospital. Goalkeeper Malcolm Webster had visited him several times, he added. Now on socialising rehab, he had asked if he could spend some time at the Abbey Stadium. I instantly agreed to have the lad with me.

Patrick started sweeping up on the terraces for an hour a week. At first he was nervous, quiet and reserved, but after a few weeks his confidence started to blossom, as did his co-ordination. By the time five or six months had gone by he was spending a couple of days a week with me and had become a bit cheeky. It was great to see the little sparkle in his eye.

Not long after, I was approached by the headmaster of Littleton House school in Girton, which taught children with various emotional and behavioural problems. They were all good kids, the headmaster explained, but some had been through challenging times and events, or had had problems at school. This touched a nerve – as I've said before, I had not enjoyed my last two or three years of schooling and felt I could relate to some of the issues.

I agreed to take some of the kids on extended work experience, and the first to turn up was Warren. The lad was a diamond, always early for work and helpful in a quiet, undemonstrative way. He always had his little tin of tobacco and roll-up papers to hand, and more often than not had a fag dangling from his lip. He also always had a smile on his face. We became good friends.

I was having weekly meetings with the headmaster, which were going very well, and everything seemed to be going according to plan or even better. As another week in paradise started, I exchanged the usual Monday-morning pleasantries with Warren. 'What did you get up to at the weekend?' I asked in all innocence, not ready for the boy's bombshell: 'My girlfriend had a baby.'

'What?' I spluttered. Warren repeated the good news, a big, stupid grin spreading all over his face. Bloody hell, I thought, you kept that quiet. You're only a young old boy and I didn't even know you were seeing a girl, let alone putting a bun in her oven.

Warren stayed with me for around a year without producing any more offspring on the sly, and then moved on to full-time employment. But he was the first of several lads from Littleton House who helped me out enormously with their work experience, and the arrangement with the school continued for at least a decade.

In fact I continued to take pupils from various schools on work experience, with varying degrees of success. Most lads were great, but we had one for whom the description 'pain in the backside' could have been dreamt up. His speciality was pushing everyone with whom he came into contact to the limits of their patience.

Some of the steel fences that were in place around the pitch – at the 'away' end, unsurprisingly – had been vandalised, and I had to call in vice-chairman Tony Douglas and his fabricator, Jack Dickinson, to carry out repairs. Jack asked if I could give him a hand but I was up to my eyes in a post-match pitch renovation and offered him the work experience lad, whom we'll call Kevin – the help Jack needed was of a very basic nature, after all.

Jack was of the old school and plain-speaking to a fault, and we were chatting over a cuppa when he poured out his thanks for allocating Kevin to the task. 'He's doing my bloody head in,' he chuntered. 'It's all "I've done this", "I've done that", not giving me a minute's peace – and not only does he never stop talking, every word he spouts is a load of bollocks.'

I sympathised, but Jack was a resourceful man and knew how to get his own back. Kevin was wearing old-style work boots with steel toecaps on the outside, as well as a welder's visor. As he welded the fence back in place, Jack asked him to press his feet against the mesh to keep it in place. It was the work of a moment for a skilled bloke like Jack to tack-weld the boots to the fence and leave Kevin having to undo his laces if he wanted to be free. There he stood, clinging on to the mesh, as I walked over to find out the cause of the commotion. 'He's only gone and welded my boots to the fence!' wailed the champion chatterbox.

Satisfied that he'd learned his lesson, Jack wandered off at a leisurely pace to fetch an angle grinder from his van. Once he was free, Pain in the Bum became a lot more respectful in the workplace.

As you might expect, the players continued to take every opportunity to improve their game when it came to wind-ups and lighthearted joking. And as you also might expect, Darler was the target for much of it.

One day I was in my little storeroom under the east stand's A block, fetching a tin of paint. I could only have been in there a matter of seconds but that was enough time for a certain Mr Turner, ambling along the corridor, to seize his opportunity for a giggle at my expense. The storeroom was plunged into darkness as Chris turned off the light (the switch was outside), slammed the door shut and turned the key in the lock. He then perfected the joke by forbidding anyone who passed by to let me out.

In the pitch dark of a stifling, tiny enclosed space, still clutching my tin of paint in one hand, I used the other to hammer on the door while yelling 'let me out!' every time I heard any footsteps in the corridor. The reply was invariably: 'Shut your row and stay in there, you little shit.'

I was on the verge of inventing the mobile phone and calling Rodney's fire brigade when Les Holloway happened to pass by and, hearing my pleas for release, turned the key and let me out. 'Why on earth did you leave your keys in the door?' he asked, shaking with laughter. 'You know what they're like.' It was yet another lesson learned.

I still got the occasional opportunity to put my boots on to make up the numbers for trial matches. In one such match a wide left player by the name of Graham Daniels played in front of me, and the game went really well for us – there was some nice link play and sharp passing. Afterwards, Graham asked John Doc where this left back called Darler had come from, and his face was a picture when he was told that I was the groundsman. 'Must be a wind-up,' he concluded, but come match day there I was in my scruffs, working on the pitch. Graham was incredulous: 'I was sure they were joking,' he chuckled.

Well, Graham earned a contract, had a decent career and stayed around Cambridge when he left United, playing for City and forging a big reputation as a coach and manager in local football. Nowadays, he's better known as the general director of Christians in Sport and director of football at United.

Playing in these games brought me a lot closer to the club's apprentice professionals. The apprentice's lot was not an easy one, and some of the things they had to do made me glad I was the groundsman.

We didn't have the luxury of a dedicated training ground in those days, and more often than not the players would use Coldham Common, at the rear of the stadium, for their sessions. The Common was not only a public sports facility; it was also a dog walker's paradise and has been used for centuries for grazing cattle and horses at certain times of the year.

The apprentices had to be in to work early in order to carry nets, pegs, steps and other paraphernalia over to the Common and make the nets ready for training. It was worse in pre-season – they also had to carry the goalposts over, for the council didn't put their posts up until late July. The lads' final task was to walk the pitch with shovels and clear the grass of cow and dog shit.

I often wonder how modern-day players would react if they were asked to carry out these vital tasks. At the time United were playing against very big clubs in the equivalent of the Championship, but there was no prima donna behaviour and very little moaning about the facilities from management or players. They just got on with the job they were paid to do.

I was now in my third season at the club. My relationship with Sharon had continued to develop and things felt really good. She seemed like the girl for me and, on one of my days off, I proved my point to myself by asking her to marry me. I would have gone down on one knee but that would have earned some funny looks in the surroundings of the lounge bar of The Fox, Burwell.

Much to my amazement, Sharon said yes. We couldn't wait to spread the news but when we got back to her parents' house later that day, the announcement didn't appear to be the happy event I was expecting. The less than warm reception we received was possibly a sign of things to come.

We started to plan the big day. The wedding would be in Burwell, we agreed, and in the meantime we managed to find a small furnished cottage to rent once we were married. But to my immense frustration, I found that there were three people in the relationship right from the early days of our engagement.

We began to move our clothing and personal effects into our house, which was a challenge given the long hours I was working. I got into the habit of popping over in my lunch hour, laying the stuff in a pile and sorting it out at weekends, but this proved unpopular with the third person. It was untidy and unacceptable, apparently.

The football club were brilliant to us. We didn't have the money to have a phone line installed in our new house, so the club agreed to stump up the cash. And John Docherty and a number of other staff members were there in Burwell on the big day.

My friend Eric was bringing his young daughter, who was a bridesmaid, but he was delayed by a road accident en route to the in-laws' house and was a few minutes late. I was highly embarrassed when this misdemeanour was met by a stinging verbal broadside from

Person Three, but otherwise the day went off without a hitch and all seemed well – pretty much perfect, in fact.

We settled into our new home in Exning near Newmarket – reputed to be the ancient capital of the Iceni tribe and therefore the home village of the Roman-bashing queen Boudicca. Did you know that?

It's fair to say that Sharon found the adjustment to married life difficult and upsetting at times, and the situation was not helped by the long hours I was working at the Abbey Stadium and my frequent absence from home at weekends – those pesky football fixtures would keep getting in the way. Things settled down but times were very tight on the money front. I remember our frustration with the old black and white TV that, even after it had taken five minutes to warm up, struggled to keep us entertained with a blurry picture that wobbled and bounced all over the shop.

After around twelve months the cottage next door, which was owned by the same couple that we were renting ours from, became available. It wasn't furnished, which gave us the opportunity to start buying our own furniture – a few enjoyable trips to the auction room and the house was filled with fittings we actually liked.

We stayed in the cottage for another year and then, with United's help, managed to get a mortgage enabling us to buy our own property. It was a middle-terrace house in Burwell, and it was an absolute dream. There was a lovely old couple living next door but they were struggling to maintain their garden, so after a few weeks I started to cut their lawn at the same time as I cut ours.

We then jetted off to Malta for our first proper holiday. In contrast to our increasingly happy home life, it was a fortnight's nightmare from start to finish. Along with half of the other people staying in our hotel, both Sharon and I succumbed to a stomach bug and spent a miserable few days wishing we'd never left home. To cap it all, Sharon then fell victim to a touch of sun stroke and was very poorly indeed for a few days. I felt helpless, unable to do much for her other than try to keep her cool. Believe me, no one has ever been more glad to get back to Burwell.

After the least relaxing holiday you could imagine, it was back to the long, hectic days of work. The pitch was still looking outstanding and was attracting admiring looks from a number of clubs and referees.

The staff at the club continued to be very supportive. Les Holloway called me into the office one day to ask if I would pop over to his house, cast an expert eye over the lawn and let him know what else needed to be done to the back garden. I ended up going back a few days later to rotavate the ground and lay turf, which instantly transformed the garden. Les, who was having a bit of a revamp throughout his house, asked if we would like his three-piece suite as he was having a new one. The chairs and settee weren't brand new but they looked it and, although we were fond of our old auction furniture, we were glad to be able to show it the door.

One thing you learn very quickly about working in professional football is that time flies by ridiculously quickly. You also have to work long, unsociable hours, often on bank holidays, and you can't book a holiday until the season's fixtures are out. All this can be very difficult for your relationship but I was lucky to have a wife who was a great cook and was pretty understanding about my work. I got on really well with her dad and brother Andrew, and spent many hours on the riverbank with the latter. Sadly, I had a few less than complimentary exchanges of views with the other family member who, it's fair to say, never really took to me.

Chris Turner had by now become a good friend, from a distance. You could never tell what he was plotting but you could guarantee that whatever it was, it was likely to be at your expense. Chris came over one morning before training and said he was having a house built in the small town of Ramsey, north of Huntingdon, and his wife Linda wanted the small back garden sorted out. Would I have a look at the job and do some turfing? Sure, I said – I would pop over one evening.

'Popping over one evening' didn't seem to suit the Turner schedule. The following day he was on my case again. 'When are you coming over to look at my little garden?' he demanded to know. It was obvious I wasn't going to get any peace and quiet until I'd driven over to Ramsey and shared my thoughts on the place's potential, so I agreed to go that evening.

What I saw made me gasp. 'I thought you said this was a small garden?' I protested. There was no top soil, there was builder's rubbish everywhere and, to cap it all, I was staring at a sizeable plot – by no stretch of the imagination the 'little garden' Turns had described. 'Well,' said the master of the house, 'what do you think?'

'What do I think? I think you're having a laugh,' I retorted, but the big man refused to be put off that easily. 'I'll make it worth your while,' he wheedled. 'You'll get a good drink if you can sort the lawn out.' He would have fifty tonnes of screened topsoil delivered so that I could prepare the ground, he insisted, and he would order and pay for the turf.

A few days later Chris announced that the soil had arrived, so I drove back to Ramsey the following weekend. As soon as I stepped out of the car, I knew something was up – the scoundrel was wearing a grin the size of Coldham Common. I edged tentatively round the side of the house to find Chris had talked someone into doing a rough levelling job on the soil with a digger – fair enough. But it wasn't the levelling that horrified me, it was the soil itself.

If this soil had been screened, it had been done by someone wearing a blindfold. Obviously sourced from one of Chris's farming mates, it looked like old carrot wash soil, but carrots weren't the only veg on show. This apology for topsoil also boasted a health-giving mix of parsnips and onions, all mixed in and begging to be chopped and made into a stew.

'Do you want a lawn or a bloody vegetable plot?' I objected. 'Just get on with it,' my tormentor replied. 'It'll be fine.'

Inspired by Chris's promise that my labours would be rewarded by a good drink, I spent the entire day raking out the soil and carting off many barrowloads of vegetables. As the evening closed in, the plot looked OK – the levels were good and all was ready for the turf. It would be delivered the following Saturday, Chris vowed, so I could lay it the following day.

Sunday came and I approached Ramsey with trepidation. I was half-expecting to find a few carpet offcuts and an expanse of Astroturf, but the turf that had been delivered was actually decent stuff. The first hour of the labour that followed was made easier by Chris barrowing the turf to me. He then made some flimsy excuse about being expected elsewhere, and left me to it. I had to admit, though, that after six hours of hard graft the lawn looked pretty good – especially considering the crap that was underneath it.

As I was loading my tools back in the car, Chris emerged from the house, clapped me on the back and announced: 'Great job, mate! Linda's really pleased with what you've done, so thanks a lot.' He stuffed a thick brown envelope into my shirt pocket and thanked me again.

After you've been turfing on your hands and knees all day, your clothes are as black as your hands and forearms, and the routine when you get home is to take off your trousers, shirt and jumper outside. As I was undressing, the brown envelope fell on to the floor; I picked it up, threw it on the kitchen cupboard and headed for the shower. It was only when I sat down to have a bite to eat that I thought about opening the envelope – and my eyes popped out on stalks like they do in cartoons. That villain Turner had done me again – my wage for three days' solid graft was twenty bloody teabags, and not even my favourite brand.

The following day, when he came in for training, I made sure to thank him for the good drink. 'Let that be a lesson to you,' he guffawed. 'In future, always make sure you name a price.'

Chris never did pay me a penny for the work, although he seldom failed to mention how good the lawn was. To be honest, being his friend was payment enough.

The fact that Chris didn't pay up was nevertheless something of a surprise, because he really looked after the apprentice whose job it was to clean the Turner boots. That apprentice went by the name of Andrew Sinton and he became another close friend, working with me on the ground after training for nearly two years. Andy got stuck into every task that was thrown at him and had a great attitude, although on one occasion his enthusiasm literally led to his downfall, and almost to the end of his short career.

Young Sinton was on ball duty one day. That meant that when a ball was kicked out of the ground, he and another apprentice would walk around to the allotments and retrieve it. A ball sailed over the wall and Andy, seeking a shortcut, climbed over the perimeter fence. As he clambered over a set of toilets he slipped and fell through the roof, landing with a sickening thud on his back. Fortunately for United fans, and those of Brentford, QPR, Spurs, Wolves and England, he was not seriously injured.

During the 1981-82 season, John Doc persuaded my mum that the Darler family home would make ideal digs for the recently signed Andy Polycarpou, a smashing fella who got on with everybody. The house quickly became a refuge for a number of players, who were attracted by the half-size slate-bed snooker table in the back room.

I recall that one evening the players had arranged to go a nightclub – it might have been Ronelles, which was housed atop the Lion Yard shopping centre and had a strict dress code. It's gone through several incarnations and now trades as Ballare. Lanky striker George Reilly turned up at our house but, realising he didn't have a jacket and wouldn't get past the club's door staff, started asking all and sundry if he could borrow one.

Andy P, being a skinny little short-arse like me, had nothing that George could have inserted himself into, and that just left my dad. He had a blazer and, although he was at least three sizes smaller than

George, the latter wasn't fazed. He wanted that blazer and he was going to have it. On went the blazer and when George presented himself for inspection it became evident that the sleeves were six inches too short and the jacket came halfway up his back. Nevertheless, it was a jacket and George duly wore it, winning the admiration of the Ronelles bouncers as they admitted him to the club.

I became really good mates with Tommy O'Neill, another one who talked me into laying a lawn for him, without the trials that I'd experienced with Chris Turner. Speaking of Chris, he was still at the club, and he was just one of an entire squad who were great to be around.

The close season had been busy. More than three hundred seats had been installed for away supporters in the Habbin terrace and new crowd barriers were fitted to the terrace areas, to ensure compliance with safety regulations. The season promised to be challenging for me. Chairman David Ruston had told me that the club's finances were precarious and there would be little money available for materials or equipment. I took this news on the chin and asked David if he would mind if I went out and tried to clinch some deals. 'My boy, you carry on,' he grinned, and the fag on his lip seemed to twitch with pleasure.

A few weeks later I had a chat with my good friend Eric Pettit, who worked for Choppen's, a local supplier of lawn care machinery and maintenance. Luckily, Eric was a keen football man and angler, and our friendship grew. He introduced me to Choppen's director Ian Heffer and we discussed a deal on machinery hire and maintenance. The meeting went well: Ian agreed to let me have any equipment the firm had in its hire fleet and help out with maintenance of our kit if Eric did the repairs in his own time.

It seemed like a good deal; in return we had to give Choppen's a quarter-page ad in matchday programmes and I had to take Eric out fishing and sort out Ian's lawn. 'It's not as it should be,' he explained. It certainly wasn't – it had more plantain than grass in it, but I didn't mind doing the job if it cemented the deal. There was another benefit to the arrangement: Eric started coming to home games and helping to divot the pitch.

'How are you getting on with your deal?' asked Mr Ruston a few days later. 'Done and dusted,' I replied, and the chairman was impressed.

The season passed quickly. John Docherty and his assistant John Cozens were as usual supportive towards me, but a big challenge was heading my way after the last ball had been kicked: on May 31 a Classic Rock concert was to be held on my beloved turf, with the aim of aiding the cash-strapped club. The London Symphony Orchestra was signed to play and guests would include England manager Ron Greenwood. Ron would be among the audience, I should add – I'm not sure he was an LSO-standard musician.

This was going to be a major headache for me. The enormous stage was built on blocks of scaffold boards that were said to be designed to protect the pitch, but I feared the worst for my lovingly tended greensward. And my fears were justified. The concert attracted an audience of nearly 4,000 and was a great success in most people's eyes, but the damage done was immense. When the concert was over it became clear that the protective boards under the stage, under the immense weight of a full symphony orchestra, had sunk so far into the pitch that they had to be prised out of the ground. John Doc was justly concerned: the pitch was in a very bad way.

We would have to recultivate the area affected to bring the pitch levels back to what they should be, it was decided amid a degree of panic, both over the condition of the pitch and the fact that the extra work would cost several thousand pounds. The area was re-renovated and seeded and hessian sheets were laid on the renovated areas to speed up germination and maintain the moisture levels – still no pop-up sprinklers in those days.

Hello to long hours of graft. We had an old Wright rain irrigator on skids, with a hose trailing behind, to water the pitch, but it took four hours to irrigate a pitch-length strip about twenty yards wide. That meant I would set the sprinkler off at ten o'clock at night and traipse back to the stadium around half-two in the morning to turn the irrigator around and drag the hoses across the pitch, ready for the next run. I had by now realised that being a groundsman generally meant you were the first person in the stadium in the morning and the last out, excluding the catering manager/barman. But I wasn't bothered in the least; in fact I loved it.

So the 1983-84 season got under way, and I was finding that being on the pitch before the kick-off, at half-time and full-time had become an intimidating experience. OK, the results were not going for United – hardly surprising given the club's financial travails and the consequent reliance on young, untried players – but I had never before witnessed personal attacks on anyone at the club.

That is certainly what was dealt out to poor John Doc, who had to endure constant 'Docherty out!' chants. I knew how hard John and the coaching staff worked, that United was John's life and that to achieve what he had on the lowest gates in Division Two – the club's highest Football League placing thus far, the best League Cup and FA Cup runs and the setting up of the youth policy – had been nothing short of a miracle.

When, in December 1983, I was told that the Doc had been sacked, I felt sick inside – he had looked after me from day one and I regarded him as a friend and mentor. John Cozens, another groundsman's friend, took over as caretaker manager but the role was short-lived and he was named assistant to new manager John Ryan, with my old mate Malcolm Webster taking charge of the youth team.

CHAPTER 5

———

CRAP DAY

Dear Ian,

*Many congratulations on serving Cambridge United for forty years –
truly a fantastic achievement.*

*When I left home in the north-east to join United as an apprentice
in July 1982, I was excited but I had no idea I would have such a
fantastic career, doing a job I loved and felt privileged to have.*

*We young apprentices worked with you on various jobs including
painting, cleaning seats and toilets and working on the pitch before and
after games.*

*I remember working all through the night with you, the other
apprentices and volunteers, armed with shovels and wheelbarrows,
to clear a foot of snow off the pitch so a game against Leeds could
take place.*

*You were incredibly proud of how the pitch looked, and rightly
so – it was always immaculate. Your enthusiasm and work ethic were
very much in evidence, and those values rubbed off on me.*

*You are a fantastic groundsman but more importantly, a really
nice guy. You should be proud of your achievements – you're a credit
to yourself, your family and the club you've served so well since 1979.*

*Every football club has unsung heroes and you are certainly one
of Cambridge United's. Thank you for the part you played in my career.
It has been a pleasure to work with you and to see you do well over all
those years.*

Andy Sinton

Cambridge United player 1982-86

Although John Ryan, who arrived at the Abbey as player-manager via a playing and coaching career that had taken in the likes of Norwich, Seattle Sounders, Sheffield United and Manchester City, came in for heavy criticism, he was brilliant towards me throughout his short time at the club.

He bought a house with a huge rear garden that was just a vast expanse of soil, so once again I ended up laying a lawn, this time embellishing my work by installing a putting green at the bottom of the garden. It was unfortunate that John, in one of his early local radio interviews, said there were quality players in the game who would be prepared to walk to Cambridge to play for him. To be fair, some of the players he was speaking to when I was round his house were big names, but they would have wanted sky-high wages that would have dwarfed United's budget.

A number of my mates – the likes of Stephen Pyle, Andy Sinton, Kevin Smith, Ray Nicholls, Keith Lockhart, Andy Beattie and Steve Clark – were now in the first-team squad. They had all done their time as apprentices and had worked with me on the pitch and in the stadium as part of their training, and I was desperate for them and the manager to do well.

Around this time John invited me to play in a practice game for the reserve team, and I made one of the biggest mistakes of my life when I crossed swords with the brilliant but fiery Tom Finney. My studs accidentally caught Tom on the back of a calf and he vented his fury by hissing, 'You dirty little punt.' At least I think that's what he hissed.

I knew I would have to watch my step, but I was unprepared for the ferocity of Tom's retribution: before a ball played into my feet had even arrived, I felt myself flying upwards like a Guy Fawkes Night rocket. I had achieved lift-off thanks to Tom's all-out assault from behind, and the only thing I could see was a vast, beautiful expanse of blue sky. Some time later, after getting clearance from air traffic control at local airport Marshall's, I re-entered the earth's atmosphere and made a heavy landing. Yes, I got the free kick; but to earn it I had had to receive payback from Belfast's finest.

After the game Tom came over and asked innocently, 'OK, son?' Which was nice. Being taken out by the Mighty Fin is a highlight of my career and to this day I remember every detail of the flight he sent me on.

We were still playing against some huge clubs and John Ryan's first game was against Chelsea. Due to their sheer numbers, half of the Abbey was given over to Blues supporters (some of my favourite human beings) and it was a game marred by truly awful crowd problems caused in part by what we in the trade term 'risk supporters' from our own city.

I remember that game – which ended in a 1-0 win for the Pensioners – especially well because it took place shortly before I lost another very close friend. When Les Holloway took up the position of chief executive at Doncaster Rovers, I was gutted.

The games came and went but none of them came or went well, and on April 14, after a draw at Middlesbrough, United's relegation from Division Two was confirmed. Relegation was a setback I'd not previously experienced, and I didn't like it one bit. A few weeks later, on 28 April 1984, we were at home to Newcastle, battling for promotion to Division One and boasting the legendary Kevin Keegan among their ranks. I was delighted when, before the game, Kevin congratulated me on the condition of the pitch, but even better was to come.

No one with more than a couple of brain cells at their disposal would have bet against a Magpies win, but the bookies hadn't reckoned on one of United's own Geordies. Kevin Smith (Stoat to his mates) scored from the penalty spot in the thirty-eighth minute and the U's held on for the 1-0 win that ended the club's – any English club's, for that matter – longest run without a League win. The last time the U's had tasted victory had been at the end of October, thirty-one long games before, when Oldham had been routed 2-1. No one around the Abbey minded much when Derby relieved us of the record in 2008.

A new season dawned with United playing in Division Three. Two more mates of mine – Kevin Massey and Mark Cooper – joined the first-team ranks and John Ryan continued his valued support for me. I was more than a little flummoxed, however, when JR – or Rhino, as he told reporters he preferred to be called – beckoned me into his office one morning to say he'd put a word in for me at a nearby golf course, where a greenkeeper was needed. John's attention was flattering and he doubtless believed that here was an ideal opportunity for me to move my career forward, but football was my game and I had no desire to leave United.

John ended up playing a few games himself in an effort to gee things up a bit. He certainly succeeded, but perhaps getting himself sent off twice in the space of four games was taking things a little too far. United's future was looking anything but secure.

A home game against York was looming but a ferocious blizzard blew in and put the game in doubt. This was serious – not only did the club need three points on the board, it was also desperate for the gate money. So it was that the ground staff, the manager and his assistant, players and volunteers including members of my family found themselves setting to work on the Friday night to clear hundreds of tonnes of snow from the pitch. We laboured all night and through to one o'clock on Saturday, and we got our reward when match referee Malcolm Cotton declared the pitch fit to play on.

So many people had worked so long and so hard to ensure the game went ahead that I was hoping the players could get a result for the two Johns. It was soon clear that hope was not enough. United went down to a 4-0 battering and, to rub salt into the wound, a number of supporters directed pithy comments towards me after the game: don't bother next time; you should have left the snow on the pitch; you should have piled the snow up in the goals – at least we would have got a point. It's not what you want to hear when your mates' jobs are on the line.

JR was sacked shortly afterwards – yet another good friend gone – and once again John Cozens landed the caretaker's job. Cozy instantly got a response out of the players, who drew the next three games.

It was around this time that my old mate Malcolm Webster struck again. Webby, in charge for a third round game in the East Anglian Cup, was in a bit of a pickle. He had a tiny squad at his disposal and, given that no first-teamers were to be involved, his side consisted of apprentices, injured players who needed a game and a couple of trialists. But what Malcolm needed most was someone to drive the team's Toyota minibus up the A10 to King's Lynn.

Having cornered me in the car park, he made me an offer I couldn't refuse. 'I know you're itching to get your boots on,' he said, quite correctly. 'Here's the deal: you drive us to the game and you can be on the subs' bench. I'll give you at least twenty minutes on the park, promise.'

To say I was excited to be getting a run-out with the lads would be to understate the case, and the old nerves were flapping as I drove the forty-five miles to the north Norfolk coast. Webby could see I was agitated in the changing room, but the only words of solace he offered were: 'Here's your kit.' I got changed and sat down, by this time desperate for a Jimmy Riddle but not daring to miss the team talk. I must have been jiggling my legs quite violently, for Malcolm demanded to know what the hell was wrong. 'I'm bursting for a slash,' was my urgent reply. Malcolm sighed and directed me through a door.

Following his directions to the letter, I was surprised to find myself outside, mingling with curious spectators beside the pitch. There were some helpful enquiries from the stand: are you lost, boy? What, are you playing on your own? Turning back to the dressing room door in some confusion, I discovered that Webby had turned the key and, silently cursing his guts, I was forced to resume my place on the touchline, the only visible sign for miles around that Cambridge United were in town. When I was finally allowed back into the dressing room, the lads naturally made the most of this priceless opportunity to rip the piss.

To be fair to him – although, frankly, I don't see why I should – Malcolm was as good as his word and I got my twenty minutes on the right wing. I was no worse than some of the others on the pitch, but we got stuffed 3-0. The following day, Evening News reporter Randall Butt wrote that United were so short of players that the club groundsman had had to make up the numbers. I thought that was a bit harsh.

My first chance to play for the reserves had come while John Cozens was assistant manager to John Doc. The reserves were due to play at QPR but were a sub short. 'Ian,' called Cozy, 'get a change of clothes and your boots and be back here in thirty minutes. You can come along.'

I always kept my boots handy in my office but I needed a decent set of clothes. With no time to get home, I had to shoot back to my parents' house and grab a pair of bro Richard's 30-waist trousers and a pair of his size 7 shoes. I was desperate to play and ignored the fact that I was a size 32 waist and took a size 8 shoe.

Breathing in, I hared back to the stadium in time to catch the minibus and clambered aboard, wincing with foot pain. It was pain in vain: the Doc appeared and enquired: 'What are you doing? Get off the bus.' Gutted.

Mr Wally Rookes … I knew it wouldn't be long before that name cropped up again.

I'd known Wally since my earliest days at United. Some people thought he was no more than a moaning old git; he was actually much worse than that. But he could be a very funny man, and he didn't give a hoot what he said or to whom he said it. His help with countless tasks around the stadium – painting, sweeping, minor maintenance, cleaning the toilets; just about anything you asked him to do – was priceless. And Wally always had a great rapport with the work experience kids. For some reason they loved working with him, and several of them wrote to the club saying what an absolute legend he was.

I'm sure other people who have to maintain areas used by the public have similar experiences, but some of the things that go on inside a football ground make your hair stand on end. Let me recount a story in which Wally was a protagonist.

Following one home game, Wally was cleaning the toilets while my assistant Trevor Ball and I were working on the pitch. We became aware that Wally was scuttling towards us, flapping his hands like a tic-tac man with the DTs and yelling loud enough to frighten the horses on the Common. 'You've got to come and see this,' he screeched. 'I ain't never seen anything like it in my life!'

We marched with the urgently beckoning Wally over to the men's toilet block behind the Habbin stand, wondering what kind of wind-up he was working on. He could spin a good yarn, no doubt about it, but this time he seemed genuinely unable to believe what he'd seen. Sure enough, the sight that greeted our disbelieving eyes was enough to make them water. There, sitting proudly in a toilet pan, was quite simply the biggest turd a human being could possibly produce.

'What a bloody beauty!' crowed Wally as Trevor pondered getting the Guinness Book of Records on the phone. We stared incredulously at the faecal behemoth, which was almost the full length of the pan and had the diameter of a full-size baked beans can. Surely no human could have passed this elephantine specimen without screaming the house down and being rushed off to Addenbrooke's for emergency stitching?

Wally had flushed the loo ten times or more, he insisted, but the shit just brushed the water off. There was only one thing to do: he would have to cut the bloody thing up into bits before he could flush it. But the turd, which we'd christened Richard and had the consistency of clay, was having none of any efforts to dissect it. It refused point-blank to surrender.

Wally thought for a minute, disappeared and came back with a road iron – one of those metre-long spikes you see holding the safety tapes around a hole in the road. Trevor and I exchanged nervous glances and prepared to flee, but our man swiftly harpooned his monstrous prey and lifted it clean out of the pan in one piece, exclaiming 'Bugger, that's heavy'.

Trevor and I lifted the lid of a manhole so that Wally could send the torpedo on its way, but it wasn't beaten yet. There it lay in the sewer gulley, staring triumphantly back at us as we swooshed gallon after gallon of water over it with encouraging cries of 'On your way, you bastard!' Finally it seemed to have had enough fun for one day and, with a revolting gurgle, disappeared into oblivion.

There was a similar event in a ladies' toilet, and naturally Wally was involved. Normally we aim to clean all the toilets the day after a game, but on this occasion the last game of the season had just been played and we were desperate to get cracking on pitch maintenance. Under burning early-May skies, we spent several days hollow-coring the pitch and then removing the cores, and it was over a week before we got round to the toilet-cleaning chores.

Wally had been off cleaning the toilets for an hour or so when he came back with that all-too familiar grin adorning his craggy features.

'Have you ever been to a tampon race?' he enquired. In response to my mystified reaction he added: 'You'd better come and have a look.'

Some of the things you come across in women's loos don't even get discussed on Loose Women. We've provided disposal bins for sanitary products for decades, but it's not uncommon for female visitors to leave used tampons draped over toilet handles for their fellow supporters to discover. Classy touch, ladies.

It was therefore with some trepidation that I strolled as nonchalantly as I could into the toilet in question. 'There you are,' said Wally triumphantly. 'Ever seen a tampon with legs? Shall we have a little bet on how long it takes to reach the wall?'

My horrified gaze followed his pointing finger. A used tampon had been discarded on the floor and, alive with maggots following a few days of warm weather, was shuffling slowly towards the wall.

It's not all about the ladies, of course. Men's toilets are often left in the most disgusting conditions imaginable, and many's the time we've had to don waterproof suits before venturing beyond the door. It was common in the Eighties for visiting supporters to write their clubs' names on toilet walls, not in nice felt-tip as you might expect but in their own faeces, or leave us a delightful gift in the form of a crap-filled urinal.

You have to have your wits about you when you're cleaning loos. We've been caught out a few times when the toilet pan and seat appear clean but when you put the lid down you find someone has left you a stinky gift. That's one of the reasons we very seldom have lids on our toilets these days. It eliminates the element of surprise, shall we say.

Where was I? In the 1984-85 season, I believe.

Changes were taking place on the board and Tony Douglas and Jack Cooke moved on. I was hugely disappointed as they had both been instrumental in me getting the job at United. The directors then appointed a new first-team manager: Ken Shellito, the former Chelsea and England full back who had also served as manager at Stamford Bridge.

Ken, always immaculately turned out, was polite to me but for some reason his outlook never seemed that positive. He fired John Cozens from the assistant manager post – another friend put out to grass – and Malcolm Webster became his assistant. That was good news for me as Webby and I had such a good working relationship, despite the constant banter and jolly japes.

To state the obvious, results didn't improve and I witnessed our second League relegation – only the third in the history of the club – when we found ourselves looking up at everyone else from the bottom of Division Three. Would this have happened, I wondered privately, if John Docherty had been given more time? There must always be winners and losers but I was learning that supporters and players can and do control team managers with their actions and performances.

We set about the end-of-season pitch renovation, putting the focus on aeration and using sports field sand rather than a soil dressing. We hollow-cored at three-inch centres to a depth of four inches, so four holes would be punched in every foot of turf, throwing out a soil plug and helping to relieve the compaction; we hammered the pitch with a Twose aerator; we followed by over-seeding and top-dressing with a hundred tonnes of sand; and once everything had germinated and settled down the pitch looked amazing. The compliments from supporters looking around the stadium while buying their season tickets were very gratifying.

A new season in Division Four started and I went back to my fancy cutting patterns – circles with diamonds, diagonal cuts with squares through the middle, curves from halfway to the corner flags. This kind of pitch creativity was still not common at the time, and visiting teams were quick to comment about the quality of the playing surface.

During the close season, Ken had signed a couple of players with whom I became friendly in Stephen Massey and David Crown, but David Moyes, whom I'd driven to the railway station a couple of times to save him getting the bus, departed after being sold to Bristol City.

Sadly, once again results on the pitch were not good enough and it was no surprise, as late summer became autumn, to hear that Ken had resigned. He'd advised me a few days earlier that the club was broke and it was time to find myself another job. The outlook seemed bleak for Ian Darler as well as for Cambridge United.

There were challenging times ahead, but what happened next was like a dream come true. The man appointed as the new team manager was my old nemesis Chris Turner, who had been working on a building site, and it came as no surprise to me that results were quickly on an upturn. The atmosphere around the club changed the moment Chris walked through the door.

CHAPTER 6

—

TURNS AND TWISTS

Dear Ian,

We met when you were searching desperately for training facilities. Our ground wasn't used much during the week, and I thought it would be good to be involved with the football club. What started out as a trial lasted twenty-five years.

You used to get phone calls from other League clubs, when they were on their way to Norwich or Ipswich, who needed a top-quality playing surface for training. Your pleas for help often came at short notice but it was a feather in my cap to be able to accommodate top-class clubs like Leeds. It was great to see the likes of Eric Cantona, Gary McAllister and Gordon Strachan on my pitches.

I love my beer, so for me to get a few cans a year, plus the occasional bottle of wine for my wife, as fees for hire of the sports ground went down well. I reckon we probably saved the club around half a million over the years.

You say I've helped you win so many groundsman of the year awards by accommodating the United players, cutting the amount of time they spent on the Abbey pitch. Not everything's about money, and helping somebody out is what life is all about.

Colin Dunne

Former head groundsman,
Christ's & Sydney Sussex Colleges' sports ground

As soon as Chris Turner had got his feet under the desk, he tasked me with finding some proper training grounds. Luckily for us, the grounds belonging to the colleges that make up the University of Cambridge are superbly maintained, and the lads in charge of them have always helped out fantastically.

Colin Dunne, who looked after the Christ's and Sydney Sussex ground, continued to help out four days a week, as he had since Malcolm Webster had asked me to help to secure training facilities during Ken Shellito's time. Colin's exorbitant fee? A few cans of beer, a bottle of wine now and then and the odd match ticket. This arrangement continued for twenty-five years, saving Cambridge United something like half a million quid at the prevailing hire rates.

And the pitches that Colin and his assistant Graham Clark produced were not only truly outstanding, they also catered for all kinds of weather. Come rain, come shine, come drought, ice, snow or plague of frogs, we hardly ever lost a day's training.

I was forever getting requests from managers at other clubs for a training ground when they were playing at Ipswich or Norwich. Dave 'Harry' Bassett was a frequent caller when he was at Sheffield United and Howard Wilkinson was often on the blower from Leeds. Colin took these requests in his stride and was rewarded by the likes of Eric Cantona and Gordon Strachan training on his pitches, but what was really great for Colin was a word of congratulation from Wilkinson. The quality of his playing surfaces, said Wilko, was as good as any he had seen.

Ron Pearce at King's College allowed us to use his field on Fridays, again in return for no more than the occasional ticket. Trevor Munns at Pembroke also helped out, along with the blokes at Trinity College.

All this vital help from willing college groundsmen didn't stop Messrs Turner and Webster asking to use the Abbey Stadium pitch for the occasional practice match and training session. Aren't I a lucky boy? The size of the first-team squad and injuries meant they often struggled to raise twenty-two players, so I got the occasional run-out along with Trevor Ball. As ever with Chris, it was seldom plain sailing.

In one of these practice matches Chris had a trialist lad playing wide right for the stiffs, while I was at right back. At one point he and I played a nice little series of one-twos that led to a juicy cross into the first-team box. Lindsay 'Wolfie' Smith headed it well clear but the ball dropped just right for me to smash a volley past keeper Keith Branagan from twenty-five yards. I was chuffed to bits but Chris quickly burst my bubble. 'No goal, you little shit,' he sniggered. 'It was offside.' Offside, my arse. After the game Keith was calling me Zico.

Randall Butt, the U's reporter on the Cambridge Evening News, asked the trialist how he thought it had gone. The lad replied that he would play with the right back any day of the week, a remark to which Chris, the self-titled King of the Jungle, took exception. 'Play with the right back?' he harrumphed. 'That's the forking groundsman!' Or words to that effect.

Graham Scarff, the youth team manager at the time, was also responsible for the reserve team that played on Saturday afternoons and – guess what? – he struggled to field a full team. So I and the two Trevors – T Ball, my assistant, and T George, the local beat bobby – still got opportunities to get our boots on. One game from that time stands out in the memory simply because the ref, feeling the winter gloom growing, asked for the floodlights to be turned on. 'No problem, ref,' we said. 'But you'll have to stop the game. Both of the ground staff are playing.' He obligingly called a short halt while T Ball ran off to the dressing rooms, retrieved his keys and turned on the lights.

Another opportunity for Trevor Ball and I to star presented itself one Saturday evening, after the first team had lost away. I was relaxing at home by flicking through the latest issue of Total Carp magazine when a call came through from the King of the Jungle. 'Can we use the pitch for some crossing and shooting tomorrow?' he asked, in a tone that suggested it was not so much a request as a demand. 'These players don't know where the goal is. Go on, you and Bally can join in if you want.'

In the morning the players duly trooped into the ground and paired off for the start of the session. Trevor was instructed to play the ball forward from the centre circle to a static player on the eighteen-yard line. The latter was then to play it back for Trevor, who would pass it out wide to me and I would supply a cross. Trevor was expected to get into the box for the strike – and at the first time of asking he slipped my pinpoint cross past the keeper, Paul Bastock.

The attacking players then took their turns. Honestly, it was more like watching the Chipperfield's Circus clowns on Midsummer Common than a bunch of professional footballers practising their shooting. Balls were flying everywhere – over the Corona End roof, into the front car park and possibly into the Globe pub the other side of Newmarket Road, into the terrace and out again, whistling past the Supporters' Club and threatening the pools office windows.

My turn came. I pinged a ball out wide for Trevor to cross and, racing into the area, drilled it without ceremony into the net.

The strikers carried on shooting and, to be fair to them, the occasional ball did end up in the net, but Turns was growing more frantic and red in the face by the second. 'Come on, hit the forking target,' he bawled. 'My wife Lynne could do better than you lot!' The session ended with him announcing that he was delighted to be managing a team whose best strikers were the bloody ground staff.

It was about this time that funny things started occurring in my lunchbox.

Every day I would bring a couple of sandwiches to work and leave the box in the groundsman's office. Hungry after a morning's graft and looking forward to getting stuck into the cheese and pickle,

I would tear open the box to find that some kind person had taken a bite out of every sarnie and carefully replaced the lid. And this was happening every flipping day.

Admittedly, my sandwich security standards were less than rigorous. We sometimes locked the room, but we tended to be in and out all the time and more often than not would just pull the door to. So I took to hiding my lunch in places I thought a sandwich thief would never look – but he or she was too good for me, and carried on munching.

Several weeks went by and I was thoroughly pissed off, not to mention hungry. One day, walking into the unlit office, I froze as I made out a huge silhouetted figure taking a leisurely bite out of my ham and mustard on wholemeal. I snapped on the light to catch the culprit in the act and found myself looking at none other than Chris Turner, blinking and grinning devilishly. 'It's you, you bastard!' I spluttered. Chris carried on chewing and, spitting out semi-masticated morsels as he spoke, observed: 'It took you long enough.'

This matter wasn't over, not by a long chalk. Contemplating revenge, I had a word with physio Peter Melville, a fellow victim of the King of the Jungle's mischief. Our plans started to come to fruition when, a few days later, Chris rolled up at work in a brand new Mercedes and parked up at the front of the ground.

When he and the players had set off to the training ground, Pete sauntered into my office, a satisfied smile on his mug and jingling a set of car keys above his head. 'Look what I've got,' he bragged. 'Found them in Chris's pocket.'

Aghast but also thrilled, I asked the pickpocket what he intended to do with them. 'We'll hide his motor round the back of Cut Throat Lane,' he suggested. I made the valid point, and I made it forcefully, that if Turns found out the identities of the perpetrators of this fiendish act, he would throttle them with those colossal paws of his and hang their corpses from a crossbar. 'He won't find out,' said Pete, and the grin spread to all corners of his face. He seemed confident, which was more than I was.

In fact I was bricking it as Pete drove the Merc out of the car park, along Newmarket Road and into Cut Throat Lane, and parked it in one of the lane's dark recesses. When the players started getting back to the ground, we hid in the front turnstile block and, sniggering like schoolboys, awaited Chris's return in the HiAce minibus.

The bus pulled in, Chris emerged and the effect when he noticed a yawning gap where his precious Merc should be was instantaneous: in full panic mode, he stalked to and fro like a more manic Basil Fawlty, holding his head and groaning like a St Bernard winded by a runaway sledge. I have to admit, it was a great feeling to get one over on the cause of so many humiliations.

But split-second timing was now crucial if we were to come out of this escapade alive. The moment Chris stepped up into the Portakabin office, Pete was off like a hare to Cut Throat Lane, hurling himself into the Merc and endangering a few cyclists on Newmarket Road as he swung into the car park, deposited the shiny new motor a few spaces away from where it had been nicked from and furtively slipped the keys back into the Turner trouser pocket.

Back in our hiding place, we watched with interest, which grew into a sense of unease and then alarm, as a police panda car pulled into the car park. Chris had obviously reported the dastardly theft of his beloved car.

He hurried out of the office, but not before the two coppers had spotted the Merc miraculously restored to the car park. 'Is this your car, Mr Turner?' a fresh-faced young constable enquired. Chris's face was a picture of mystified incomprehension and he put a finger to his lips as his brain ticked over.

It was time to retire and we crept away, stifling our laughter. The King of the Jungle never did get to the bottom of the mystery of the missing Merc.

This act of revenge helped me to relieve some of the pressure of the embarrassments Chris Turner had heaped on my head, but the comfort was short-lived.

The next episode of the saga came during a spell of crappy weather and heavy snow. I was inside, carrying out a repair on a toilet, when someone knocked on the outer door. I know I should have exercised some caution but I wasn't thinking. On opening the door I was greeted by Chris with a snowball as big as a space hopper raised above his head. It crashed down on my bonce with immense force, and I can tell you honestly that I've seldom experienced as much pain. If that wasn't bad enough, I was also soaked to the skin.

'Got you, Darler,' said Turns simply as he turned on his heel and swaggered off down the corridor.

I was bloody fuming but not too muzzy-headed to be unable to plan my retaliation. I knew Chris normally walked underneath the police control box, which in those days sat at the north end of the east touchline, to get back to the car park at the front of the ground. Clambering on to the flat roof next to the control box, I spent an age in rolling up a huge snowball and waited, wet through, freezing my bollocks off and shivering like a dog, for the enemy to appear.

I was just about to say 'Sod this for a game of soldiers,' and head for a warm shower when a shouted greeting drifted over from the Habbin terrace, on the other side of the ground. 'See you in the morning, Ian!' yelled Turns, wrapped up snug in a nice warm overcoat and making his way home via an unaccustomed route. The bastard had sussed me out.

My initial reaction was to curse and gnash my teeth – the oversized git had done it again – but then I stopped and thought a bit. I'd probably had a lucky escape, I realised: I might have killed the bugger if I'd dropped half a hundredweight of snowball on his skull from height.

———————————

I was still good friends with the apprentices and was often called into the match officials' room, which Chris, Webby and Graham Scarff used for their ablutions, so I knew Chris's post-training routine to a T.

Woe betide the kids if the big man's bath wasn't ready when he returned from the training ground. After a good, long soak the King of the Jungle would jump out and cover himself from head to toe with Johnson's Baby Powder. The act of dressing never varied: the first items of clothing to go on were always his socks, pulled up as high as they would go.

My office was still being ransacked, my lunchbox was still being tampered with and I was still hungry – for revenge, mostly. As the days and weeks went by, a fiendish plan took shape in the Darler brain and I couldn't help convulsing with laughter whenever I thought about it.

One day, after waiting for the lads and coaching staff to head off to the training ground, I crept into the officials' room armed with a sharp pair of scissors. My heart was racing as I reached down to one of Chris's training shoes, extracted a sock, cut the end off and carefully returned it to its resting place. Now I'd had some practice, the second sock was a little easier.

Malcolm Webster was in the daily habit of dropping into my office – at the other end of the main stand to the officials' room – for a lunchtime cup of tea. That particular day I was eating what was left of my sandwiches when he appeared in the doorway with a stupid grin on his chops. 'Chris has gone mad down the bottom,' he chortled. I knew what was coming next. 'He's getting dressed after his bath, pulls on a sock and it goes up to his thigh. He's storming round the dressing room asking who's responsible.'

Inside I was crying with laughter but I managed somehow to keep a straight face. Just as well, too – Malcolm could read me like a book.

The following day I repeated the surreptitious sock surgery, and when Malcolm appeared in my office for his cuppa his face was as red as a Liverpool shirt, tears were rolling down his cheeks and he was running his fingers through his luxuriant bandido moustache. 'Whatever's the matter with you?' I asked innocently. 'Someone's only cut the toes out of Chris's socks again,' he guffawed.

There was no way this time that I could hold back the laughter and Malcolm twigged immediately. 'It was you, you little sod!' he gulped. 'Damn right,' I replied. 'It was payback.'

Webby could see the funny side but he was also worried. 'Ian,' he said, 'you've got to own up. Turns is really mad – he's going to have the players in for training on Sunday unless someone puts their hands up, even if they win.'

I confess I hadn't really thought this part of the scheme through, but I now knew I had to face the Jungle King's wrath. Calling on the Darler fighting spirit, I marched boldly down to the dressing rooms and knocked on Chris's door. 'What do you bloody well want, you little shit?' he growled as I inched into the room.

'Chris, it was me,' I admitted.

'What was you?' he demanded, looking me up and down like a tiger sizing up a nice juicy deer.

'I cut your socks up,' I mumbled, expecting the tiger to pounce and my guts to be used to decorate the room like some gory kind of Christmas tinsel.

'Oh, OK,' said the tiger, lowering his voice. 'Thanks for owning up. Now get out.'

This unexpected reaction was extremely worrying; I would have preferred the tiger treatment there and then. I knew in my heart of hearts that this was not the end of the story, and wasn't very heartened by Malcolm's grim 'good luck, mate' when I told him what had happened.

I was on my guard for weeks and Chris's placid behaviour continued. 'Everything OK, boy?' he would ask every morning, following up with a kindly 'Bless you, boy.' I knew he was the complete professional and, when there was a job to be done, prank mode would be switched off instantly. But still, something wasn't right. It was too damn quiet, as they used to say in the cowboy films.

We had a home game in the offing. The pitch was saturated and there were several areas of standing water. Some serious forking was required, and I went to my store shed in search of fork, waterproofs and wellingtons. It was there that the shape of Chris's retribution became clear: the toes of my wellies had been neatly clipped off at the bridge.

I took my medicine. Off came the socks, on went the wellingtons and out I went, toes and a goodly expanse of feet exposed, to get some forking in.

Chris wandered out to see how the work was going and doubled up with gales of laughter when he beheld me forking away in the open-toed wellies. When he could catch his breath he drove home his message: 'Never mess with the King of the Jungle, son.'

The staff Christmas party, to be held at the Caxton Motel, was approaching and club secretary Phil Hough asked me to tell Trevor Ball the details. 'What's the dress code?' I asked. 'Smart casual,' he replied, 'but wait a minute. Tell Bally it's fancy dress and there'll be a cash prize and a bottle of champagne for the best costume.'

To my astonishment, Trevor believed every word and asked what Phil was going to wear. He'd had taken the bait, I told Phil later, and he let all the other staff in on the joke. If Trev asked about the dinner, he told them, they were to make something up about their outfits. Phil, who was quite a sizeable lad, told Trevor he was going as Friar Tuck.

The dinner wasn't mentioned for a few weeks, until one day Trevor said his mum (who was by now in on the prank) had been working hard on his outfit. She'd made an Andy Pandy suit, he announced proudly as I disguised a giggle as a coughing fit.

His mum phoned me at work: could I pop round to her house when Trevor was at the stadium? When she came to the door she was laughing so hard that the tears were flowing, and I soon saw why: Trevor would be modelling the most amazing Andy Pandy suit it's possible to imagine, decorated by anything and everything connected to the festive season: crackers, baubles, tinsel, the holly and the ivy, you name it. The three wise men were probably on there somewhere, but not if they were that wise.

Trevor's mum, between laughing and coughing fits, then said he'd had a brainwave: surely, if he were to have a chance of carrying off the prizes, his suit should have some flashing lights on it?

The plot thickened. I informed Trev that my wife Sharon, who was six and a half months pregnant with our son Liam, was going as the Virgin Mary. But there was a downside to Phil's genius scheme: I had offered to drive Trevor to the motel and couldn't give the game away by turning up in my usual suit. I managed to get hold of an ankle-length, long-sleeved Arab dishdasha, which would conceal the whistle I would be wearing underneath.

The big day arrived and we picked Trevor up, drove to Caxton (ignoring the grisly sight of the seventeenth century gibbet nearby; I don't think it's much used to display the rotting corpses of executed criminals nowadays) and parked up. As Sharon and our victim made their entrance, and as I struggled out of my dishdasha in the car, a wave of loud and raucous cheering burst out of the building.

'Bally,' enquired a solicitous Phil, 'why on earth are you dressed like that?' Trev was unflappable. 'Don't you worry about me,' he grinned. 'Wait and see what Ian looks like.' It was unfortunate for him that I chose that moment to waltz in flaunting my dress suit.

He still saw the humour of the situation. Not only was he a good sport; not only did he get his hands on the cash and the champagne; he also drank enough to give the original Andy Pandy a poor reputation as a toddlers' TV idol. Time to go home, time to go home, Bally is waving goodbye.

No one, not even a respected member of the local constabulary, was safe during the King of the Jungle's reign of terror.

I've already mentioned PC Trevor George. He worked the local beat and was also the Cambridge force's football liaison officer, and his dual role meant he spent several hours of every week at the stadium. The banter between him and Turns would at times spill over into utter stupidity.

During one of Trevor's visits Chris noticed that he hadn't locked up his bike – a bad example of crime prevention in action if you ask me. Sneaking into the ground staff's yard, Chris found a length of blue rope that was ideal for his purpose – hoisting Trevor's pushbike up at a fair old height inside one of the floodlight pylons.

PC George would happily admit that he was never the quickest to respond to radio calls, but there was no denying the urgency of the message that came through to the football club's control room that day: he was required to respond immediately, if not sooner, to a serious incident. Trevor could move quite rapidly when he needed to, and he raced outside with a steely, determined look on his face. That soon changed to horror, and then panic, when he realised his bike was missing, presumed nicked.

The King of the Jungle, who as fate would have it happened to be loitering outside the control room, at first seemed as concerned as the pride of the Cambs Constabulary. 'What's the matter, Plod?' he asked. Trevor had been around the Abbey long enough to pick up some of the groundsman's lingo. 'My forking bike's gone missing and I've had a shout,' he howled.

Realisation dawned quite quickly and he whirled round to face the K of the J. 'Where is it? he demanded. 'Where have you put my forking pushbike?'

Chris reacted coolly. 'Let's have a game of hot and cold,' he suggested. But Trevor was in no mood for games. 'Stop pissing about and tell me where you've put it,' he snapped, his face white with fury.

'Trevor, Trevor,' replied Turns with a patronising smile. 'My dear Plod, calm yourself! You'll do yourself a mischief. Now, do you want your bike or not?'

The seconds were ticking by, a small but amused audience was gathering and Trevor came to the sickening conclusion that he had no choice but to play Chris's game.

'Cold,' announced Chris as his victim hopped about like a squirrel robbed of his nuts. 'Colder! Warmer! Very warm, hot!' Trevor was standing slap-bang under the pylon and his face had by now changed colour to a nasty shade of puce. Not once did he think about looking upwards, until he spied the telltale blue rope tied off on a pylon strut and the game was up. 'You twat!' he swore as his trusty steed was lowered to the ground.

Chris saved his punchline for the moment his dupe leapt aboard and started pedalling furiously away. 'What's the hurry?' he shouted after the retreating figure. 'Has someone nicked a cake from Nell Gwyn's shop?'

Trevor's reply was the old two-fingered salute. I'm sure they don't teach that at police training college.

CHAPTER 7

—

THE WISDOM OF BECK

Dear Ian,

As I started my first game for United, the furthest thing from my mind was the state of your pitch, but little did I know that over the next thirty years a lot of my time would be spent on that fantastic surface.

During our association, as a player, supporter and manager, your ability to produce a pitch of Premiership standards has been second to none. It's as good at the end of the season as at the start although, knowing the perfection you require, your opinion may be different.

What you were required to do to the pitch during John Beck's tenure helped our style, so it wasn't too bad for us. But I can only imagine the torture you went through seeing your beloved area of grass turned into Blackpool beach.

The dignity you showed, when you had created something of beauty and were asked to go against your principles, was extraordinary. Lesser men than you would have walked away.

John Taylor

Cambridge United player 1988-92 & 1996-2004, manager 2001-04

The end of the 1993-94 season was on the horizon when I was called to the office to receive some excellent news. The club had been told that our pitch had been judged one of the top three in the Football League. We would be receiving a visit from an independent judge who would decide the winner of the Groundsman of the Year award. Yes, though I say so myself, the pitch did look in top condition for the time of season.

The inspection was carried out by Dr Steven Baker from the Sports Turf Research Institute. Naturally, he gave nothing away during his visit, but it was subsequently confirmed that we would be awarded the top accolade. Was I chuffed by this recognition from my greenkeeping peers? Just a bit.

We were nominated again two years later and, although we failed to win the title this time, received a commendation. But we were back in a posh hotel four years later when we were again awarded the Groundsman of the Year title.

Chris Turner, football club manager and prankmaster general, loved his cricket. Capable of playing at a good standard himself, he was always talking about his batsman brother-in-law Wayne Larkins, who appeared in thirteen Tests for England and was also, incidentally, no mean footballer, having been on Notts County's books in his youth.

One morning Turns rolled up to work announcing that he needed eleven players for a charity match in the village of Bluntisham, and a team was quickly assembled. Club secretary Phil 'KitKat' Hough was a bit handy with a bat; United fan and radio sports all-rounder Mark Saggers, who had played at Minor Counties level for Cambridgeshire, was wicketkeeper; and I was informed that I was playing – not asked, just informed – because Chris was aware that I was OK with a bat in my hand. I can't quite recall if I mentioned at the time that I hadn't played for several years.

The night of the game arrived to the familiar sound of merciless banter and piss-taking flying around the pavilion, despite the presence of wives and girlfriends. The United boys went in first and Chris – who else? – opened the batting with KitKat. I, down in the scorebook at number four, was eagerly awaiting my return to the crease.

Chris and Phil put on a good few runs for the first wicket before the latter was bowled. Batsman number three didn't last long, bowled by the last ball of the over, so I soon found myself heading out to the wicket. Chris seemed to be taking the contest very seriously: he came to meet me halfway to the square and gave me a good talking-to. 'Back me up,' he urged. 'I'll take the batting.'

He took guard and, tapping the first ball of the next over towards square leg, roared 'Yes!' I responded to his call and sprinted down the wicket towards Turns – who hadn't moved an inch and was beaming from ear to ear (which in Chris's case was quite a distance). 'No!' he yelled, loud enough to wake the dead.

I stopped on a sixpence, turned and hurtled back to my crease but it was hopeless – I was run out by a country mile and the bastard's laughter was ringing out loud around the ground.

Run out without facing a single ball, I mouthed 'you twat' at the perpetrator of this foul deed, but his mirth only increased. Then came another call from the big man – 'Ian!' I turned, foolishly thinking he was going to apologise, but his parting shot as I turned again and trudged back to the pavilion, swearing vengeance under my breath, was: 'Thanks for coming.'

He wasn't finished yet. Mark Saggers, batting at number five, got exactly the same treatment, run out without facing a ball. Mark is a lot more polite than me. 'Why,' he wanted to know, 'would you do that,

Chris?' The only answer he got was a reappearance of the mischievous grin, as wide as goal posts.

At the end of the match, I need hardly add, everything was back to normal; as far as Chris was concerned, we were all good mates. 'I thought you said you could bat, Ian,' he murmured. 'My Lynne could have done better than that.'

The quality of the playing surface had been drawing attention, and it made the headlines when United played Coventry in the Littlewoods Cup on 22 September 1987 and Sky Blues gaffer John Sillett went public on the subject. '"Better than Wembley" was the accolade for the Cambridge United pitch from Coventry manager John Sillett, and he should know,' read the Evening News report. 'Having led Coventry to FA cup glory at Wembley only five months before, Sillett said the pitch was superb, the best he had seen for a very long time.'

John's praise didn't end with his comments to the press. He then asked Colin Proctor, a supporter since 1947 and a prominent member of the Vice-Presidents' Club, how many staff looked after the pitch. Colin pointed to me and Trevor. 'What?' spluttered John. 'Just two lads produce a surface like that? Unbelievable.'

I was surprised a few weeks later to hear that a new head groundsman was being sought for Highfield Road, and astonished when I was invited to an interview. I was honest and open with the United directors, told them about the interview and asked their permission to attend. It was granted promptly.

So it was that I found myself one day in the Post House Hotel in Crick, near Rugby. Nervous? Please bear in mind that I'd only ever attended one other interview. I approached the reception desk surreptitiously wiping my sweaty palms on the seat of my suit trousers,

110

and my nerves grew throughout the few minutes I had to wait for John Sillett to appear.

I need not have been so anxious. John was welcoming and friendly and exhibited a bubbly personality. 'Now then,' he assured me, 'you're my man but we've got some other fellas to interview before you. Get a bite to eat and a drink in the restaurant. I'll come and get you in an hour or so.'

To be honest, I didn't feel much like eating or drinking, and the hour dragged. At last I was called up to a suite to meet four or five club officials, who included the vice-chairman Ted Stocker OBE. John, sitting opposite, gave me a reassuring smile as the questions started. Can you tell us how you produce a surface like the one we saw a few weeks ago? How much do you spend? What machinery have you got?

I was growing uneasy as the questioning went on. There were one or two sighs around the table to start with; then came the laughter, which was initiated by John. 'Told you so,' he told his fellow interviewers, then turned to me. 'I've already told them most of the things you've mentioned. They didn't believe anyone could produce a pitch better than Wembley with a staff of two, a staggeringly low budget and basic machines.'

I was feeling a lot more comfortable now, and the interview changed direction to 'We would like to offer you the position of head groundsman at Coventry City.' Ted read out what they proposed to offer me and my chin bounced off the floor – the salary would more than double what I was earning at United. They agreed to provide free accommodation for the first three months of my employment, with an extension to six months if I paid half of the cost; they would pay £2,000 towards my solicitor's fees and £1,000 in disturbance allowance; I would be working with an annual pitch budget equivalent to around six years' spending at the Abbey Stadium.

It wasn't that I didn't trust anyone around the table but my mate Chris Turner's words, impressed on me a day or so before, were clattering around in my head: get it in writing, son. I was nervous about asking for written confirmation but Ted immediately took out a pen and wrote the details down on headed paper. 'Welcome to Coventry City,' he said, handing it across the table.

John asked if I would follow him back to Highfield Road to have a look at the pitch. Once at the ground I was taken up to the directors' box and from there experienced a flashback to what I'd seen that first time at United: once again a game was in progress and once again the pitch was bloody awful.

John thanked me for attending the interview and said he was pleased I'd been offered the job. And with that I headed home. I'd had a pleasantly warm welcome at Coventry and they'd all seemed such nice blokes. But as I made slow progress down the M6, doubts started flooding into my brain. Would the new role mean that I wouldn't have to beg, steal and borrow to produce a good surface? Would it mean I wouldn't have to buy my own machines to use on the pitch, as I did at the Abbey?

The following day Reg Smart, who had succeeded David Ruston as United chairman, came to ask how I'd got on. When I told him I'd been offered the head groundsman's job, he said: 'We can discuss it over lunch.' A little later he was back in his Mercedes and whisked me off to a pub in the nearby village of Horningsea.

Lunch at the Plough and Fleece made a nice change from squatting in a dingy office eating whatever Chris Turner had graciously consented to leave me. Over a highly acceptable steak and chips, Reg wanted to know what Coventry had offered and, when I told him what the employment package covered and what wage was on the table, he laughed out loud. 'Who are you trying to kid?' he chuckled. 'They wouldn't offer to double your wage with all those other benefits.' But he was quick to apologise when I reached into my pocket and produced a copy of the offer. 'Hm. So what do you want to do?' he asked.

'I'm very happy at United and would like to stay,' I assured him.

There was now a hint of panic in Reg's voice and he looked flustered. 'We can't pay you anything like what they're offering,' he protested, 'but I'll speak to the other directors.'

I'd never seen Reg look like this before, but I think he knew he was getting a good deal with me. Following the awful Valley Parade fire in Bradford in 1985, in which fifty-six people lost their lives and at least 265 were injured, I'd taken on the role of stadium manager alongside the head groundsman title, but I'd had no pay rise reflecting the extra responsibilities.

Later that day Reg came back with a revised contract offer that was still a million miles away from what Coventry were proposing. But, he said, if I stayed at the club the offer would benefit me in the future. At that point I broached a subject I'd been mulling over for some time. If I agreed to stay at the Abbey, could I run my own business in my own time? Reg couldn't see a problem with that and the deal was done. I was very happy to be staying in Cambridge.

The following day I phoned Coventry to say I wouldn't be taking them up on their amazing offer. They wouldn't enter into a wage auction, they stressed. I explained that it wasn't about money; it was about happiness and circumstances. I was going through an upsetting break-up with Sharon and had a son who was only fifteen months old and was my life. I just couldn't contemplate being away from him. What's more, I just loved being in Cambridge with all my football club and fishing mates.

Steve Fallon, United's legendary centre half who had served with huge distinction for just about twelve years and nearly 450 games, had become the team manager at Cambridge City. He called me with some concerns about the Milton Road pitch.

Once the envy of clubs far and wide, it had received fierce criticism after being relocated following the redevelopment of part of the ground to form the Westbrook business centre. On a very tight budget, I carried out some end-of-season maintenance jobs for Steve and managed to produce a surface that was OK – at least it looked like a football pitch.

I was flattered by the letter of thanks I received from Steve. The work I'd done, he said, had within two seasons transformed the pitch from one of the worst in City's league to one of the best. It's always nice when people are happy with your work, and I've always believed you should do the best possible job for anyone. It was also nice to do a favour for the club that had dominated my youth.

I felt that, since the appalling debacle of the mid-Eighties and with the invigorating arrival on the scene of Mr Turner, United were generally on the up in most areas, on and off the pitch. But there were weak spots.

The catering arrangements in the lounge areas were severely limited, and catering managers came and went. My ground staff team, as at most stadiums, would clear the rubbish from outside the kitchen areas as a matter of routine, but there was one occasion when our efforts went astray.

A few hours after we'd cleared the black bags away as usual, my assistant was gobsmacked to find the catering manager clambering around in a refuse skip, sifting through the rubbish and muttering to himself. 'Have you lost something?' he asked. 'Carrots,' mumbled the disgruntled kitchen supremo. 'In a black bag. Must have been thrown out.' We all knew what the insides of those skips looked like, and we didn't eat at the club that evening.

The next catering manager came up trumps when the club staged a sporting dinner in one of the lounges, with rack of lamb on the menu. The evening was going well and the waiting staff were busy serving up what looked like delectable plates of succulent lamb. Then the food ran out.

I was one of the unlucky thirty or so guests who were left drumming their fingers and staring into space while the sound of rumbling stomachs rose in crescendo to drown out the polite chatter and clash of cutlery on china from the other tables. After an eternity, the waiting staff emerged once more from the kitchen, bearing steaming platters of the dish our chef had rustled up to replace the missing lamb.

Look, I've got nothing against the Pukka Pie. I won't hear a word against the Pukka Pies company or its wide range of gourmet treats. The Pukka Pie is a fine product in its place, but that place is in a steamy-windowed chippy or on a football terrace on a chilly, misty Saturday afternoon. That place is not at a prestigious sporting dinner for which we'd had to smash our piggy banks in order to buy tickets.

We didn't think the meal could possibly get any worse but we were underestimating the kitchen genius's talents. When the apple pie with custard was served up we found it to be frozen solid in the middle, and one guest emphasised the point by banging his dessert on the table and announcing that he'd discovered a substance harder than diamond.

The catering manager was of course apologetic, and over the next few days offered a number of excuses. None of them cut the mustard and he soon found himself packing up his knives and departing the Abbey Stadium.

I've mentioned no names so far, but I've no hesitation in shining a light on the next manager to take over the catering department: step forward, Julie Wright. She was like a breath of fresh air, changing the club's entire catering set-up, knocking the hygiene side of things into shape and meeting all the environmental health requirements in double-quick time with the minimum of fuss. Any defects were rapidly identified and food standards went from poor to top-quality in a kitchen that was, to say the least, very basic. Julie was a joy to work with.

Her influence was to the fore when it came to solving a puzzle involving members of the part-time staff that had been plaguing us for some time. Matchday stewards had been complaining to me that the drinks served at the away fans' end were revolting and just about undrinkable. This mystified Julie, who used the same products throughout the stadium, but when she set to work to root out the problem she found it stemmed from just one of the away end's tea bars.

Together we hatched a plan to watch the area on CCTV at the next fixture, and kept a close eye on a monitor before and during the game. Nothing unusual or untoward seemed to be occurring, but then the half-time interval came along and we gathered round the monitor, stunned by what we were seeing.

A figure appeared on the terrace and started picking up all the used and discarded cups. His task complete, he scurried back to where he had come from – the tea bar in question. We watched as he carefully washed and dried the cups and were then able to make out the staff pouring half of the contents of new, unused cups of coffee, tea and hot chocolate into the relevant washed and dried cups.

So that was their game – when the stock-check took place at the end of the game, there were found to be more cups than there should have been left on the shelf, and the staff were able to walk away with the value of the extra cups in cash. If they were up thirty cups, for example, they could whip thirty times the value of a drink out of the till, so at £1 a cup they would be pocketing £30. Naturally, the services of the staff in on the scam were quickly dispensed with, but we would never have been aware of their wrongdoing had Julie not been so proactive.

Another sign of her impact on the catering standards was the fact that we on the ground staff happily started eating the food produced in the tea bars and lounges. Confirmation of her impact came when Julie's mouth-watering and legendary bacon rolls secured United the top ranking in the 1998 Colman's Football Food Guide. But this gave rise to another story.

Some of Julie's part-time catering staff would arrive at the ground on a Friday afternoon or early on a Saturday morning to help set up the tea bars for a match. One woman in this group, after giving birth to a beautiful bouncing baby, would bring her pride and joy with her and would work her way round the stadium, pushing the gurgling newborn in a pram and loading the tea bars up with chocolate, rolls, sausages and bacon. I would often have a peep into the pram and enquire after the baby's health. 'Yes, baby's doing well, thank you,' the mother would say.

One fine day I was walking around unlocking the exit gates while the group were loading up the tea bars. 'How's baby?' I asked as usual. 'Not very well,' came the reply. 'Oh dear,' I sympathised, 'hope it's on the mend soon.'

An hour or so later I caught up with the women again. 'I'm surprised you brought baby out if it's poorly,' I remarked to the mum. 'It is very quiet.'

'Yes, I know,' she replied. 'As I said, baby's not well.'

Glancing into the pram, I said: 'I think it's worse than you realise.' There was no poorly baby returning my gaze, but there were five kilos of bacon wearing a crocheted bonnet.

Julie was nearby and heard some of the conversation. Mother was sent packing and the rest of the staff realised they would have to be on their toes, even if one of their number had been rasher than they would ever be.

Chris Turner had been taking giant strides with the team and we were making good progress. Eventually his impact on every aspect of the club's operations was recognised when he took on the additional role of general manager, and John Beck came in as part of the coaching team.

When he first took control of team affairs, John was brilliant bordering on genius and his ideas were years ahead of anything else happening in the country at the time. The players' diets were a huge part of Becky's game and peak fitness was essential. He brought in a stats analyst in Neil Lanham who provided John with data on every aspect of a game: the number of tackles players won, the number of times they lost possession, the number of times play broke down, the location of the loss of the ball.

This level of attention to detail, although commonplace today, was unheard of in the early Nineties. John, with Gary Johnson as his assistant and a team largely assembled by Chris for absolutely zero outlay, continued to earn outstanding results.

With John taking charge of so many aspects of playing matters, Chris was able to take some time off and embark on the occasional holiday. I'd booked a week away with my new partner Lisa in a hotel in Bugibba, northern Malta, and I happened to mention it to Chris a couple of days before we were due to fly from Luton. 'I'll see you beside the pool,' said the King of the Jungle. 'Yes, of course you will,' I replied, and thought no more of it.

Let me interrupt my flow for a minute or two to tell you about Lisa and her family. Having met her at work, I'd been with her a while and we'd been away on holiday a couple of times. On our first trip to Spain we stayed in a hotel with a good-sized pool but I didn't take full advantage; as I messed about in the shallow end, I would tell Lisa: 'I wish I could swim.' The saintly lady spent three days trying to teach me the basics and encouraging me into the deep end, but on the fourth day it was so hot that I just had to put an end to the charade: diving over her head, I swam an enjoyable few lengths, to be met by a few choice words. Well, you have to have a bit of fun, don't you?

Lisa made a massive commitment when she got involved with me. My son Liam was very young but she took the new responsibility in her stride, treating my pride and joy as her own. She was the epitome of professionalism at the club and, forming a formidable team with the likes of club secretaries Steve Greenall and Andy Pincher, worked alongside me for twenty years before being made redundant.

I struck it lucky with her parents, too – they accepted the arrival of Liam and myself as if it were the most natural thing in the world, and we were made very welcome in their family. I also found a new friend and prank victim in Lisa's sister Michelle.

Having just about finished cleaning her car one day, Michelle found she couldn't reach high enough to rinse off the roof with a bucket of water. She really should have known better than to ask me to help. It took her a few days to exact revenge for a thorough soaking, but when it arrived it was a good 'un. While working on the pitch irrigation, I carelessly left a hose lying about and shouldn't have been surprised to find my car full of water.

Lisa's mum was another great one for the prankery. I called round one evening to pick Lisa up and found her mum sitting in a chair, holding her stomach and looking pained. She'd had the gripes all day, she explained, and I sympathised. Her reply came in the form of the loudest fart I'd ever heard, from man, woman or elephant. Not knowing where to look, I felt my sympathy growing but in the next instant, as she produced a whoopee cushion from under her bum, was feeling a right prat.

Once in Malta, we wasted no time in checking in at the hotel and checking out what it offered – a nice-looking seafront pool with a handily placed bar would be where we would be spending a fair chunk of our leisure time, we decided. The pool area was overlooked by a pavement with the kind of metal handrails you see so often at seaside resorts.

We'd been in our Mediterranean paradise for three days, were enjoying ourselves no end and were happily soaking up some rays by the pool when our peace was shattered by the sound of an unmistakable voice at almost unbearable volume.

'Oi, Grumpy!' boomed Chris Turner. 'What are you doing with that old trout?'

We both looked up. As a matter of fact, everyone around the pool and for half a mile around looked up. Out in the Med, a dolphin popped up to see who was making the row and if he was doing it on porpoise.

Chris and Lynne, along with Peterborough United director Alf Hands and his wife, were leaning over the railings intent on a little top-volume banter, which continued for an hour. Chris then buggered off, but not before threatening: 'I told everyone I'd keep an eye on you – I'll be back!'

The following day Lisa and I travelled to the fortified town of Mdina, which is known as the Silent City. The trip on one of Malta's famous, colourful vintage buses was something of an ordeal – a smooth, air-conditioned journey it was not – but we arrived safely and I thought it was time I played a little game with Lisa.

'You know no one is allowed to speak in the Silent City, don't you?' I asked, and she took this useful local information on board. We strolled around for thirty minutes or more with not so much as a peep out of her, and I was enjoying a rare period of peace and quiet. I kept smiling at her and she smiled back, but not a word passed between us. When we reached the top of the Silent City and Lisa noticed other tourists chattering about the weather or what they fancied for lunch, she turned to me, a mystified expression on her face, and pointed.

'What are you pointing at?' I asked. She instantly twigged that she'd been stitched up, and the first words out of her mouth for half an hour were: 'You arsehole.'

Despite Chris's threat that he would be keeping an eye on us, he didn't turn up again that week, but when we returned to the club his humour was still much in evidence.

Becky was also proving himself to be a very funny man, besides being a very good footballer and an outstanding coach, with a spot-on impression of Norman Wisdom doing his 'Mr Grimsdale!' routine in his repertoire. In his next breath he'd be 'doing' Bernie Winters, the only comedian to make a career out of saying 'Eeeeeee!' and threatening to smash someone's face in.

I had several good days out with Becky on the side of a lake, although it was laboured at times. Yes, we went fishing together, but I was expected to supply all the gear and then listen to his phone ring constantly for five or six hours. But he was great company.

In the run-up to one of the two FA Cup quarter-final games to which John led United – either at home to Crystal Palace in 1990 or against Arsenal at Highbury in 1991 – a TV company asked John for an interview somewhere away from the stadium. He chose to be filmed fishing the river Cam opposite my old stamping ground, the Pye sports ground, and together we hatched a plan: I went down a couple of hours before the interview and caught a few fish, then John arrived to take over on the riverbank. Fish! Camera! Action!

The cameras had been turning over a couple of minutes and John was successfully resisting the temptation to showcase his Norman Wisdom when the interviewer, retching and covering his nose, called a halt. 'Whatever is that terrible smell?' he wailed. Becky and I were crying with laughter: the TV man had stood in a big, sloppy pile of dog shit and had been spreading it all over himself and the riverbank for some time.

Changes took place at the club during the 91-92 season: Gary Johnson was moved sideways to make way for a new coaching assistant in Gary Peters, and the atmosphere started to change. The day after a cup game, for which the pitch had looked amazing as usual, John called me into the office and told me that the surface was too good for the style of football United were playing.

The apprentices, who were still working with me several afternoons a week, couldn't stop talking about some of the dodges the management had them performing in order to give United an advantage.

In those days the home club used to supply the warm-up balls used by the visitors. Our kids were instructed to put the away team's kick-about balls in the bath overnight and then place them in front of the convector heaters in the dressing room. This made them as hard as concrete and as heavy as medicine balls, and just as bouncy. At half-time there was another treat in store for the visitors: there were no energy drinks around in football at the time, but the tea in the away dressing room made a good substitute after being laced with vast amounts of sugar. There was no chance of visitors cooling down during the interval, for the heating was cranked up as high as it would go and the windows were welded shut.

Meanwhile, their managers and bench staff would be seething about the position of their dugout – I'd been instructed to have it moved to a position just ten yards outside the south end's penalty box. The highly pissed-off visitors found it difficult to communicate anything to their team from that vantage point, and to make matters worse the dugout roof was lowered so that those sitting in the back row could only see half of what was happening on the pitch.

I was instructed to reposition the marks on the goal line ten yards from the corner flags to eight yards, to enable our lads to close the ball down. I found this strange as United never took short corners

– the ball had to be knocked into the box at every, and I mean every, opportunity – and the visiting players would also be standing just eight yards from the ball.

Before a match against Plymouth Argyle, Gary Peters instructed me to turn off the electricity in the away dressing room, thus denying the visitors the use of the ghetto blaster they used to get their players in fighting (and possibly dancing) mood. I refused: it was a requirement that power be supplied for the physio's use. Nevertheless, unbeknown to me, someone took it upon himself to sever a cable later that day. I can't explain why the fuse board, admittedly of the old style, didn't trip out.

Whoever the culprit was, his scheme was foiled because on match day the Plymouth dressing room was bouncing and the mice were putting earplugs in – the Pilgrims' ghetto blaster was battery-powered. The following day I called our contract electrician Glen Gawthrop in and was horrified when he told me that, although the cable had been cut, it was still live. To this day I dread to think what might have happened if a player had leant against it.

Becky had by now employed a new kit man in the slight, moustachioed, immaculately turned out figure of Roger Parker. He'd served plenty of time in the military, and it showed. You half expected him to march in as if on to a parade ground, take our salute and conduct a thorough inspection of the ranks. Roger's motto was evidently 'a place for everything and everything in its place', which was music to my ears. The kit man's area was spotlessly clean and, for goodness sake, the tumble dryer vent was cleaned out each and every day.

Roger was a dream to work with and always happy to help out. But he liked to get everything squared away in the morning so that he could head off to the Supporters' Club bar for a lunchtime drink knowing he had forty minutes or so until the end of the dryer or washing machine cycle. It was noticeable that Roger became more forthright and plain-speaking after these little revivers.

We'd planned a fire drill for three o'clock, or 1500 hours as Roger would have termed it. The alarm was activated and all but three of the staff duly gathered at the fire assembly point. I joined Roger, who hadn't missed his regular appointment at the bar, in searching the building for the missing second-year apprentices, and we soon made out their unconcerned voices emerging from the away dressing room. Roger entered sergeant-major mode, burst through the door as if making an SAS-style entrance and screamed: 'So don't you fuckers burn? Get your arses up to the assembly point!' Everyone at the club grew to like Roger and forgive his lunchtime tipple routine.

By now Julie had moved on. The new catering manager tried hard but, to put it kindly, struggled to meet the requirements of the job. Just about every meal came out of a cook-in-sauce bottle and the kitchen was not at its most hygienic, but at least the kindhearted lady would always offer the staff something to eat.

It became more apparent that, a bit like Mr Partridge, the dipsomaniac children's entertainer in the holiday camp sitcom Hi-de-Hi!, Roger's normally tolerant manner could change after drink had been taken. One day, on his return from the Supporters' Club, the catering manager asked if he would like anything to eat. His frank reply, voiced at parade ground sergeant volume, was: 'My dear lady, the only thing I would eat out of your kitchen is a fuucckkiing banana, and that's because it has a skin on it!'

His victim soon departed – she simply couldn't cook, which I've always found to be a shortcoming in a catering manager.

I'm not sure who had the next brainwave: two sets of large sprint check boards arrived at the stadium, four feet high and eight feet wide on large steel A-frames. I soon found out that they were to be placed facing each other on the pitch, some fifteen or twenty metres apart. The players were required to run at one of them then check, turn and run back to the other board, and the plan was clearly to destroy the playing surface on the central part of the pitch, making it difficult for visiting teams to pass the ball.

I found this utterly heartbreaking. I and my ground staff had worked so hard for so many years to ensure the club had a good playing surface. Everything the club achieved during Becky's first spell at United has been well documented – the amazing FA Cup runs, the rise in consecutive seasons to what is now the Championship, the topping of that division and coming so close to taking part in the Premier League's inaugural season. I can only salute those achievements, but I can and do question some of the antics that occurred and the tactics that were employed.

The most bizarre occurrence in my forty years at Cambridge United came when John called me into his office and reiterated that the pitch was too good for his style of play. His players would, he said, now train on the pitch each and every day and I was not to put right any damage incurred.

I was dumbfounded. 'In that case, John,' I enquired, 'what do you want me to do all day?'

'You like fishing,' he replied. 'Go fishing.'

Naturally, I was worried that I would lose my job under this regime – groundsmen who spend all day on the riverbank tend to be unemployed groundsmen. I pointed this out to John who, to give him credit, signed a letter confirming his instructions and emphasising that the pitch was no longer my responsibility.

The ground staff did on occasion try to replace the divots at the end of a training day, but one day we were confronted by a member of the coaching staff, who told us in aggressive tones to get off the pitch. One of my volunteer staff members who challenged his actions in the same manner quickly found himself on his arse.

This sorry episode had two positive results. First, while the pitch suffered, my match fishing results improved no end. Now that I could fish one day a week on whichever river I was due to compete on the following Sunday, I could get to know the spot like the back of my hand. Second, the letter John had signed became a party piece wherever I went – no one could believe how bad the pitch had been allowed to become, and everyone scoffed when I announced that I'd been told it was too good.

In my opinion, the determination, or desperation, to win at any cost then went a stage too far.

We were playing Port Vale at home and I was, as always, the matchday safety officer. There had been problems with United and Port Vale 'risk' supporters having a go at each other and a running battle was under way at the front of the stadium on Newmarket Road. The so-called Vale supporters invaded the Globe pub opposite the ground and used pool cues and chairs as impromptu missiles to be hurled at their rivals. The two groups were beating seven shades of shit out of each other and the police were working their regulation-issue socks off to stop the brawls and keep the factions apart.

Meanwhile, a city-centre pub had reported that their pool balls had gone missing and a display of glass grapes had been swiped off the bar. Tension was still high as the game kicked off, and the pool balls and glass grapes made their reappearance when they were flung on to the pitch. It goes without saying that we didn't need anything to occur that would further inflame the situation.

The interval was upon us and half-time scores from around the country were being read out over the PA. Supporters of both clubs were listening intently, for the scores in other games were crucial – Port Vale were fighting relegation while we were pushing for promotion. From the control room we couldn't work out what had happened to provoke it, but serious crowd disorder suddenly broke out on the away terrace – there was angry shouting and jeering and fists were being waved. We sent extra stewards and police officers on to the terrace to find out what had happened, and what we were told took some believing.

The PA announcer had been provided with false scores and had duly read them out. As announced, they meant that Port Vale were in a relegation spot.

Whoever had made up the scores and had them passed to the announcer hadn't reckoned with the radios that some Vale supporters were listening to, and the word that they were being duped quickly spread along the terrace, making it a very uncomfortable place for any steward or police officer. To my mind, this was a must-win-at-any-expense tactic that backfired badly, with the potential of causing injury or worse.

Another occasion that stands out in the memory was the time I was instructed to make the playing surface as small as possible. We were obliged to break out all the concrete around the posts, move the goals forward and re-cement them in so that the pitch length was reduced to just a hundred yards. At the same time, the touchlines were pulled in so that the playing surface was no more than fifty yards wide. The result was a kids' pitch.

I think the one and only game that took place on that mini-surface was against Birmingham, and we got beat. And of course, all lines had to be moved back to their former positions – the reduced surface didn't comply with the regulations for FA Cup matches.

Becky's time managing the team wasn't all dissatisfaction and dissent, not by a long chalk. The players that Chris Turner and he had assembled were a fantastic set of lads and we had some great times with them.

The likes of goalkeeper John 'Legend' Vaughan, the Kimble twins Alan and Garry, midfielder Gary 'Hedgy' Clayton, rock-hard defender Liam Daish and his centre-back oppo Phil Chapple, John 'Shaggy' Taylor, the one and only Steve Claridge – what a great bunch they were. And no one could accuse them of not looking after their own.

That was confirmed one evening after a home game, when Lisa and I were in Browns restaurant in the city centre. The match had fallen on the day of the Varsity Boat Race and the restaurant and bar area were full of undergraduates who had been drinking all afternoon.

In these enlightened times the University is becoming a little more diverse, but back in the day any townie could spot a student a mile off: he would be the one wearing the same clothes as his dad, speaking a strange tongue halfway between a drawl and a bray and answering to the name of Jonty or Septimus. The ancient sport of grad bashing, perfected over centuries of Town v Gown conflict, has been on the wane for some time, but it's fair to say there's still not too much love lost between the two sides.

On the day in question, some of these foolish, over-entitled young grads were at the staggering stage of intoxication and one of their number barged into me, spilling his beer over my shoulder. He then had the brass neck to accuse me, in a raised and what he believed to be a threatening voice, of pushing him.

I wasn't worried and I had no reason to be. Liam Daish, as intimidating a figure off the pitch as on it, stepped in. Taking a firm hold of the fella's clothing, he enquired politely if he had a problem and, although I've never seen anyone literally quaking in their boots, I came close that night. The incident was closed and my aggressor was scurrying back to his college room, as fast as his wobbly legs would carry him, for a change of underwear. I was grateful I'd done Liam the odd favour such as running him to the railway station when he first joined the club.

Former plasterer Gary Clayton was another of my favourite blokes. Every day he would greet me with 'All reet, young-un?' in broad Sheffield, and he would often sneak out for a quick fag before training.

I have great admiration for John Beck and what he achieved at the Abbey, even taking into account everything that happened to my beloved pitch. I genuinely think that if he had continued to work with Gary Johnson they could have been the new Clough and Taylor. John is hyper-talented and ahead of the game in so many areas.

Above, at the age of three, I'm already happy with a ball at my feet;
below, a year later, I'm looking for the throttle control on my first mower

My first pitch inspection came at the age of twenty months;
I'm giving Cambridge City's surface at their lovely old Milton Road ground the once-over

With Lisa and Ruby during the drinks reception
before my Cambridge News Lifetime
Achievement Award in 2015

A ball was seldom far from my feet,
even on my first day at Arbury junior school

At twenty-one months, Liam was already showing signs of wanting to follow in his dad's footsteps

Proud smile as I cuddle the newly born Ruby in Hinchingbrooke Hospital's special care baby unit

A special day in 2007: Lisa and I tie the knot

The family that has been a source of help and support throughout my life: above, mum Jill and dad Keith; below, the Darler boys, from left, son Liam, me and brothers John and Richard

Early days at Cambridge United's Abbey Stadium in 1979: above, on my first day as head groundsman –
the youngest in the Football League – I pose topless for the Cambridge Evening News photographer;
below, in conversation with John Docherty, my first team manager who was ultra-supportive

In 1989, following the Hillsborough disaster, I discuss the implications with chairman
Reg Smart (second left) and representatives of the police and local authority

Award winner: left, Jewson groundsman of the year in 1994 and,
right, the Institute of Groundsmanship's unsung hero in 2015

More awards ... the Cambridge Evening News lifetime achievement presentation in 2015 ...

Dream Team winner Ian Darler of Cambridge United (right) is congratulated by Turf Business publisher Keith Dalton at Chelsea's Stamford Bridge

... Conference groundsman of the year in 2010 ...   ... and Dream Team winner at Chelsea in 2005

Fishy business: Angling Times photo shoot in 1974 ...   ... Ruby's first carp ...

... Liam, winner of the Cambridge
Charity Fund Raisers' fishing series ...   ... and me with a winning haul

A couple of the Abbey Stadium pitch designs I've dreamed up over the years:
above, I must have paid attention during some school geometry lessons after all;
below, a Christmas tree design that attracted national media interest

Managers I've worked with: ... Gary Brabin, the hulk with a kind heart ...
Chocolate Finger King Gary Johnson ...

... love-in with Joe Dunne ...   ... Roy McFarland, the perfectionist ...

... calm and collected Colin Calderwood ...   ... and the always-supportive John Taylor

Clockwise from above: EFL special award for long service presented by chairman Dave Doggett;
police area commander's award from Superintendent Vicky Skeels in 2014;
Ruby and niece Yasmin with their charity book presentation

Cambridge Charity Fund Raisers presentation to Tom's Trust in 2017

My assistant Mick Brown and I receive the man of the match award
after the home game against Luton Town in March 2018

My amazing first boss, Bill Scott, with his wife Elsie

Best-man duties on Liam's wedding day

Some of the training matchday stewards have received over the years: an exercise in patient removal from stands

The Duke of Cambridge kicking a ball about on my pitch as he records a
BBC programme that launched the Heads Up mental health campaign

Catching up with old friends at the Cambridge United Hall of Fame induction ceremony and dinner in 2018: above, Andy Sinton, United's youngest League player when he made his debut in 1982; below, goal-scoring hero Alan Biley

Above, I'm on the left, carrying out a winter pitch inspection with (from left) Phil Hough,
Mike Bullivant and legendary manager Chris Turner;
below, back on the straight and narrow in more clement conditions

CAMBRIDGE UNITED F.C.

Registered Office and Ground: Abbey Stadium, Newmarket Road, Cambridge CB5 8LL
Telephone: Cambridge (0223) 241237 Fax: (0223) 247874 Registration No. 482197 England

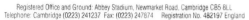

JB/dk

17th September, 1992

Mr.I.Darler,
Stadium Manager,
c/o Cambridge United Football Club,
Abbey Stadium,
Newmarket Road,
Cambridge CB5 8LL

Dear Mr. Darler,

This letter is to confirm my instructions given to you in a meeting held
in the Officials Room on the 17th September, 1992, with myself, Gary Peters
and Ian Darler.

I stated the pitch is too good for the style of football Cambridge United
play. We need to produce a surface which will benefit us. I confirm the
pitch will now be used almost every day for training, also that the doggy
boards will be used down the centre of the pitch in order to destroy the
sward.

The pitch is also to be watered heavily, the only areas I require grass on
the pitch are in the four corners, the pitch is now not the responsibility
of the Cambridge United ground staff.

I confirm that these instructions are to clarify any misconceptions to any
persons within or outside the club regarding the condition of the pitch.
It will be my responsibility and no blame will be made toward Mr. Darler
or his groundstaff.

Yours sincerely,

John Beck
MANAGER

Life President: D.A. Ruston F.C.C.A.
Chairman: R.H. Smart   Vice Chairman: D.A. Ruston F.C.C.A.
Directors: G. Harwood, J. Howard, R. Hunt, G. Lowe, R. Smith
Company Secretary: Steve Greenall   Team Manager: John Beck
Commercial Manager: John Holmes
Supported by Cambridge City Council

Official Club Sponsors:

FUJITSU

The global computer & communications company

The 1992 letter from manager John Beck that confirmed my
Abbey Stadium pitch was too good for his team's style of play

CHAPTER 8

—

YOU'RE NICKED!

Dear Ian,

I managed to find a way to your heart and persuade you to let us use the pitch for training through my love of Cadbury's Chocolate Fingers. If I went on a trip I could go through a couple of packets quite easily and quite often I had packets in the car. I would use them to smooth negotiations.

Maybe some of my health problems were due to them but you'll be pleased to know I've stopped eating them. I didn't like giving them up – it was like losing a best friend – but at least my weakness wasn't cigarettes or drugs.

You certainly know how to prepare a pitch. Even in the days when John Beck required a poor pitch, it was always a credit to you. You wouldn't touch it for a few days and people would say 'where's the forking groundsman?' Becky would say: 'Don't worry about him, we don't need him.'

You were a major part of our success of the early 90s by knowing how to prepare the pitch, whether it was good or bad.

Gary Johnson

Cambridge United assistant manager 1990-91, manager 1992-93 and 1993-95

After John Beck left the club, Gary Johnson was in charge for a few games before being sidelined once again; in came Ian Atkins as team manager. A number of people at the club were not that keen on Ian, although I was fortunate as he was always pretty good and supportive to me. But there was one occasion when he made my blood boil.

I and the rest of the ground staff repaired the pitch after a Saturday home game because heavy frost and snow were forecast for the coming days. I was extremely discumnockerated when the players started training on the pitch just as the frost was coming out the following day, making an unholy mess of the surface. To make it worse, the sun came out while frost was still on the surface, and by Monday the pitch had black footprints all over it where it had been scorched. In fairness to him, Ian did apologise.

I think it's fair to say that Ian and Gary failed to hit it off. Amazingly, Gary was told not to attend home games and was apparently sent out to watch unimportant, irrelevant games in the South-South-West Cherry Hinton League, or something. Or was he?

Gary hit upon a neat little ruse. Calling Lisa to ask for a ticket, he explained that he would be slipping into a home game unnoticed, under heavy disguise: sports jacket with the collar turned up, baseball cap pulled down over his face and dark glasses. It was so effective that when he arrived at the ticket office on match day, Lisa didn't recognise him and he had to ask several times before giving up and whispering: 'Lisa, it's me, Gary! Give me the flipping ticket, will you?'

Having known Gary for quite a few years, I can say with certainty that he went through this rigmarole for one simple reason: he loved working at United.

After Ian left the club he was very complimentary about me and the ground staff, and he gave me his home phone number, saying: 'If you ever need anything and you think I can help, give me a call.' A lot of people say that, but Ian meant it. Almost a decade later I called him to ask if he would ask around his contacts in football for bits and pieces I could use in one of my charity events. I was chuffed by his reaction. Thinking back to his time at Everton, he said: 'I can let you have one of my shirts signed by the squad,' and he was as good as his word. When they went under the hammer at a charity event, the shirt was snapped up by former United club secretary/finance manager Steve Greenall, who is a diehard Evertonian.

The board duly gave Gary Johnson the role of team manager. Gary is a true gentleman, has remained a good friend for twenty-five years or more and was a dream to work with, as long as the pitch we served up was of a high standard.

Well, no one could really complain about the pitch because it was then that I won my first Groundsman of the Year award, which saw me in the unfamiliar surroundings of a posh London hotel. I was presented with a very nice crystal trophy and £200-worth of holiday vouchers, which I shared with Trevor Ball.

Gary found there were two ways he could get me to let him use the pitch for training. The first was to allow Trevor and me to have a run-out; the second was to call me to his office for a cup of tea and a box or two of Cadbury's Chocolate Fingers. The working relationship remained intact until the day he left.

While carrying out the matchday safety officer aspect of my job, I'd become good friends with a number of the police officers. I'd also turned out for the police team in the occasional Thursday League game, which made me an easy target for the inevitable banter.

One Saturday, when the U's were playing away, Lisa and I were wandering around the city centre and found ourselves in the HMV store. Lisa was delighted when she found a CD she'd been after and, while she queued to pay, I watched the world go by through the window. Among the crowds wandering past were PCs Dave Carson and John Aveling, who spotted me and, after a quick discussion, leaned around the door, leering. I was uneasy; if ever two police officers were up to no good, it was these two.

As one man they burst into the store screaming: 'Stay there, sir! Don't move! We've been looking for you. Hands behind your back!' With that they snapped the cuffs on my wrists and hustled their captive, now resembling Billy the Beetroot, out of the shop.

'You bastards,' I snarled, not unreasonably, as we passed a shocked checkout queue that included the wide-eyed, nonplussed Lisa.

'Dear, oh dear,' said Dave. 'Swearing at officers. That's a serious offence.'

But once we were outside the shop they took the handcuffs off and gave in to the hysterical laughter they'd been suppressing. By the time of the next home game the following Saturday, the world and his or her live-in partner knew the scandalous story of the HMV arrest.

During the same week there had been a murder in the public toilets on Jesus Green. The police were searching for a suspect and asked if the club would display some 'Have you seen this man?' posters around the ground. We agreed, but with the posters came a plan for vengeance. On the quiet, I enlisted the aid of Trevor George, our police liaison/ intelligence officer.

The police were at the stadium early on the Saturday morning and lost no time in putting their posters up. I was certain that quite a few spectators that afternoon would spot the wanted man: the moment the posters were up in the area that Dave would be working later that afternoon, I snuck in and glued his photograph, supplied by Trevor, over them.

When the spotters arrived for the game there was a fair amount of piss-taking over the previous Saturday's incident but I was happy:

I knew what the afternoon had in store for PC Carson. The turnstiles had only been open a few minutes when he was made aware that he had become the wanted man. Needless to say the posters were soon replaced by the genuine article and the piss-taking was reversed.

It's strange how the football world works. I've run across Barry Fry many times – when he was manager at Barnet and again when he was manager, then chairman, then director of football at Peterborough – and he's asked me more than once if I would be interested in the Posh groundsman's job. He may well have been paying lip service but I'll confess I was surprised when a phone call came through one evening at home and the unmistakable voice came down the line.

'Hello, it's Barry here,' it announced. 'Barry Fry.' Well, I'd already worked out that it wasn't Barry Manilow.

'Can you help us out with our pitch?' Barry croaked. 'It's forking awful at the moment and we're struggling to get our games played. I know you run your own business and you've done some work for other clubs.'

I booked some time off, went to have a look at the London Road pitch and could see what Barry was talking about – it was so compacted it resembled concrete, with all the moisture trapped in the top twenty to forty millimetres, and it was giving off a mighty stink – it was totally anaerobic. The pitch was so wet that using any tractor-mounted equipment was out of the question, so over a Friday, Saturday and Sunday, when Posh were playing away, we set about putting in a series of sand bands by hand. The pitch started to dry out very quickly.

On the Sunday we were cracking on with the work when the sweet tones of the Fry foghorn carried over from the main stand. 'Oi!' bellowed Barry. 'Do you old Cambridge boys want a Sunday lunch?'

He got an enthusiastic response and, in what may be a first for a football ground, the three of us sat down in the centre circle to be served roast beef, Yorkshire pud, roast potatoes and all the trimmings by a chuckling Barry. I thought about asking if I could inspect the wine list but didn't want to push my luck.

I didn't charge Barry or Posh for my work on the pitch. A grateful Mr Fry said: 'If you ever need a favour, let me know and if I can help I will.'

A few weeks later he was on the blower again, asking if I could drive up the A1 again to meet him and Phil Neal, his assistant manager at the time – they wanted me to carry out their close-season pitch renovation. I had the meeting, gave some advice, followed up with a report and left it at that.

A couple of days later my home phone rang at an ungodly hour of the morning and, fearing something serious had befallen a family member, I hurtled downstairs. 'Hello,' sang an unfamiliar voice, 'it's Peter Boizot. What a beautiful morning! The sun's out, the birds are singing ...'

I interrupted Mr Boizot, who was Posh's owner, to ask if he was aware it was 5.45am.

'Is it?' he replied. 'Terribly sorry. But the sun's out, the birds are singing ...'

Eventually I managed to extract from the Pizza Express entrepreneur what he wanted from me: a meeting with him and his board at London Road to discuss pitch maintenance.

At the meeting some criticism was directed at the incumbent groundsman, to which I didn't respond. I did say, however, that no one could maintain the playing surface to a high standard with the extremely basic equipment the groundsman had at his disposal. The board asked me to provide a list of the kit that was required and promptly bought it all: tractor, aeration equipment and lightweight mowers. I was then commissioned to carry out the renovation.

We set about the work and by the start of the new season the Posh pitch was as good as the Abbey Stadium's. General manager David

Kerr wrote a complimentary letter saying what a terrific surface we'd provided at a very competitive price. Which was nice.

Back at Cambridge, the board had granted me a testimonial year, which started a few months after the completion of my work at Peterborough. I was looking for a guest speaker for a sporting dinner I was planning, and I thought I'd take Barry up on his offer of a favour. I was blown away by his reaction. 'Yes, my son,' he said, 'let me have a couple of dates and I'll book it in.' To my question about his fee, he replied: 'Nothing. I owe you.'

Barry was born to give after-dinner speeches. On the night he covered his entire career and the antics he'd been involved in, and talked at length about the great George Best, with whom he'd played in the Manchester United youth set-up and managed when Bestie turned out for Dunstable Town.

'What do I owe you?' I repeated when he'd done. 'Nothing, mate,' came the reply. I did send quite an expensive bottle of vintage whisky to London Road, mind you.

It was around this time that my old angling friend Percy Anderson reappeared in my life, and that I was made aware of something I hadn't known about him: he had played for Cambridge United.

Percy had been a talented forward who made his United first-team debut in 1950, when the U's were playing in the United Counties League. After a handful of games he came to the attention of the big boys and was snapped up by West Brom. Failing to make the grade at the Hawthorns, he had a spell at Stockport County, for whom he made his only Football League appearance, before returning to Newmarket Road. There he scored seven goals in twenty-nine games for Bill Whittaker's heroes.

Percy wasn't just an expert angler and footballer; he excelled at just about any sport he tried. Take him on at indoor or outdoor bowls, snooker, pool or table tennis and you would soon be standing back and admiring the man.

I listened, enthralled, as my hero recounted the story of one of his last great goals at the Abbey. He wasn't always a crowd favourite, he told me, and during the game in question, playing at centre forward, he was on the end of some stick. He was also on the end of a headed clearance and let fly with an instinctive volley that screamed into the net, whereupon he ran over to his critics in the crowd, turned his back and dropped his shorts to reveal the Anderson arse.

Whenever he visited me at the stadium, Percy took great delight in re-enacting the moment. Running out of the players' tunnel clad in his customary baggy grey tracksuit bottoms, he would wave to his imaginary fans, run into the penalty box and either finish a make-believe flowing move with a diving header or simulate the famous 25-yard volley. Galumphing around with his arms in the air with Jimmy, his malodorous little Yorkshire terrier, in hot pursuit, he would then run behind the goal and bare his scrawny arse to the non-existent crowd. My protest of 'you can't do that here!' would invariably be met by two fingers.

A lot of ex-players have a habit of returning to the club, and Percy was a regular visitor, usually to talk about fishing or on the scrounge. When he turned up early one morning hoping to touch me for some fertiliser for his lawn, I said: 'No problem. I've got some microgranular feed in my van – take it. There's enough for two applications: one now and one in six weeks' time.' Percy thanked me and went on his way.

The following week he was back, looking his best – the usual grey sweatshirt with egg, sauce and tea stains down the front – and yelling like a madman. 'That bloody shit you gave me has killed my lawn,' he ranted.

Curious to see what had gone wrong, I went to his house in Fen Ditton and one look was enough to solve the puzzle. You would see more grass on a badger's bum than he had on his lawn. 'You plonker,' I smiled, 'you've put all the fertiliser on in one go.'

Percy shuffled his feet uneasily. 'I thought it would thicken the lawn twice as quick if I put it all on,' he pleaded. I ended up having to do a lawn renovation job.

He turned up the next day at the stadium, a big, soppy grin spread across his mush, and presented me with a bloody great bundle of peacock quill and Benny Ashurst stick float blanks – something really special in angling circles. 'Thanks, son,' he said. 'I really messed up.'

I'm not sure they were adequate compensation for the numerous ways in which Percy carried on haunting me over the coming years.

We continued to take children on work experience and always did our best to make them feel welcome. Some were hyper-confident; others had little or no self-esteem; some had had difficult starts to their young lives. I always tried hard to give them the opportunity to work in as many interesting aspects of groundsmanship as possible, but there were always a few who let themselves down.

One day-release work experience lad, whom we'll call Jack, was pretty laid back as well as a little scruffy and generally unkempt. He seldom brought anything to eat, so I would pack up an extra sandwich for him.

On a never-ending quest for riches, the ground staff filled in a football pools coupon every week. At lunchtime on a Thursday Trevor Ball would take the money we'd all chipped in out of the 'pools cup' and down to the shop, but one week the cup was empty. Trevor's enquiries revealed no one had touched the money and we thought no more of it, but the following week it was missing again.

We knew the cash was in the cup the day before Jack came into work. The following week I got some trailblazer (bright green dye) out of my store and painted the underside of all the banknotes in the cup, telling Trevor and the other ground staff what I'd done. Fast forward to break time, ten o'clock on the Thursday morning.

Trevor, Wally Rookes and I filed into our office and, doing our best to keep straight faces, sat down and waited for the kettle to boil. Jack came in and sat down next to Trevor, and I kicked off the interrogation.

'So what have you got to tell us about the money that's been stolen out of this office over the past couple of weeks?' I wanted to know.

'Nothing,' Jack blurted out. 'It's nothing to do with me.'

'Have you been in the pools cup today?' I probed. No, he hadn't, he insisted.

'Then perhaps you would care to tell the jury,' here I nodded at Trevor and Wally, 'why you look like the Incredible Hulk.'

He'd obviously panicked when dipping his fingers in the cup: he had dye all over his forehead and his nose, and his hands were covered in it. I know they say some people have green fingers – an advantage in our game, you might think – but it didn't bring Jack any luck.

I told him I'd painted the pools money and advised him to have a look in the mirror. I then laid out two options for him to consider: we could call PC Trevor George and he could account for his actions; or he could pay back the money and forget about any further work experience. He went for the second option and we got all our money back.

It's a shame when kids let themselves down. True, we can never know everything they're going through in their lives, but you can't work with a thief in your midst.

Most of the children were little stars but one of their number, who seemed advanced for his years, liked nothing more than bragging about a girlfriend he said he had. Matt would drone on about what they'd done the previous night, what they were going to do at the weekend and how often. After a few days he was doing our heads in. We were always sensible when we had kids with us but this one overstepped the mark when he asked Wally when he had last had sex.

Wally, an ex-soldier, certainly had more stories under his belt than this young lad, but was reserved and kept schtum. Trevor and I were impressed with his self-control, but we had a feeling it wouldn't last if Matt kept up his vainglorious boasting.

Sure enough, the following lunchtime he was at it again, describing various girlfriends' anatomy in great detail. And then he asked Wally if he'd had sex the night before. Big mistake.

This time Wally played the youngster's game and requested more information about what he got up to during his nights of passion. It became obvious that most of what he'd claimed was the product of an over-fertile imagination.

Wally then threw down his trump card. 'You seem experienced,' he told the poor lad. 'Tell me, what is a clitoris and where would you find it?'

The reply was confident. 'My mum's got one,' Matt declared – so far, so good.

'It's got a pink flower and it's climbing up our garden fence.'

The delighted laughter erupted like water from a burst pipe as Wally said patiently: 'No, mate. I think you'll find that's a clematis.'

Matt went a little red about the chops, and that was the last time we heard anything about his imaginary private life. I think the poor lad thought his tales made him appear grown up; quite the opposite, in fact.

My work with the matchday stewards intensified in 1997, with more regular training sessions covering every possible aspect of any event that could occur at the stadium.

The staff, who had been selected to take part in a trial along with their counterparts in Leeds, Bradford and Scunthorpe with a view to acquiring a qualification in matchday event stewarding, waded through an amazing amount of work. The six modules took months to work through: all stewards took part in a classroom activity at the stadium once a week, were given homework to complete by the following week, were involved in simulations of incidents and took a series of exams.

Their commitment was outstanding and I was seriously proud of what they achieved. Cambridge United became one of the first four clubs to be recognised as having qualified stewards.

Even after this, training was full on for all the eventualities that might see staff being called into action. Their hard work and commitment were never more noticeable than on an Easter Monday afternoon when United were playing Southend. Let me run you through the events as they happened.

The game kicks off at 3pm. Just six minutes later a radio message is received from the main stand supervisor requesting medical assistance – a male supporter has collapsed and from a distance it looks possible that he is fitting. Less than a minute later he reports back: patient is unconscious and possibly not breathing; has lost control of bodily functions and urinated himself.

3.07: club crowd doctor Steve Jones and paramedic David Monk are dispatched and the stewards' training kicks in as the patient has to be moved to an area where resuscitation can be carried out. He is carried over the seats at speed to a rear walkway at the top of the stand, an area pre-designated as an emergency treatment area.

3.09: stewards keep area clear for medical staff to work on patient; CPR being performed. Defibrillator en route; patient not breathing.

3.09: steward supervisors confirm public diversion is in place.

3.10: defibrillator is used; CPR continues.

3.15: David Munk and Dr Jones still performing CPR; defibrillator used again; pulse located.

3.17: Ian Darler is at patient's location, checking staff welfare, dealing with family members and friends of patient. Alf Walker, head steward and deputy safety officer, covers the control room.

3.17: stewards at Newmarket Road entrances direct ambulance to medical emergency location.

3.20: patient is responding to treatment and being transferred on to a spinal board. Preparations to move him down rear staircase into ambulance.

3.26: ambulance departs Abbey Stadium en route to Addenbrooke's Hospital. One of the patient's sons accompanies him; other family members still at the stadium are taken to the briefing room and are comforted by Cambridge United control room staff and club chaplain Stuart Wood. Club doctor updates close family on condition of patient and provides a phone so that the patient's son can call his mother.

3.37: Alf Walker and other staff involved in the incident stand down for a drink and discussion; welfare of staff is checked. The incident has clearly affected supporters who had been in close proximity. All staff except one female say they are fine to continue working; the female steward is tearful, is stood down and is looked after by Stuart Wood and Ian Darler. She later asks to return to duty; this is agreed but she is monitored throughout.

A full debrief of all staff involved in the emergency is carried out after the game. All staff are informed that the patient is still alive but remains critically ill; he had been clinically dead for several minutes during the incident.

Ian Darler congratulates all staff on a tremendous team effort. All agree that the in-depth training the supervisor stewards have received from Bob Brotchie, Steve Howard and other medics from the East Anglian Ambulance Service over the years has contributed to saving the patient's life.

I was very happy to confirm the following points:

- Good, early, accurate communication of incident from steward supervisors
- Good early identification of patient's condition
- Quick extraction of patient from seated area to medical working area as prearranged at training sessions
- Stewards kept a good working area between public and patient
- Good communication between CUFC staff, medical team and police
- Good relayed updates to control room
- Good care and assistance offered, with information to family and friends of the patient.

All staff involved in the incident were spoken to the following day to ensure they were OK – they had witnessed and been involved in a distressing and serious medical incident.

It was not until several hours after this event took place that I was made aware that the patient was the father of one of my fishing mates, whom I used to pick up and take to matches most weekends. The patient made a full recovery and to date has had another thirteen years of life with his family and friends.

This is the time when you appreciate fully all the hard work and commitment your staff put into their training year after year – and it wasn't the last incident of its kind. There have now been three similar emergencies at home first-team fixtures: all three patients suffered heart attacks and were clinically dead but, thanks to the amazing work of the medical teams and stewards, all three survived.

This was simply outstanding work, and I could not have been any prouder of all the staff involved.

My own training in CPR techniques proved invaluable the day after my son Liam's wedding, at which I'd acted as proud best man. The following morning at breakfast my dad, Liam's grandad, suffered a heart attack and I had to spring into action, dealing out a cardio thump into the bargain. I didn't mind at all, of course, but I was bit miffed at missing out on a cooked breakfast.

You know that odd, creeping feeling that something is about to go badly wrong? In my time as matchday safety officer I've had weird premonitions several times.

The first happened before an Easter Monday game. During the pre-match steward briefing I told anyone who would listen that I was worried that something untoward was about to happen – we were going to have to deal with a heart attack, I insisted. Sure enough, this was the occasion I've described above.

On another occasion I told the staff about my horrible feeling about a fire breaking out in the stadium. It wasn't long before a steward who was driving along the A14 called in to say that the north-east floodlight appeared to be on fire. Scrambling to action stations, we found that a fire had indeed broken out at the top of the pylon, 120 feet off the ground.

Do humans really have a sixth sense? My money's on 'yes'.

Another example of good, positive action from the stewards reacting to an emergency situation happened when we were playing Stoke City one roasting hot summer.

With the temperature in the low thirties, a number of supporters' coaches arrived late at the stadium because of a traffic accident and a series of roadworks. The delay had forced the fans to sacrifice the usual stop at a motorway service area, so they had not eaten and, more importantly, had not been drinking.

The game got under way and was progressing just like any other until just before half-time. That was when a visiting supporter collapsed on the terrace, and he was followed quickly by another ... and then another, and another.

Our policy if we have one incident of this type is naturally to deal with it. If we have two in the same area and the second is identical to the first, our concerns heighten. That day, with five or six incidents of a similar nature occurring within minutes of each other, the alarm bells started ringing like the clappers. Supporters were dropping like ninepins.

The medical team were concerned that the wave of collapses could have been the result of some form of contamination or food poisoning, but the real cause soon became clear: the very high temperature, the Stoke supporters' location under a steel-clad roof and the fact that some were dehydrated had combined to create the perfect storm: the area they were standing in could best be described as an oven.

As soon as the cause of this nasty incident had been identified, the staff set about passing dozens of large bottles of water into the crowd, and carried on ferrying the precious liquid to those who needed it for twenty or thirty minutes. And the grateful response from the Stoke fans was astounding.

Again, I was proud of the highly organised, professional job my stewards and medical staff had done – they had nipped a potentially more serious situation in the bud. But the most gratifying response to their actions came after the game.

We hadn't known at the time, but the TV presenter and comedian Nick Hancock, a diehard Potters supporter, had been among the crowd. After the game he called Radio 5 Live's phone-in to say what an amazing job the United staff had done in helping his fellow fans in a truly awful situation.

CHAPTER 9

—

TESTIMONIAL TRIALS

Dear Ian,

When I first met you, you were very young and I wondered if you were up to the job. I need not have worried.

Before you arrived, stewards didn't have tabards and weren't given any particular places to stand – we found our own spots. After your arrival, I began to realise how a ground should be run, and your enthusiasm helped to bond the team.

You did a deal with the Post Office, and their old orange jackets became Cambridge United stewards' first uniforms. Before you came, communication consisted of walking over to the next steward. You managed to get radios, and what a difference they made.

You introduced NVQs, which at first nobody thought they could do, but we soon realised we were wrong.

When we carried out dress rehearsals for evacuations, it felt as though they were really happening. Being stuck in the middle of a hostile crowd in the bad old days was daunting, but because of the training we knew what to look for and how to deal with it.

A lot of the stewards have been here fifteen, twenty, twenty-five years, and that tells me how much they feel valued as part of a team.

You're also one of the kindest people I know. When you leave us, you're going to be a huge miss.

Alf Walker

Matchday head steward at Cambridge United

The next person to step into the team manager's role was Tommy Taylor, whom I would describe as the Cambridge United BFG. He is indeed a giant of a man with a heart to match and a warm, caring nature. He later looked after all the apprentices in a club house that was renovated by chairman Reg Smart's building firm.

While the renovation was going on, my staff and I were instructed to landscape the garden and gravel driveway, and it quickly turned out to be a popular job. During the first visit Tommy's wife Pat invited us to eat with them every time we visited and the food she served up was fit for the gods. Tom and Pat treated the apprentices as if they were their own kids, and they lived like lords.

Tommy's own lads attended first-team home games and one of them, Lee, offered to wear the Marvin the Moose mascot suit. The moose looked spruce and did a brilliant job entertaining the crowd for a few months, until one day the U's supporters on the North Terrace saw fit to dish out some moose abuse. Rather than call a truce, the moose turned and made a discreet 'wanker' gesture towards his critics. It was seen by a number of people and the next thing we knew the moose was loose, sent out to grass, and a new Marvin impersonator was climbing into the suit.

I was good mates with Reg Smart, who looked after me royally once we got to know each other, but there was one decision I think he got wrong: not offering Tommy a contract – the manager had his team playing some lovely stuff. Others obviously thought the same because someone broke into the boardroom, smashed the photos of the board members on the walls and generally made a right mess of the place.

After Tommy left the club for Leyton Orient, Reg asked the entire staff to a meeting in the boardroom: he had an announcement to make. Reg told us that the board had decided to employ a big-name manager and Roy McFarland was introduced.

By now I was thoroughly used to getting to know new managers and their requirements and ideas. As Roy spoke, dressed immaculately in a tasteful suit, my attention wandered and I found myself thinking about my first ever trip to Wembley back in 1973. Roy had been in the England team that, to the horror and disbelief of the nation, was knocked out of the World Cup qualifiers by Poland that awful night.

I pulled my focus back to what Roy was saying: he would always be sure to work with every single member of the staff, and he wanted a good surface to play on. I was of course delighted, and we happily delivered a top-quality playing surface that received a commendation from the Football League issued by Dr Stephen Baker of the Sports Turf Research Institute.

Roy was a football manager of pure pedigree, and just as importantly he was at pains to make every single person at the club feel important. He would take the trouble to speak to everyone he ran across, be it senior employee, supporter or volunteer sweeping the terraces. He would often take to the running track around the pitch in the afternoon, proudly wearing an England tracksuit complete with badge, and in his late forties could still keep up a cracking pace.

Roy's belief that every corner of the club should be clean, tidy and organised was music to my ears and it was no surprise to me that he managed to sweet-talk the chairman into undertaking a full renovation of the dark, dingy and less than hygienic dressing rooms and bathrooms. At no cost to the club, we and some of Reg's employees set about stripping the plaster from the dressing room walls and the tiles from the bathroom areas, and removing the plasterboard ceilings. It didn't go entirely smoothly; it couldn't have gone entirely smoothly with Catweazle (remember him?) a willing member of the volunteer crew.

One lunchtime Cat, misguidedly thinking he would be helping out, took it upon himself to set up some steps in the home bathroom and pull the nails out of the ceiling joists with a claw hammer. When we came back from lunch we found he'd fallen off and smacked his head against a urinal, shattering it into a dozen pieces – the urinal, not his head. The latter was in a poor state, though, and Catman was whisked off to A&E at Addenbrooke's. There he said he'd had an accident at work and we soon therefore had a visit from the Health and Safety Executive. He shouldn't have been in the dressing room of course, but we duly received a warning – the site should not have been left unattended.

Once the renovation was complete, with Catman mostly out of the way, the dressing rooms looked fantastic. In my forty years at the club, he has without doubt constituted my biggest area of risk and the flood of Cat-related disasters showed no sign of drying up.

Roy was ultra-professional in every aspect of his job. He had the priceless gift of making you feel at ease and his charm always got the best out of his players, the ground staff and the office employees. He also displayed huge compassion and understanding of life's trials, as he showed towards Bill Cawdery, a staff member whose contribution to the club had been enormous. After being diagnosed with cancer, Bill underwent treatment for what seemed like an eternity but Roy would visit him in Addenbrooke's almost to his dying day.

He was also a brilliant storyteller and held everyone at the club's Christmas dinners and social events enthralled with his stories of his England days, Sir Alf Ramsey and the squad's activities. These included visiting London Zoo where, Roy modestly pointed out, the players drew more attention than the animals. The 2018 World Cup in Russia made me think again about the McFarland era at United – the feeling around Gareth Southgate's player-management philosophy bore similarities with Roy's.

Lisa and I, on holiday in North Devon one day, spotted a photo on a hotel wall – the legendary Roy McFarland sitting on the bonnet of a yellow Ford Capri. Naturally, the first thing I asked him on my return to work was if he'd been a model at any time in his life. As soon as I mentioned the car, he instantly recalled the full story.

Roy had great success over five years at United, including winning promotion to League One in 1998-99, so the chairman's decision to take him on in place of Tommy Taylor was more than vindicated, but I still feel there was unfinished business with Tommy.

It was a sad day when Roy's time at the Abbey came to an end. It was natural for him, on his last day, to walk around the stadium and thank every single employee and volunteer for their support and help. If the board made a mistake, it would have been in not offering to pay Roy a retainer to keep him at the club as an ambassador. He's a true gentleman, a professional every minute of the day, considerate, highly respected and a good friend to all.

John Beck returned to the Abbey for a second spell as manager. This time round I didn't have to endure the indignities of his first spell in relation to the playing surface; we were respectful to each other throughout, but the relationship never got going this time around.

When John left again, it was time for a supporters' favourite to take over the managerial reins. John Taylor, known to supporters as Shaggy for his youthful resemblance to the slacker character in the Scooby-Doo cartoons, had formed a mutual admiration society with the fans over two spells as a player, and held the record for goalscoring since United had first made it into the Football League in 1970.

While his playing career had been winding down, he'd been working behind the scenes with the reserves and assisting the manager, and was the supporters' overwhelming favourite for the job of team boss. And his promotion to the post came like a breath of fresh air. He asked me to produce the best-quality pitch possible – he wanted to play football that would attract the supporters.

Always considerate and the perfect gentleman to the ground staff, John asked me before the new season to make the pitch as long as possible; he felt it would benefit his style of play. The length was to be increased to 120 yards, so out came the concrete around the goal posts again.

The extension, however, caused a few problems. The new area of the pitch didn't have adequate drainage or any irrigation facilities. What was even more tricky was that it was the south end of the ground that provided the new yardage, so with the new South Stand in place, at least fifty yards of the pitch were constantly in shade during the winter months. Frost became a nightmare.

John worked his socks off for the club and, when the results went against him, never once blamed the pitch or his players. Whenever John returns to the stadium on match days he receives a hero's welcome, and that's fitting for someone who gave his all. It was a great shame that his spell as manager didn't work out.

The team management arrangements that followed were, to say the least, bizarre. On April Fool's Day 2004 it was announced that Claude Le Roy would be the new team manager, and more than one supporter instantly suspected an elaborate but desperately unfunny joke.

Claude arrived at Newmarket Road with an international reputation few people could match. Starting off in the French game, he'd performed miracles in football backwaters, lifting Cameroon to a prominent position in world football, raising the profile of the Senegal and Malaysia national teams, working in Shanghai and for AC Milan and Paris Saint-Germain. What on earth did he think he was doing in Cambridge?

It took a few days for Claude's position to become a little clearer. His views on the game were valued by the French TV mega-channel Canal+, to whom he was still under contract, and it turned out he wasn't United's new team manager after all. It had all been a misunderstanding; he was at Cambridge to assist a colleague, the up-and-coming Hervé Renard, a David Ginola lookalike who enjoyed great popularity among the club's female staff.

On Claude and Hervé's first day, training took place at the stadium. 'This is a nice training centre,' said Claude in his excellent, accented English. It fell to me to explain that this was the first-team stadium, not a training camp.

Hervé was an engaging and thoroughly pleasant fella who did his best to improve his English and was always dressed to kill in the latest Paris fashions. With Claude nowhere to be seen, having departed to coach the Democratic Republic of the Congo, he teamed up with Dale Brooks, who had been John Taylor's assistant and then acted as caretaker manager.

Between them they reshuffled the pack and Hervé used his contacts and knowledge to recruit players from French-speaking countries. I'm told their lack of English was a challenge at times, although a variety of tongues can be heard in pretty much every senior club's dressing room nowadays – and boy, did we play some exciting passing football.

It's no surprise to me that Hervé has gone on to enjoy massive success as a coach of African national teams and at French clubs. It's often been said that, for him, Cambridge was simply the right club at the wrong time.

Steve Thompson replaced Hervé as manager, and he was tasked with saving United from relegation out of the Football League to the Conference as financial turmoil engulfed the club and its supporters.

Renard and Thompson couldn't have provided a more striking contrast in their approach to the sartorial arts if they'd tried. In contrast to Hervé's crisp white dress shirts and neatly pressed trousers, Steve turned up to anything from a training session to a meeting with the board in unimpressively baggy jogging bottoms.

Let's just say that things didn't go well for Steve. He insisted on training on the pitch more often than not – 'We need to stay up and we need to train on the pitch,' – which, as in John Beck's first stint, hammered the surface to the point of submission and a lingering death. I didn't object but I have to say that, having witnessed the lads training and seen the lack of organisation in the team, I also saw the writing on the wall.

United were duly relegated out of the Football League during May 2005. It was a sickening experience personally and a devastating blow for the club. I will never forget, to my dying day, the awfulness of the complete, grief-stricken silence that enveloped the Abbey when the ref blew to end the match that decided the club's fate. The dedication and unwavering commitment of the men, women and children who had lifted United from the obscurity of a boys' Sunday school team in 1912 to the undreamed-of heights of the Football League just fifty-eight years later was undone at a stroke.

Not only was the club back in non-League, it was also in administration. Budgets were cut, staff including Steve Thompson lost their livelihoods when they were made redundant and former Norwich player Rob Newman, who had assisted Steve, was drafted in to pick up the pieces as manager. Working with Tony Spearing as his assistant, he started to augment the four senior players who were still under contract and assemble a squad. The two of them, provided with a tiny budget, worked twenty-four hours a day to tempt players to the Abbey.

It was during Rob's time as manager that one of the representatives of supporters' trust CFU who helped to staff the club, Heather Wilkanowski, requested that the board award me a testimonial match to reward my twenty-five years of service. I was at a loss as to how to organise the game until my old friend Malcolm Webster came to the rescue.

By now the goalkeeping coach at Ipswich, Webby asked the Tractor Boys manager Joe Royle if he would take a team to Cambridge for the testimonial. As luck would have it, Joe had been one of those who had written to the club praising the high standard of the Abbey's playing surface, and he agreed instantly. We settled on a date – the game, on 13 July 2005, would be the first of the new pre-season.

The weeks flew by and before I knew it I was being introduced to the crowd by former club secretary Steve Greenall, who then passed me the microphone. I thanked the loyal supporters for their attendance and then returned to the fifty guests who were having a meal with me in the lounge that night, including six invited mascots from Cambridge and six from Ipswich. I hadn't charged the kids a penny as I thought it would be good to offer a few youngsters the opportunity to fulfil their dreams.

At half-time I was stuffed – I'd had a three-course meal, a pint of lager, three glasses of wine and two cups of coffee, and was giving the digestive system a breather. Heather suddenly appeared from behind a pillar, bearing a United shirt with 'Darler' printed on the back. 'Here you go,' she said simply. I was grateful for the gift and thanked her profusely. 'No, you don't understand,' smiled Heather. 'You're playing in the second half.'

I made my way to the dressing room, wobbling slightly and feeling the food and drink lying heavy on the stomach. Pulling on the size 8 boots that had been found for me and struggling into the shirt, I made my way outside, where the second half had already kicked off. I felt and looked like Billy Bunter, the Fat Owl of the Remove. The shirt was so tight it appeared to have been sprayed on.

As the final twenty minutes approached, Rob woke me from a light snooze in the dugout and asked where I wanted to play. Rubbing my eyes and letting out a soft burp, I replied 'Out wide' and sure enough, the next time the ball went out of play I was on my way on to station myself wide left on the Habbin stand side.

I was amazed to receive a lovely warm reception from the United and Ipswich supporters. But as I reached the far touchline the welcoming applause vanished and the young, twinkly-eyed right back said, 'Hello, grandad.' That was all the motivation I needed. All memories of the vast amounts of food and booze disappeared and I felt twenty again and on my toes – I knew this little shit was going to be on my case at the first opportunity.

The first ball came my way and, just my luck, it was in the air. I'd never been a great enthusiast for heading in my playing days, but I remembered the 'grandad' comment, jumped and was surprised to find that I'd beaten the full back to the ball. That set the fans in the Habbin off with a wave of rapturous applause and encouraging shouts.

With the exception of a few established United players, the team that night was made up of trialists and hopefuls, some of whom were fairly crap. U's left back Stuart Bimson (not one of the crap ones, I should make clear) passed down the line to me and I turned inside and whacked a pinpoint ball across to the opposite side. It was a decent ball but the lad out wide was looking at the sky and never moved, and Twinkletoes at right back took the opportunity to remind me of the great age he perceived me to be.

The rain had persisted down earlier in the evening and my beloved pitch was a tad greasy. A few minutes later a ball was played over the top and I and the full back set off in pursuit. He got there first of course, but then he started fannying about and showboating, running his foot over the top of the ball and all that malarkey.

I may not be the biggest bloke but I must have looked a bit like an oil tanker looming into view as I approached and, like that oil tanker, I was finding it took a while to come to a halt. As I closed in on him he tried a little shimmy but I was already sliding in hard and fast in true Tom Finney style, aided by the slick surface. I took the ball. I also took the player, who ended up writhing on the running track to an ear-splitting cheer from the United faithful, who until that point had not had much to get excited about.

The match officials were kindly running the game at no cost to me, and Darren Debden was reffing it. To this day I feel my Finney Special was a fair challenge but Darren had other ideas and sprinted over to say: 'Thanks, Ian and goodnight, Ian. You can leave of your own accord or I'll be forced to send you off.' I decided I had best make my way off, making it look like a substitution, but I was gutted.

After the game I went down to the visitors' dressing room to say thanks to the Ipswich lads. As I walked in I was greeted by a loud cheer and listened as the lad who'd called my age into question received a lesson in what not to do. It seemed he'd been told in training not to piss about with the ball; he would end up getting injured or giving the ball away, or both. I listened as the coach stressed that if a grandad could take him out, anyone could.

I felt very honoured when I read some of the articles in the testimonial match programme. John Seymour wrote: 'I have known Ian Darler for many years and he never ceases to amaze me with the standard of playing surface he and his team produce year after year. He has an amazing way of making £1 do £10 worth of work, such are the constraints he has had to endure over the years.

'How is he so good at his profession? I don't know, just ask Sir Alex Ferguson, Sam Allardyce, David Pleat, John Sillett and many, many other illustrious football managers whose teams have graced the Abbey Stadium pitch over the years. If Ian can produce the standard of surface we have at the Abbey, what could he do with the endless resources of the big clubs like Old Trafford, Anfield, Highbury etc?

'Ian has had opportunities to move on over the years but has chosen to stay at the Abbey. Loyalty indeed. Ian also organises events to raise money for much-needed equipment for his team of safety stewards. Annual fishing matches are just one of the events that enjoy large support due to the man's popularity.'

The blush-inducing articles continued with a contribution from Alan Millard, a matchday supervisor for forty years. He wrote that his first meeting with me was when I was introduced by Reg Smart as the new man in charge of the stewards. 'I had been a steward for several years, but following the Bradford fire tragedy and the Popplewell inquiry, things had to change,' Alan wrote. 'Ian was deemed the man for the job. As well as continuing with his groundsman and stadium manager duties, he then had matchday safety officer duties.

'Following the Hillsborough disaster, ground safety and stewarding underwent further changes. Reports had to be read and implemented by Ian, and the grass still had to be cut, aerated, marked out as well. The stewards, under Ian's supervision, had to undertake proper training which led to FSQ and NVQ qualifications, both of which were professional qualifications – all this coming under Ian's duties as a volunteer safety officer. Then there is all the paperwork, which his partner Lisa has assisted with, meetings to attend, new stewards to interview and train, pre-match briefings to prepare with the police and, yes, the grass still needs cutting. The list is endless but somehow he still finds time to go fishing.

'I know Ian takes great pride in the professionalism of his stewards, and that is only down to one man, Ian Darler. He works us hard at times, the word complacency is not in his vocabulary. We all appreciate what he does and what is required from us and I am sure I am a better person for having worked with him for the past years.

'The last person to have a testimonial [John Taylor] was named The Legend by Cambridge United fans. I believe Ian is also a Cambridge United legend who is held in great esteem by many people both inside and outside the football club.'

Reading these two articles brought a lump to my throat. I was staggered by what people I'd worked with for decades had written. I was even more amazed by what club chairman Roger Hunt had written.

'I have known Ian for seventeen years and his dedication to this club and the professionalism he has always shown is second to none,' said Roger. 'He has always been more than the groundsman.

'Every season Ian would sit down with the directors to argue his case for a realistic budget to enable him to provide one of the best playing surfaces outside the Premiership (and in my opinion even better than some of them), and for as long as I can remember the only time he came close to getting a proper budget was in the early Nineties. Usually he would be sent away with a very small budget and told to do what he did – beg and borrow from local friends and suppliers, with whom he had a tremendous relationship – and as always, come the start of the new season our pitch would look fantastic and be a pleasure to play on.

'Ian's dedication and loyalty is an example to us all … I will finish with the wording of the sign Ian had alongside the pitch: Grass grows by the inch and dies by the foot – KEEP OFF. This says it all about Ian: the pride he takes in doing his job is second to none.'

Reading these words just about finished me off and I was overwhelmed by emotion. I had never had any idea how the club looked on me, and I found the tributes humbling.

A highly enjoyable evening passed by very quickly, but things took a nasty turn in the following forty-eight hours. My testimonial bank account had been set up at a Lloyds branch managed by a friend of mine. Two days after the game he was on the phone asking when the testimonial funds would be deposited. I could feel the panic rising through my body from the feet up, but reckoned he was on a wind-up. 'No,' he replied, 'we've not received any funds.'

The money taken on the turnstiles had been collected by the same security company that collected the League game funds, but something had gone badly wrong. Andy Pincher, the club's company secretary at the time, contacted the company, to be told that they were allowed to drop deposits at Barclays Bank but not at Lloyds. Gutted.

Andy moved heaven and earth to help me sort out the problem. The money was traced but it emerged that it had been passed on to another bank. For several days it moved from bank to bank like a late-night drunk trying to find his way home. At one point we managed to pinpoint the money but it was then sent on its way to yet another bank when the sort code and account number could not be identified. Andy finally came up with some good news and some equally bad: the funds had been located but when they arrived in the testimonial account a lot was missing. At this point the police became involved.

I remain frustrated and angry that, despite much hard work by a lot of people, some of the cash was never found. I had committed to donate £2,500 to East Anglian Children's Hospices and I honoured that commitment even though the funds raised were less than we'd expected.

I was privileged to visit a hospice and came away with my eyes opened to some new realities. On a discreet tour of the facilities to see how the money would be used, I saw some of the children with life-limiting conditions and their parents cherishing every remaining minute with their little ones. It was a heart-breaking experience that stays with me to this day and made me fully conscious of how fortunate I've been, first with Liam and now with Ruby.

The testimonial year's events continued with an evening of music and entertainment in the Supporters' Club. Paul Mayes, the club chairman, kindly offered to put on the event and flogged most of the tickets, while I made a small contribution to the sales. I'll always be grateful to Paul and the club, but perhaps I should have done a little research before the event.

We'd advertised the evening's main attraction, a group glorying in the name of the Space Cadets, on posters all round the stadium and in front of the Supporters' Club. I thought the band looked a little unusual but, hey, that's kids today, right? As guests started to arrive they couldn't help noticing the presence of a number of wheelie bins dotted about the stage, but I didn't pay them much attention.

We settled down for a cracking evening's entertainment. Down went the lights, the music started … and the Space Cadets burst, as one man, out of the bins. It was impossible not to notice that they'd omitted to get dressed. Stark bollock naked, they clambered out of their bins and, descending from the stage, one of their number attempted to insert his loathsome man-prong into a female guest's ear. Taking a dim view of this invasion of her personal space, she and her husband hastily gathered up their things and made for the exit, and I can't say I blame them.

As this scene from a low-budget Seventies porn film was being enacted, I was standing, aghast, at the bar. I glanced at Lisa. 'If he comes over here,' she declared. 'I'm going to punch his lights out.' Dozens of the audience, struggling to believe what they were seeing, were turning their heads towards me, shoulders shrugged and hands raised. I knew what they wanted to ask: what the hell have we done to deserve this?

On dragged the performance and out streamed the guests, several of them asking for their money back. It was at this point that Paul confessed that ticket sales had not quite covered the cost of the group. I believe I covered my face with my hands.

I asked Paul to get the Space Cadets to clothe themselves during the interval – it was the least they could do. We ran a small auction that didn't go at all well, and what little profit we made had to be used to pay off the group.

The musical element of the second half was terrific, I'll give them that, but it was enjoyed by a half-empty room – most of the audience had gone home in a huff. To cap it all, I was then faced with a group of young women who'd obviously spent more time than was wise at the bar, and were livid that the Space Cadets had got dressed. Paul admitted afterwards that he hadn't realised the group normally performed for hen parties.

Dozens of friends and family members were there that night, to my profound embarrassment – a discomfort that is still, fifteen years on, brought up in conversation by delighted piss-takers. On the whole, I'm glad we put on the testimonial events but disappointed that the income didn't recoup anything like the money I'd laid out over the years for the football club.

CHAPTER 10

—

SETTING STANDARDS

Dear Ian,

As a manager, the first person you're keen to meet when you're new at a club is the head groundsman. He has to understand your needs and, in turn, you have to understand his – you're both working for the same outcome.

You and I got on straight away. At times I asked for things that were a little bit cheeky but you were always brilliant in meeting our needs. You would even always find us a ground for training away from the Abbey.

I respected you as a person: you take pride in your job just as I take pride in mine. There was mutual respect, we were friends and we had a close relationship.

Whenever I come back to Cambridge with another club, I always know the pitch will be perfect, even if it's the last game of the season.

Gary Brabin

Cambridge United manager 2008-09

It's thirty-two years since Reg Smart asked if I would consider taking on the additional role of matchday safety officer as an unpaid position, alongside those of stadium manager and head groundsman, and thinking about putting together a proposal for a new stadium safety structure. My proposal was accepted by the local authority's trading standards department, which was being run by Lloyd Wilson. Lloyd, extra helpful from day one, has continued to help the club up to the present day – when he retired from the local authority I persuaded him to join the matchday control-room staff.

As Reg said, the safety officer role would be a challenge. At the time there was little teamwork between the club and the police, fire and ambulance services. The police were in control of the stadium on match days and were in truth acting as stewards, although the club did have a handful of stewards who were really just football fans. My first job was to convince the police that I was serious about sorting out the differences between them and the club and improve communication between the two parties.

I arranged a meeting with Superintendent Michael Dean at Parkside police station, which overlooks Parker's Piece, at the meeting point of Cambridge's university and town areas. I'll admit to a few nerves as I sat, heart pounding, in his secretary's office, but that doesn't explain why I did what I did when I was told that Mr Dean was ready for me. To this day, I can't justify my actions.

As I walked towards his office I reached into my pocket, took out a white handkerchief and waved it around the door before entering. A stern raised voice from inside dispelled any hopes I might have had that this light-hearted gesture of surrender might break the tension. 'If you think that's funny, Mr Darler,' intoned Mr Dean, 'you'd better think again.'

He gave me both barrels about the various measures the club had agreed to put in place but not delivered. I let him have his say and then assured him that I would act on his instructions. 'Well, we'll see,' he replied. I felt like I'd been back in front of the headmaster at Chesterton School.

As the weeks went past items were steadily crossed off the list of improvements to be made, and after a few months I received a message that Mr Dean would like to see me again. Off I went to Parkside, feeling the same old trepidation as I waited to be summoned into the headmaster's study. This time, though, the superintendent came out to greet me and asked if I would like tea or coffee. The meeting went better than I'd dared to expect, and he was complimentary about the changes we'd made.

We talked about the new matchday control room that Reg Smart had placed on the roof of the former dressing rooms and toilets in the north-east corner of the ground, and in fairness I could understand why Mr Dean hadn't been best pleased with the club in days gone by. You would have been hard pressed to squeeze a constable, his truncheon and his dog into the previous control room but, while the new Portakabin couldn't exactly be described as spacious, we made it work.

The drawbacks to this accommodation weren't apparent until winter rolled in. The Portakabin's windows were not double-glazed, so in cold weather we had to use shammy leathers on the condensation to make portholes through which we could peer. Our frequent wiping efforts would be met by cheery waves from the supporters in the home end, returning our greetings.

Summer brought a new problem: opening the windows would bring one of two delicate aromas into the room, depending on which way the wind was blowing: either the stench of the rivers of urine passing through the toilets below or the fatty reek of the burger bar behind the control room.

Although we'd made good progress, it's horrifying today to think that I was still the only person able to open the exit gates on match days – I was the sole keyholder. That procedure, however, was about to change.

Saturday, 11 May 1985 should have been a day filled with celebrations for Bradford City supporters, who had followed their team to the summit of Division Three. Instead, fifty-six of those supporters died in British football's worst fire disaster.

Forensic scientists found that the fire in Valley Parade's antiquated wooden main stand may have resulted from a match being dropped or a cigarette being stubbed out in a polystyrene cup. Whatever the cause, Mr Justice Popplewell's report on his enquiry into the disaster shook up the field of stadium safety and brought about drastic and much-needed change, at a time when many grounds still had timber structures of the Valley Parade type.

Naturally, the local authorities, particularly the fire service, stepped up their work in this area. It always helps if you have a personal connection with those handling the work, and when the time for a fire inspection arrived I was pleased to hear Cambridge's fire chief, Brian Saddington, greet me with the words: 'I used to play football with your dad.'

The initial inspection brought about big changes: fire extinguisher certification was introduced, half-hour fire doors were fitted all through the stadium lounges and dressing rooms, fire alarms were installed throughout the main stand and conditions were imposed in the laundry room – it could not be used on match days as the gas tumble dryer and washing machines posed a potential risk. Safety policies were rewritten to include a great deal more detail and contingency plans were drawn up with all the emergency services.

My role was now significantly more challenging but it was also exciting, and I knew we had to raise our game. We'd been working hard with our stewards, who generally responded well to the changes we had to make, although a few threw in the towel when I told them that being a matchday steward didn't mean they could watch the game. I became friendly with another fire officer, Alan Pilsworth, who took me under his wing and gave up hours of his own time to train stewards in fire prevention and extinguisher use.

Alan and his colleagues carried out inspections on match days and it became routine for each fire service watch to visit the stadium, both during the week and on match days. They produced schematic drawings of the stadium showing high-risk areas like generator rooms and power houses, and carried out drills simulating fire incidents. Tenders set up on Coldham Common to pump water out of Barnwell Lake became a frequent sight, bringing back memories of Rodney Slack and his colleagues rolling their hoses out over the Common in my early days at the Abbey.

It was hard work but the stadium was becoming a far safer place to be.

While all this was going on, the games were coming thick and fast, but we could now call on a greatly improved matchday set-up in the control room. The ground commander, normally the highly organised Inspector George Jones, was supported by Sgt Andy Galligan on the radio and PC Trevor George as the football intelligence officer. My team was developing and, although at times during games I still walked the stadium to ensure my staff were performing their new roles diligently, I knew I had top support in the form of head steward Alf Walker, who was always active in ensuring stewards did their jobs.

Steward briefings and debriefs became regular occurrences. We'd never had them before but I understood how important they were, and I needed to know if my staff had anything to report and likewise if supporters had any concerns. The police also had debriefs, of course, and in one of these meetings it emerged that at times during games they couldn't contact me – stewards didn't have radios in those days. I was surprised to be issued with a police radio; I hadn't seen that coming when I first sat down with Superintendent Dean.

Some of United's games at this time were big fixtures and the ugly face of hooliganism was still showing itself far too often. All football matches are categorised for risk and high-grade fixtures, which were quite common, would see Inspector Jones out in the stadium with a superintendent taking his place in the control room. It can be busy in the box, with a number of people all doing their jobs simultaneously, so good teamwork is essential.

The superintendent, who would normally be familiar with the stadium, would monitor the crowd from the control room constantly to enable him or her to make decisions. This was vital for fixtures like a certain home game against Millwall – there had been a number of nasty pre-match incidents involving risk supporters of both clubs in and around the city. Our normal superintendents were not available and as the game got under way our new officer in charge was showing little interest in the game. In fact she was knitting.

Sgt Galligan and I were obliged to run the fixture, constantly monitoring the crowds, but as it progressed it became obvious that the crowds were becoming more engaged, as we say in the trade. We were all on our toes, concentrating on a potentially troublesome situation, when an exclamation from the superintendent sent us to action stations.

'Oh no!' she sang out, and her tone suggested a degree of anger, concern and frustration.

We scanned the terraces in vain, looking for the slightest suggestion of disorder. 'What's the problem, Ma'am?' queried Andy urgently.

'I've dropped a stitch,' replied his superior.

This was obviously a grave situation but I could see, from the gestures and grimaces Andy was making in my direction, that he was far from gruntled.

I should stress that in thirty years of performing the matchday safety officer role, this was the only time I've come across a ground commander who was less than totally engaged with the role.

The club was still having a problem finding training grounds. Eventually an opportunity arose in the form of the Cambridge Evening News sports ground at Porson Road, but the downside was that it would involve me, for the fella who had managed the site for decades had been taken ill and was unlikely to return. I was asked if I could take on the management of the ground, which had three football pitches, four tennis courts and a cricket square.

A deal was done with the newspaper: I would manage the site in my own time at evenings and weekends, through my private business. The ground, which had not been maintained for months, was a right mess but I was grateful for the opportunity: I needed the extra money to pay maintenance for Liam following my divorce.

After a few weeks I managed to get things shipshape with the help of my mate Eric at Choppen's, who lent me some heavy-duty mowing kit, and a few volunteers including Lisa and her father, who spent many an hour driving mowers over the surface. As the club couldn't afford three sets of goalposts, I had to call in a favour from a mate who owned a fabrication company, and he came up with six goals and boxes in return for a few match tickets.

The Porson Road ground hosted the Thursday League fixtures of Cambridgeshire Police and a United team mostly made up of youth and injured players, and that was great for me. Both teams were often short of players and that gave me the chance to strut my stuff on a pitch I maintained, and although I was only (officially) signed on for the Police, I managed a few run-outs for the U's.

The arrangement with the News lasted for a couple of years until the newspaper made a number of redundancies and gave up the sports field, which was taken on by a private school. I was disappointed after all our hard work on what was now an excellent surface.

One day in late 1999 Reg Smart sauntered over and asked me to attend a meeting, without mentioning what it was about. I was mystified but intrigued when it emerged that the matter on the table was the proposed redevelopment of the Abbey Stadium, the first phase being the replacement of the Allotments End terrace at the south end by an all-seater stand.

It soon became obvious that a number of people sitting around the table had limited knowledge of the workings of a sports stadium and what would be required in order to make the most of the facilities. I didn't hold back: in my view neither the design of the proposed new stand nor its location were practical.

I explained what I meant: it would be far from ideal to install just one set of turnstiles at the south-west corner of the ground as problems would be posed if we decided to admit home and away supporters to the new stand. Yes, there could be separate toilets and catering outlets, but offering only one set of turnstiles would not be compliant with the guidelines. The club asked the local authority and allotment holders if it would be possible to take a few more metres of the allotment land, which would have allowed the turnstiles to be sited at the rear of the proposed new stand, but the suggestion was rejected.

Several heated discussions took place over the location of the new control room and medical centre. On the first set of architect's drawings they were sited several metres behind where they are now, meaning some areas of the stadium would not have been visible and we would have had to rely on CCTV. I felt that was not only ridiculous but also very costly. Reg and I got our way and the drawings were changed.

The scheme was approved, demolition work started on 6 June 2001 and as it progressed Reg spent weeks at the ground, at first managing the clearance of the old terrace and then overseeing the relocation of the two floodlight towers at the south end. His attention then turned to construction of the external rear wall – hollow blocks filled with steel beams then mass filled concrete, then the installation of a large concrete reservoir drainage pipe at the rear of the structure.

As it happened, this drain was never used as the architect had specified a high-level reservoir. I wasn't happy about that at the time as I felt it would be difficult to maintain and was a ticking financial time bomb, and my concerns turned out to be valid. In 2018 the club engineer condemned the reservoir: it was leaking and rusting and in a generally dodgy condition. It had to be relined and strengthened, and to this day it's not practical to maintain.

The final drawings for the build were approved and a contractor was appointed. I was not involved in that side of things and Reg was preparing to move home to Thailand within a few months. Club director John Howard took over management of the development and I became friendly with several contractors and sub-contractors. What I learned from them was very interesting.

They told me the contractor was trying to spend as little as possible in certain areas. It's not unknown in the building trade. When I was speaking to the electricians in the new stand's undercroft one morning, the site foreman was talking to other subbies in the room next door, and we all clearly heard him say: 'Give them fuck all.'

We ran into the foreman outside, whereupon I let him know that we'd heard everything. He replied: 'We've already overspent.' I found this excuse difficult to understand as the scheme was a design-and-build project.

The stadium redevelopment masterplan originally included the replacement of the Newmarket Road end terrace and the Supporters' Club by an all-singing, all-dancing, cutting-edge structure, and to accommodate it we would have to extend the pitch fifteen metres southwards. But as the work progressed the extension specification was changed.

We'd planned to extend the drains and irrigation system but that idea was shelved because of its cost. The pitch contractor provisionally booked to carry out the construction work was also dispensed with. He was to have created a playing surface on what had formerly been the south terrace and the work was due to involve 600-plus tonnes of root zone which was a soil-sand mix. This was reduced and I was allowed a mere 300 millimetres of root zone. To my disgust, we were forced to lay this material on top of crap soil that had been dug out of the old terrace's footings and included kerbstones, bricks and probably a few dinosaur bones.

Never mind my concerns; the old rubbish was simply buried. The kerbstones still cause problems. When we're aerating we often find ourselves on bucking bronco rides – excuse my language – as the machines bounce on hitting the stones.

My good friend Malcolm Peacock of A Peacock & Son Land Drainage came to the rescue and helped Trevor Ball and me to install a new main drain in the pitch extension, along with eighty-millimetre lateral drains at five-metre centres. The club didn't have to pay a penny, thus saving more than £7,000.

The seed germinated and came through, and to our relief the extension looked like a playing surface. But it was suffering from a lack of water – we had just a hose at our disposal for this area – and it was also in shade for the best part of the day: not ideal.

The day came when the contractors finished the build (at least they said they'd finished) and handover day arrived. The unveiling of our shiny new stand, control room and medical centre promised to give us a day to remember. Local dignitaries were expected for a look around at 10.30 in the morning, and the thing I needed least that morning was Percy Anderson turning up for a chat.

I was finishing preparations in my brand new control box when I noticed Percy ambling up the running track with his faithful but stinky terrier Jimmy in close attendance. I probably clutched my brow in exasperation. One man and his foul-smelling dog mounted the stairs with some difficulty and strolled in, with Percy announcing: 'Just walked the towpath by the Pike & Eel.' He inspected my precious control box closely. 'Looks good, son,' he assured me.

Much as I enjoyed passing the time of day with the old boy, I didn't have time for his compliments. 'I can't stop today, Percy,' I told him. 'I've got the opening here in an hour's time.'

'OK, son,' he sniffed. 'I know when I'm not wanted.' And off he trotted, Stinky Jimmy in tow.

They'd only been gone a few seconds before my nasal organs came under vicious assault from an overpoweringly offensive odour. 'Fork me,' I muttered, gagging and choking, 'what the fork's that smell?'

It didn't take long to work out that Percy and his accursed mutt had painstakingly walked a prodigious amount of doggy doo into every inch of the control room carpet and all down the stairs. It was as if the entire canine population of Battersea had relocated to CB5 for a fortnight's training in bowel evacuation.

Time was running out; the mayor was probably lifting the chain of office over his head at that very moment. Within seconds I was on the phone to Peter Cozens, who had laid the carpet, for some more tiles, and cursed when he told me he had none of the same colour in stock. Peter was forced to leap into his van and bomb over to the Abbey with a varied collection of grey-colour tiles.

The site foreman, arriving in the box for a last-minute check, reeled back, trying to plug every one of his facial orifices. 'What the ...?' he managed to gasp as we flew around with scrubbing brushes, buckets, cloths, bleach and disinfectant, sprayed litres of air freshener into the affected areas and helped Peter throw down his multi-coloured tiles.

Percy was back the very next day. 'Flippin' 'eck,' I exploded, 'you got me in trouble yesterday!'

I've seldom seen him so untroubled, although I noticed Jimmy was trying to hide a smirk. 'I never had shit on my shoes when I got home,' the old bugger pointed out.

'Because you left it all here!' I remonstrated, although I was by now seeing the funny side.

Percy put a comforting arm round my shoulders. 'Don't worry,' he said, 'they wouldn't have noticed.'

Once I had some keys in my hand we set about familiarising ourselves with every square centimetre of the new stand. That process included snagging, the process of checking a new building for faults that need to be rectified. We found plenty to keep us going.

Rain water was flowing freely through the building's electrics, the undercroft had leaks in several places and the reservoir on the roof creaked when it was full of water, forcing us to install overflows. The lighting in the seated area remains a nightmare to this day. Every time we need to replace a faulty light we have to hire a scissor lift and run it over the grass – ridiculous when you consider that stringent working-at-height legislation was in place at the time of the build.

Some of the snagging has never been dealt with. I was raising concerns from the start but they were dismissed. I have more problems with this stand than any other part of the stadium and, worse, after just fourteen years of life, it's already starting to show structural issues. Because it has only one turnstile block we still have a knotty problem to solve every time the club wants to seat home and visiting supporters in the same stand.

Luckily, there are always distractions to take your mind off mundane difficulties. Percy was still a regular visitor to the stadium, even though he was by now suffering from a serious lung condition. One morning he rolled up and said someone had dropped out of a fishing match at Dents Farm in Hilgay, out in the Norfolk fenland. Did I fancy it?

Not half. Percy had been fishing these matches, run by Cambridge tackle dealers Tim and Sid Cooper, for several seasons. They were light-hearted affairs but were attended by some top anglers.

I hadn't seen the lake before and Percy was happy to dispense his wisdom on how to fish it. He then proceeded to give me and everybody else a bloody good hiding, bagging a number of good chub and large carp. At one point I walked down to find out what he was using for bait. Seeing my approach, he cast his pole line just as I arrived.

'You're doing well, Percy,' I observed.

'Not bad, son,' he replied and sat back, paying scant attention to his float. A few minutes later he lifted his line out of the water, and I was surprised by what I saw. 'Your bait's gone, I said.

'No it hasn't,' was Percy's reply. 'I took it off before you got here.'

I was puzzled. 'What are you catching on?' I enquired politely.

'Can you keep a secret?'

'Yes, of course I can.'

'So can I,' he said. 'Now fork off and let me get on.' I forked off.

When the match was over I remarked to my mentor: 'I really struggled on the beefsteak bait on the hook and minced beef in the feeder you told me to fish.'

'That's funny,' he said, 'so did I when I tried it the last time I was here.'

The old scoundrel had had me over good and proper. Soon everyone in East Anglia had heard the story and the piss-taking was long-lasting and merciless.

I ended up fishing two of the series at Dents. Due to Percy's growing health problems, I would carry his tackle, set his box up and get his kit out of the rod bag. One day I'd taken the tackle from the van to the bank, set up Percy's gear and got on with fishing the match as normal. Four hours into the match, a bloke came and sat behind me.

'Are you mates with Percy?' he asked. 'He doesn't seem too well. Will you go and see him?'

I hurried over and found Percy struggling. To my anxious questions he replied: 'The cold air's hurting my lungs and chest. I feel like I'm going to pass out.'

I managed to get him back to the warmth of the van and went to pack away his kit. By the time I got back he'd perked up a bit. 'Thanks son,' he said gratefully. 'I did feel ill.'

'I could see that,' I told him. 'But you are a little bastard. I was winning that match. You want to bring more food and a hot flask of drink, and put a pair of ladies' tights on when it's cold.'

A huge grin spread across Percy's face. 'You bloody fool,' he rasped. 'That's forty years you've waited to get your own back, from when you passed out as a youngster down on the Cam. It seems like yesterday.'

I got Percy home, made him comfortable and phoned his daughter Tracy to let her know about her dad's poorly spell. He missed the next match because of the cold, but from that day on he referred to me as Doctor Darler.

It was only a short while afterwards that I lost a very dear friend, when Percy passed away in Addenbrooke's.

Lee Power supplemented his short spell as club chairman with an even shorter stint as team manager, and who should turn up to assist him but my old mucker Chris Turner. I hadn't seen Chris for a while and, naturally, I was on my guard after all the grief he'd given me over the years. I soon realised, however, that something wasn't quite right.

On his arrival every morning he would ask me to take him down to the changing rooms – he couldn't remember how to get there, he told me. It took a few days for me to understand that he wasn't having me on.

But if his geography was a bit off, there was nothing wrong with his coaching sessions or his one-liners in reply to moans about having to run around the track. 'Why are we doing this?' questioned one player. 'Who does he think he is?' Big mistake.

'You're running because you're not fit and your results are shit,' Chris boomed. 'Now get on with it.'

Lee and Chris were great to work with but their time filling the manager's role was soon over and, in September 2006, Jimmy Quinn was the next to take his place in the gaffer's chair. He was another manager who was OK with me, as was his assistant Willie Wordsworth. They managed to get United to the 2008 Conference play-off final against Exeter, but promotion back to the Football League was not to be.

I was away from the club on the day of Gary Brabin's appointment as manager. A few of the lads at the fishing event I was attending told me the news and added: 'Good luck – you'll need it. Everyone says he's a real hard nut.'

I should have learned by then not to take what people say or what you read in the press as gospel. My first meeting with Gary could not have gone better and we hit it off from the start.

Gary can handle himself and has a physique resembling the proverbial brick shithouse, but he and his assistant Paul Carden were simply amazing to work with. Considerate to a fault, they had a complete understanding of how much work goes into playing-surface preparation.

Brabs gave his all in everything he took on and defeat on a match day cut him to the quick; he would really beat himself up about it. One Sunday morning following a Saturday game I went into the stadium around seven o'clock to work on the pitch. I found the dressing room doors open and the lights on so I crept in cautiously, only to find Gary washing the kit so that the two old girls who normally did the washing could have a day off. On the side was a bunch of flowers for them.

'What on earth are you doing here?' I asked the big man. His reply was that he was frustrated and annoyed by the previous day's result, and this was his punishment.

The lads at the college training grounds continued to help the club out on a daily basis, providing top-quality pitches at no cost to United. It was a massive help to Gary, Cards and me. And the two Scouser pals were always highly complimentary about the playing surface.

I was massively impressed by the way they got the best out of their squad, and not a bit surprised when they took the team to Wembley for the 2009 Conference play-off final against Torquay. I was equally gutted when we got beat. They had worked incredibly hard under a lot of pressure, especially in the early days when there were constant rumours about other managers being interested in their jobs.

Paul took over as caretaker manager when Gary left, and the amazing working relationship continued for a few weeks, until chairman George Rolls – there was rapid turnover in the chairman department around that time – appointed Martin Ling as team manager. That appointment will be remembered for ever as like something out of a third-rate sitcom.

On the day the management news was due to be announced, three candidates – Alan Lewer, who had helped out at the club for a short while, Liam Daish, a fans' favourite and good friend of mine, and Martin Ling – believed they had been offered the position. To add another twist to the farce playing out around the club, Liam and Martin turned up at around the same time.

Did Martin get the job because he arrived at the stadium first? I know from speaking to Liam a while after the event that he was massively disappointed. He told me the truth of what happened that day but the time for that story to be made public is not yet upon us.

I was pleased with my first meeting with Martin. He told me what any groundsman wants to hear – he wanted to play attractive football and needed a good surface to play it on. I had a good working relationship with him but he often appeared to be a slightly nervous sort of fella, albeit with a sharp sense of humour. That was a bonus, because humour was essential to appreciate some of the things that went on in and around his appointment.

To say the least, the club was going through a trying time and results went nothing like according to plan. Martin departed and in 2011, with United staring into the abyss of relegation to Conference South, director of football Jez George stepped in as team manager, with Nolan Keeley assisting him. Every game was a battle, and even when we hadn't played well I would call Jez afterwards from my car to offer support and highlight a few positive aspects of the game. At times that was difficult; we were often very poor.

There was a sense of despair and doom around the club, for relegation would surely have taken us close to extinction. But hard work and unity will always bring rewards. Everyone stuck together and we scraped together enough points to avoid the dreaded drop.

By now the club had a training facility at Clare College's sports ground in one of the city's leafier areas. It provided an ideal headquarters for the week's work and a very good surface for the lads to play on.

Following the relegation scare, Jez stepped back and Richard Money came in as team manager. Richard is his own man and I have to say that I didn't really have a proper conversation with him until after the home FA Cup fixture against Manchester United in January 2015.

The fantastic job Richard did in getting the club back into the Football League in 2014 has been well covered in the media, but there are a few things from that time that stand out for me.

The club hadn't spent much at all on the first team pitch, despite my warnings that problems were developing in the drainage system. No funds were available to upgrade the drainage, and that led eventually to the surface waterlogging quickly after a short spell of rain. You might have a regular, planned aeration programme, but if your drains are blocked you've got a real challenge on your hands.

The problem at the Abbey is exacerbated by the fact that its subsoil consists of the blue gault clay that sustained a brickmaking industry in the Newmarket Road area for many years. When fine clay particles from a subsoil filter into porous pipes, they will eventually set like concrete. Inspection of the drainage system confirmed that water was sitting on top of the pipes instead of running through them.

We had a new chairman, Dave Doggett, who saw the problem at first hand and was supportive, agreeing that at the next close season we could carry out the renovation that was desperately needed. In the meantime, with finances as tight as a camel's sphincter in a sandstorm, we were obliged to do what we could to ensure that games went ahead.

With a first-team match due to be played one Saturday, the preceding Wednesday saw a prolonged downpour visit our little corner of Barnwell. The pitch was left in an unstable, unplayable condition and it was too wet to apply a top dresser – it would have buried itself. So we worked hard over the next forty-eight hours to shovel the best part of forty tonnes of sand on to the surface, following up by rubber-raking the entire pitch by hand.

This measure tightened up the surface and by the Saturday it was hardly noticeable that all that sand had been applied. The pitch looked pretty good, the match was played and the gate receipts went into the bank. The manager saw things differently, however. In his post-match radio interview he stated that the groundsman had, for some unknown reason, decided to cover the pitch in sand and it had affected his team's performance.

I found Richard's comments deeply disappointing. We'd worked so hard to get the game played at all, knowing full well that it would have been off had we not set to with shovels and forks. With payday approaching, that would have put heavy pressure on the chairman.

A meeting took place the following week between Jez George, Stewart Jeffs, a sports turf representative I'd worked with for decades, and myself. We explained the problems with the pitch but, despite our advice, we were told that no more sand was to be used. It was a classic case of someone with very little knowledge of pitch maintenance getting involved.

The pitch continued to struggle with some areas becoming waterlogged after a tiny amount of rain. It came to the point that I was forced to put in a few sand bands by hand in the north-west corner of the pitch, where they were unlikely to be seen by the management. I knew this was the only way to improve the surface – I'd done a similar job at Peterborough years earlier – and sure enough, within just two days the area we'd worked on had improved dramatically.

I asked to see the chairman, who looked at our work and agreed it had transformed the pitch's stability. OK, it didn't look pretty but it reduced the risk of losing games.

The chairman joined me, my staff and volunteers for a couple of weeks as we set about putting sand bands in by hand. It's not something you're likely to see at Premier League grounds, but you have to do what it takes to get games played within the resources available to you.

We laid old advertising boards back to back across the pitch, with forty-millimetre gaps between them, and two people with edging knives would cut out a trench forty millimetres wide. This was then dragged out with drag hoes that had been cut down to 35mm width and the root zone was removed to a depth of 150mm, until we hit the clean gravel that sits on the main drains. It was a mammoth task but the more work we carried out, the dryer the pitch became.

At home one evening after another long, hard day, I had one of those A-Team moments – you know, when Hannibal manages to knock something life-saving together out of a comb, two rubber bands and some sticky-backed plastic. Or is that another TV programme? Anyway, I was doodling away on a scrap of paper, trying to come up with something that I could have knocked up and put on the three-point linkage of the tractor, cutting the amount of manual work and speeding up the process at a stroke.

I love it when a plan comes together. After several hours of doodling I had something down on paper that looked like it would work. The following day I got in touch with a mate who worked in steel fabrication. He came over, had a look at our design attempts and announced that my sketch had some mileage. Two days later he arrived at the stadium with the prototype of a tractor-mounted sand band cutter.

The moment of truth was upon me. I climbed on to the tractor and, with fingers, toes and everything else crossed, dropped the cutting discs into the ground and pulled forward. The air was blue when the cutting discs buckled under the pressure – we had designed them to run parallel to each other and they were trapping the spoil.

Off came the kit and away went my mate to beef up the discs and have them set at different angles. He returned the following day with prototype two, and this time joy was unconfined as it cut through the turf as clean as a whistle. 'Job done!' my mate cried.

I was forced to cut short his celebrations. 'Hold your horses,' I said. 'Now we've got the disc cutters working, I need to fit a leg and a shoe on the bottom to lift the soil out of the ground.'

It took several more attempts to get the modification's depth and angle right, but once it was sorted the kit worked like a dream. We lowered it into the ground, the discs cut the turf and a spade on the back of the kit removed the root zone and laid it to one side, ready to be collected. The mini-trench was then back-filled and compressed with sand and the capillary draw we achieved worked very effectively.

The end of the season was approaching and we were asking for quotations for a pitch renovation from a number of companies that dealt with fibre sand pitches. Why fibre sand? We'd played away on a firm, fast fibre sand pitch and it had worked well for us. The quotes ranged from £35,000 to half a million and I'm sure you can guess which option we went for.

The top 30mm of the pitch was taken off with a Koro Field Top Maker (look it up and prepare to be amazed) and new 80mm lateral drains were installed at five-metre centres and gravel bands at metre centres. We applied 380 tonnes of fibre sand and cultivated it into the top 100mm profile, then overseeded the whole shebang.

Though I say so myself and even though the work had been carried out on a shoestring, the pitch looked in cracking condition come the first game of the season. It would make Cambridge United 'pass masters', Richard Money told the local media. It didn't even look as though a game had been played on it, and it would suit teams who wanted to get the ball down and pass.

Richard's comments came as something of a nice surprise as this was the first time we'd received any compliments from his management team. The acclaim was short-lived, however.

We'd been playing on a grass height of 25mm in League games, and the pitch had played fast and proved very stable. The operations manager then passed on the news that the director of football and team manager wanted the grass cut shorter, down to 18mm. 'You're having a laugh,' I protested. 'No,' he said. 'You've just got to do it.'

I got Craig Lalley from Mansfield Sand in for a meeting to make the management aware that what they were proposing was far from good practice. Craig arrived with a letter stating that 18mm was too short and that a sensible height of cut should be reinstated.

It emerged that Richard had picked up a seed company brochure that stated the seed I was using could be cut to a height of 18mm. That didn't mean you could play professional football on that height of grass, I explained, but my pleas fell on deaf ears and we played on 18mm for several months.

As the colder weather began to creep in and the pitch began to struggle and cut up, I raised the subject of the height of cut with the management again; there was a greater risk of losing games to frost if we didn't raise it, I told them. This time I was allowed to increase the height.

That was a challenge. By that time of year the grass had just about stopped growing.

CHAPTER 11

—

LIFE-CHANGING

Dear Ian,

I started off as a matchday steward, became head supervisor of the away section and then deputy safety officer. I took over from you as matchday safety officer. Fulfilling that role has opened my eyes.

How you managed it alongside your other duties – stadium manager and head groundsman – I will never know.

Among many other aspects of the job, you have to be an agony uncle. The number of calls, emails and texts I get every day – people wanting to talk about domestic matters and so on – is unbelievable. You're a listener and support your staff.

Your best qualities are undoubtedly your commitment – you give a hundred per cent and nothing less – and the professional way you do your job.

I simply can't believe the time, the effort and the amount of your own money you've put into Cambridge United over the years.

Andy Pickard

Cambridge United matchday safety officer

I remember the date vividly, although at first it seemed like any other day at work. It was 6 August 2013. I was replacing divots on the pitch when my volunteer secretary Carol phoned to ask if I could go to the club office and collect an advertising sign that had just been delivered.

I put down my fork and made my way to pick up the sign, checking the corridors in the office were clear as I went. I took great care in picking up the thin metal sign, which was about five feet by two, and was careful how I carried it too – these things can be bloody sharp, as we'd often found when fitting them around the pitch perimeter.

Meanwhile, in the couple of minutes that I was in my office, someone placed some cardboard boxes along my exit route from the building. I never saw them.

Tripping over the boxes, I nosedived forward and hit the deck. It was over in a second but I remember feeling, as if in slow motion, the sign's sharp edge heading towards my face and throat as I was falling. A thought flashed through my mind: if I fall on that my time could be up.

The last thing I heard before the darkness descended on me was an almighty crash. Then marketing manager Julie Clark was holding my head and telling me to lie still.

I'd smashed my head on a wall and terrible pain was slicing through my hip and stomach. Some teeth were broken and there was blood all round my mouth and neck. Gingerly, I felt my throat to see if I'd cut it open.

A first-responder paramedic was on the scene within minutes. He gave me morphine for the pain and stabilised me, and an ambulance crew then whisked me off to Addenbrooke's, where more tests were carried out. Before I was discharged several hours later, I was told I was passing blood.

There followed a night of terrific pain and precious little sleep, and by the morning I was wondering if I'd had a stroke. I had no feeling in my right arm and three fingers of that hand, and the neck pain was excruciating. The problem, which later proved to stem from a neck and back injury, plagued me for months, until I underwent an operation to burn out the nerves.

It would be months following the medical procedures before I could return to work. Even then I was very limited in what I could do and had to get friends to help out.

I knew after a few weeks that something besides the physical damage was very wrong, but I couldn't put my finger on it. I just tried to get on with things.

In January 2015 every small club's dream came true for Cambridge United: a home draw in the third round of the FA Cup against the world's biggest club, Manchester United.

It was fantastic for the club and supporters but a bloody nightmare for me.

I would have to prepare the pitch in what I knew would be sub-zero temperatures. Still at that time matchday safety officer, I would need to schedule a series of meetings with the local authority and police. A number of staff had just started working at the club and had no knowledge of what working big games required.

The BBC announced that it would show the game live on TV on the evening of Friday, January 23. Manchester United, in particular safety officer Phil Rainford, were tremendously helpful. The security team visited the stadium to ensure everything was as it should be, and they planned a Friday-night dry run with the team coach from Bedford Lodge in Newmarket, where the team was due to stay, to the ground. I often drove to and from Newmarket, where my parents lived, and I felt the timings the dry run would produce would be misleading.

At my suggestion, Phil agreed the dry run should be carried out so that the bus arrived at the Abbey a couple of hours before the scheduled kick-off time. So, accepting the chance to see how the other half lived, I climbed into the luxury bus for the drive to Bedford Lodge, along with police tactical advisor Duncan Norman – something of a Bobby Charlton lookalike – and one of the Man U security team.

We arrived at the hotel and set off on the return trip. It took ten or fifteen minutes to clear the main drag through Newmarket town centre, and already the bus driver was saying the timings would have to be changed. It would be worse still on a Friday evening, we assured him.

As we inched along the road in the Man U-branded coach, Duncan's Charltonesque hair style was attracting a great deal of attention from car passengers and on the pavements outside, and some admirers even started to wave. Duncan thought it only proper to wave back.

The journey took fifteen minutes longer than the original estimate, so a revised schedule had the team leaving twenty minutes earlier than first proposed – for their safety, we had to get the players into the ground before the turnstiles opened.

By now I'd realised that we might face problems with counterfeit tickets. I'd browsed the internet the day after the draw and, to my amazement, found two websites selling match tickets. This was surprising because at that point the club hadn't had any printed. Gathering as much information as possible, I navigated both websites in the guise of a customer until I got to the checkouts. My investigations revealed that tickets were being offered for sale in an imaginary 'Stand D', with rows and seats that did not exist. I passed the information on to the relevant parties, who confirmed that I'd found fake overseas sites trying to make a fast buck.

We knew we were facing a battle with Mother Nature. Temperatures were forecast to drop as low as minus seven and frost could have put the fixture in peril. The BBC, anxious not to risk losing such a high-profile live match, asked us to cover the pitch with a balloon and pump hot air under it, and I complied with joy. I also took the opportunity to give the pitch a drink in the form of liquid feed, which perked up the grass and improved the colour for the TV cameras.

Before we knew it, the big day was upon us. The Beeb's Match of the Day host, Gary Lineker, and his pundits were casting admiring glances at the surface and commenting on how good it looked. In view of what happened after the game, their opinions were helpful.

It remained bitterly cold and we had to leave the balloon inflated later than we'd planned. That meant I couldn't mark out the pitch until around five o'clock, less than three hours before kick-off. Several of the photographer boys seized the chance to snap a groundsman marking out a pitch wearing not scruffs and wellies but a rather natty suit, though I say so myself. 'Bloody hell, chaps,' I mused. 'If you came here more often you'd see this is nothing unusual.'

I'd spent many hours doing my safety homework for this fixture; it was, after all, United's biggest home game for a very long time. Phil Rainford provided a raft of information and I reckoned we were ready for whatever might come along. But as the time ticked by it became clear that we had an exceedingly busy evening ahead of us.

Phil had kindly arranged for ten of his stewards to help out, and I was chuffed when he commented on how professional we'd been in the build-up. All the safety authorities were there – the local people, Martin Girvan from the Sports Ground Safety Authority, a friend for two decades who gave me masses of information, and FA crowd advisor Barry Norman, who normally dealt with the security around the England team.

I feel I now have some understanding of how it must have felt to be a medieval peasant in a city under siege. Every single thing that we'd anticipated could happen did happen.

Supporters tried to force their way in all over the stadium: attempting to surf over the turnstiles, climbing over walls and even the Supporters' Club roof, and invading neighbouring residents' properties. Genuine fans reported that they'd had tickets snatched out their hands.

Near kick-off, groups of Mancunian supporters stormed the south turnstiles, breaking them and causing them to spin freely. This resulted in the monitoring system showing capacity had been reached in the South Stand. The lessons of Hillsborough remain fresh in any matchday safety officer's mind, and I decided to close the turnstiles, not allowing any more spectators into that section of the stadium.

On the night, taking into account that we had more than fifty-five forced entries and ejections, the safety side of things went as well as we could have hoped, and we received some very gratifying comments from the safety representatives. And the match ended in a goalless draw, setting up a huge payday for the club in the form of a replay at Old Trafford.

During the storming of the turnstiles one of my stewards had been injured, pinned against a bridge that crosses Coldhams Brook and leads to the gates. But it was what happened after the game that would later cause me serious problems, while also perhaps helping me to find a path out of them.

During his debrief, the injured steward described what had happened and showed me his injuries. He said he'd been so scared at one point that, pinned against the bridge's steelwork and struggling to breathe, he thought he was going to die.

Those words echoed in my head and refused to die away. I'd felt precisely the same thing during my mishap with the metal advertising sign.

I'd known that all was not well in my mental processes from a few weeks after the accident, but it wasn't something I wanted to talk about. As I finished the debrief, I felt dark shadows closing in around me.

There was much to do after the game: the debrief with police, the de-rigging of the TV equipment and a multitude of other tasks, and I didn't get away from the stadium until one o'clock in the morning. Despite all the little jobs, I had some time to myself in the control room, during which I sat and cried uncontrollably. For a long time I'd been experiencing worrying symptoms: plagued by recurring, nightmarish thoughts about the accident, I'd become familiar with tingling lips, hot flushes, the shakes and acute feelings of distress.

I'd noticed that since the accident I'd become reserved, quiet and non-confrontational, avoiding situations that would require me to fight my corner, and that was not like me. Before the accident, while always happy to help anyone out, I would have my say if I felt I was in the right. Now I felt I had become like a limp, wet lettuce and would do anything to avoid confrontation in any form.

I arrived home at 1.45am on Saturday morning and by the time I'd had something to eat and drink it was half-two. I was back at the stadium for seven o'clock to enable the TV riggers to get their gear packed up ready to move on to the next Cup game.

I was writing up the paperwork from the game in the control room at 7.45am when the stadium director burst through the door, and he was buzzing. 'What a great night!' he enthused. 'What a great result!'

The dam burst and the tears came flooding out again. 'Great night?' I managed to blurt out between huge, shoulder-shaking sobs. 'Are you kidding?

'I had a steward who was badly injured, it was so full on it was like dealing with a game from the early Eighties, I didn't get a chance to have a drink from midday Friday until 1.45am this morning, I'm really struggling and I can't carry on like this.'

I know now that the cocktail of drugs I was taking to combat the pain from my injuries and various surgical procedures was a major contributor to the way I was feeling. Waking up every day in pain and discomfort takes its toll. Little was I to know that I would be diagnosed with post-traumatic stress disorder and would undergo harrowing, intense therapy that would challenge me to the very core of my soul.

As if I didn't have enough problems ... the day after the Man U game I was made aware that their manager, Louis van Gaal, had complained about the pitch. I found that mystifying when his backroom staff had had nothing but praise for the surface, but my surprise and gratification when the media came out in support of me, the pitch and Cambridge United was enormous.

I've never had the pleasure of meeting Mick Dennis, at that time the football correspondent of the Daily Express, but if I ever do I'll shake his hand. I'll always be grateful for his support in the story published four days after the game, from which I'm quoting large chunks below.

Under the headline 'Louis van Gaal is the loser in this pitch battle', Mick wrote:

'Let me tell you about Ian Darler. He's the man whose life's work was gratuitously insulted by Louis van Gaal.'

The 'supremely arrogant' van Gaal was, he said, dismissive of all the hard work I'd done and too self-absorbed to offer any congratulations to United. 'Instead, a predictably familiar bleat about the referee was embellished with a needless and inaccurate moan about the condition of the pitch. And that traduced Darler's achievements and efforts.'

I'd been United's head groundsman, and sometimes the only groundsman, since 1979, Mick pointed out, and '... for some of those thirty-five and a bit years, the club were in administration and even when they were technically solvent, they were often skint. In fact,

Darler reckons he has spent about £30,000 of his own money over the years on lawnmowers and the like, so that the club's financial woes did not prevent him from providing the best possible playing surface.' With the exception of the first John Beck spell, I'd mostly produced turf of which anyone would be proud, the article said, and in 2010 I'd won the FA's national groundsman of the year award.

Mick declared: 'The pitch was pretty much perfect at kick-off on Friday night. It cut up a little before the end, but that is what happens when you play on proper grass, rather than the £800,000 hybrid of natural turf and synthetic fibres they have at Old Trafford.

'That's the wonder of the FA Cup, surely, that teams like United, for whom money is no object, have to play clubs who scrimp and save and who are kept alive by the dedication and commitment of volunteers and loyal club servants. In the background at all the "little" clubs who enjoyed surprise Cup triumphs at the weekend there will be men and women who have toiled for decades – some for very little reward, some for none at all.

'But it is a reward of sorts when clubs like the United based in Cambridge play a club such as the United based at Old Trafford. It's a once-in-a-lifetime experience full of completely justifiable pride. If the underdogs then grab a good result, well, it is magical for all of us. It reminds us why, for all its wanton extravagance, the battered old game can still amaze and move us.'

Mick's moving piece went on to say that Ryan Giggs understood this and had made a point of congratulating the U's players. Van Gaal was fortunate that the main media focus wouldn't be on him that week, for there had been bigger Cup upsets over the weekend.

It concluded: 'But I hope that someone at United tells lucky Louis that his graceless remarks in Cambridge told us more about his unattractive personality than he intended – and that they paid no regard at all to a good man whose service to the game deserved better.'

Following van Gaal's outburst, our head coach Richard Money stepped into the debate, saying the ground staff did an excellent job on a minimal budget. I appreciated that, and thanked Richard for his support; it was the first time I'd seen this side of the man – an almost shy, thoughtful and caring side.

The follow-up report from Chris Whalley of the FA blew me away, while Barry Norman's account contained much detail and, more importantly, showed that our safety team, stewards and medics worked to a very high standard.

Although our stadium was dated, Barry wrote, it was clear that a great deal of effort was made to maintain it to the best possible standard. I probably had an unrivalled depth of experience at this level and presented as an excellent ambassador for the club and its safety officers. My briefing of the background to the match, preparation and event management plan and my documentation were all of a very high standard. The stewards' briefing, which had cascaded from me via supervisors, was appropriate and effective and encouraged dialogue.

Barry reported that the dry run I'd organised for the Man U bus had led to the visitors correctly leaving their hotel earlier than planned. My decision to close the South Stand's turnstiles was, in his view, the right one. He concluded by saying that the policing and stewarding were of a high standard, co-operation between police and stewards had impressed him and my grip of every aspect of the event management was a testament to my skills, experience and unrivalled commitment.

Wow. That brought a lump to my throat. It also showed how much commitment my staff had given me over the years, not just for this one big game. Many had been with me from the old Division Two days. I was even more blown away to receive a complimentary email about the report from the club's CEO.

Jez George wrote: 'I thought I would share this report with you all. It's the high level of excellence that we aspire towards across the whole club and every part of our operation. Absolute professionalism whether it's from senior staff, junior staff, part-time staff or matchday staff. If we all demand excellence and settle for nothing less, our behaviours and our standards will permeate down to everyone. That is what happens with Ian's staff on match days.'

Van Gaal's comments provoked amazing support from groundsmen's organisations. Sports Management magazine said the fact that I hadn't reacted to the criticism was an example of why I was considered among the best in the business, and went on: 'Far be it from him to allow himself to be put on a pedestal, however. He'd much rather advocate recognition for groundsmen and the groundsmanship industry as a whole.'

The Institute of Groundsmanship's chief executive, Geoff Webb, wrote that when I revealed I'd spent £30,000 of my own money on the pitch and equipment over the years, I'd demonstrated the dedication of groundsmen for whom the role wasn't just a job but a passion. 'People like Ian make this industry stand out,' said Geoff.

It was enough to bring back the tears.

The playing side of the club evolved again and Richard Money left for pastures new, making way for Shaun Derry. This coincided with the introduction of a new management and reporting structure that I found strange. In future, I was not to deal directly with the team manager (or head coach, as he was now titled); I had to speak to a line manager about pitch requirements. In turn, the team manager/head coach could not speak directly to me and had to communicate through the same line manager.

This was unfamiliar territory to me, but I didn't question it. I had enough on my plate. Awaiting further surgery and doped up on high painkiller dosages, I was finding day-to-day life terrifyingly difficult.

But we continued to provide top-quality surfaces for Shaun and I had no complaints from him. We acknowledged each other on match days and he was always very civil.

There was one occasion when we did manage to speak man-to-man. Shaun asked if there was any chance of making a pre-match adjustment to the pitch, and I replied that I had no problem with that at all but I couldn't carry out his request without the line manager's approval. Shaun's face, which always reminded me of Simon Callow, formed into an accurate representation of the famous actor expressing disbelief, and I sympathised. Anyway, the three-way consultation took place and the changes were made.

I'd made the management aware that I was struggling and that I had to undergo more surgery. I'll be honest: I was disappointed that no assistance in any form had been offered when I'd asked for it some months earlier, and I was left to fend for myself.

I was expected to be off manual work for six weeks but I'd planned the appointment so that it would cause as little disruption as possible to the club. I wouldn't be able to cut the pitch for six weeks, but I reckoned I would be back at the club within a couple of weeks to run the office side of things and act as matchday safety officer, and cope with other paperwork at home.

The operation went ahead but I struggled with the after-effects of the anaesthetic and was kept in Spire Lea Hospital for twenty-four hours. I was glad to get home but the feeling didn't last. I was feeling very unwell, coughing up blood and green sputum, and the doctors were concerned that there was a possibility of a blood clot on a lung. There was a series of tests and scans to endure, at the end of which they found that I'd picked up an infection, possibly caused by intubation (the insertion of a tube into the body) during the surgery.

I'm not exaggerating when I say that this experience was a life changer. I struggled for months with pain from the hip surgery and seemed constantly to be on antibiotics for the lung infection. I would finish each course believing the infection had gone, only for it to make itself felt again a week or ten days later.

One day, in the middle of a challenging physiotherapy session aimed at helping the hip recovery, I broke down and wept. I just couldn't cope with feeling so poorly and my frustrations at not being able to get on with my life poured out of me in a torrent. I was experiencing frequent torrid flashbacks to the accident, although I kept them to myself. They were wrecking my sleep patterns and when I did manage to drift off I was restless and sweating, sitting bolt upright in bed and shouting.

Lisa kept asking what was wrong with me. I couldn't tell her. How could I begin to tell anyone what had turned a proud, strong, fit man striding confidently through life into a shambling, shuffling, weeping, twitching and trembling excuse for a human being?

My physio had set me a number of exercises, some at home and one involving a short walk through the village streets on crutches. It was while I was struggling on one of these excursions that a solution revealed itself.

All the excruciating pain, grief, mental torture, feelings of inadequacy and frustration could be over in seconds, I realised. All I had to do was to step out in front of a car.

It was thirty seconds before I was able to banish the destructive thought. It was enough to think about what effect my suicide would have on Lisa, Liam and Ruby for me to snap out of it. I demanded of myself: what the hell is wrong with you?

I returned home shaken and called my GP, only to break down while I was on the phone. An emergency appointment was made for me at the surgery, and there I answered a series of questions about my state of mind. Everything around the accident had caught up with me, I sobbed. From the first day I'd struggled with pain and discomfort.

I was told that what I was experiencing was not uncommon and I was put on the list for an appointment at CPFT, which provides physical and mental health services for adults and older people.

Several weeks, during which I continued to battle the lung infection, went by. It had knocked me for six and some days I was so poorly that I struggled to get up the stairs. And without me being aware of it, I had become snappy, raising my voice and generally being unaware of what was going on around me. I can now see, and admit, that I was very scared.

The appointment with CPFT came through and I had to summon every scrap of courage I had left in order to attend. But at least I was acknowledging that I couldn't get through this nightmare on my own and needed help.

At the first appointment the therapist asked me to recall, in minute detail, every second of the accident and its aftermath. I found it incredibly difficult to relive an incident that had devastated my life, but I managed to struggle through.

I told her that I'd fallen over some boxes at work, suffering a number of injuries including a cut head, broken teeth and damaged hip and elbow. The ambulance crew had given me morphine. I'd been passing blood and feeling generally unwell, and the following day I'd woken with no feeling in three fingers and unable to move my neck. This had led to several medical procedures to remove nerves in my back and neck to relieve the symptoms, and then three procedures on my right hip, while taking a cocktail of pain-relieving drugs. Since the bang on the head, I said, my memory had been shot to pieces, which bothered me massively. My assistant Mick Brown had noticed the change a few months after the accident.

There were a few things I couldn't talk about as to do so would make me feel ill, set my lips tingling and send me into a panic.

I couldn't tell the therapist that I was carrying a very thin piece of metal Dibond two feet by five when I fell, or that as I was falling all I could see was the razor-sharp metal in front of my face, or that I was thinking if I fell on the sheet it would cut my head off and I would die. I couldn't tell her that when I came round from the bang on the head I had blood in my mouth and on my face, and could remember running my fingers around my throat, thinking I had indeed landed on the metal.

I attended these appointments for several months before being referred to a consultant psychiatrist, Dr Louisa Mann.

A psychiatrist? Had it come to this? I had little knowledge of what a psychiatrist actually did and didn't have a clue what to expect. Attending my first session with Dr Mann was one of the scariest moments of my life.

The appointment involved a number of tests and a series of questions, and then Dr Mann told me she would refer me for a brain scan due to my loss of memory. She also said she believed I was suffering from depression. I did not accept her conclusion.

I went back for several more appointments and each one was more difficult than the last. Time after time Dr Mann asked me to consider medication to help me sleep, but I declined. Then one day I said the solution to the whole sorry affair was simple: I just needed to 'man up'.

Wrong answer, but it was a turning point.

It wasn't easy, but Dr Mann convinced me that trying to 'man up' wasn't a helpful approach. Finally I surrendered to her advice. Finally I accepted that I was suffering from depression. Finally I agreed to take the antidepressant mirtazapine.

From then on it was plain sailing, if you believe that plain sailing consists of paddling around the world against the clock in a leaky canoe while half-starved sharks circle menacingly and you haven't a clue where you are or where you're going. In fact, the next few weeks were some of the toughest of my life.

The thought of setting foot outside the house filled me with fear. I would avoid anywhere there were likely to be other people, which is pretty much everywhere. I would take the dog for a walk without noticing anything on the way, and later not realise I'd been out.

My assistant Mick, whom I've known for thirty years, drove past when I was on one of these walks. He was waiting patiently to see me when I got home, and said he hadn't recognised me. 'I thought it was an old fella in his seventies,' he added.

A number of very close friends starting coming round to see how I was. I appreciated these visits but found them enormously difficult, tiring experiences. My matchday medical officer and deputy safety officers visited several times and, to my surprise, one of them revealed that he'd been through depression himself and knew exactly what I was going through. One of my most loyal friends, a matchday steward at the club for forty years, came round and told me he too had suffered terribly during his depression.

While these reassurances went some way towards persuading me that depression is a distressingly common disease, I'm sorry to say that at the time they were like water off a duck's back. I couldn't see a way out of what I was feeling; I had no interest in anything; if somebody had presented me with a million pounds and asked what I would like to do with it, I would have replied 'nothing'. My life had no meaning and even less purpose.

But I had another huge surprise when one of my visitors, before I'd said a word, described my symptoms in precise detail and said he'd also been through a rough spell. I wasn't alone, he stressed. He was a serving police officer and real hard nut who was always the first to put his head above the parapet and deal with crowd disorder – the last person I would have suspected of suffering from depression. His revelation had an impact on me and I found it so much easier than usual to talk to him.

I struggled to sleep, I told him, and more often than not when I did get to sleep I would wake an hour or two later reliving the accident or feeling like I had the devil sitting on my shoulder, taunting me. I felt utterly useless, I had no energy or enthusiasm for anything, I was scared of my own shadow, I was unsociable, I felt everyone was judging me, I was snappy with loved ones ... no doubt about it, depression is a dark place to be, full of terrors and there's no sign it will ever improve. Depression is a killer.

The psychiatrist appointments kept coming but I was finding the waiting room intimidating. I dreaded seeing anyone I knew. It sounds ridiculous now but at my lowest point I couldn't get out of the house, so I was set a challenge by Dr Mann: going to the Co-op twice a day to start engaging with people in public places.

I found myself cheating. If the car park was busy I would wait until it was quiet, and I would have the right money ready in my pocket for a quick exit at the till. There were times when my lips felt three times their real size, I had the shakes and panic attacks were common. Having dealt with large crowds at work for decades, I found these especially hard to deal with but there I would be, struggling to breathe, convinced I was having a heart attack and was going to die.

———————————

At one appointment a colleague of Dr Mann's was in the room. Dr Kim asked if I would return to the clinic with a family member or friend. I couldn't bring myself to ask Lisa as I knew I'd already put her through hell, so I asked my good friend Andy if he would come.

We were both asked a series of questions and Andy said I'd had an amazing memory before the accident; something had changed since then. Once again, I was asked to relive everything that happened on the day of the accident and as I recalled the events of those awful hours I broke down in a flood of tears. Dr Kim asked why the tears had come, and for the first time I talked about the flashbacks to that terrible moment when I thought I was about to die. It was likely that I was suffering from PTSD as well as depression, Dr Kim told me.

There followed weeks of exhausting therapy with Isobel Wright that involved reliving the accident several times a week while holding a Dibond metal sheet, as well as exercises to be completed at home, and the trips to the Co-op continued. But I found it impossible to go anywhere near the Abbey Stadium and I couldn't bring myself to watch football on TV.

In the latter part of the treatment for PTSD, Dr Kim asked me to relive the accident on the council sports pitches on Coldham Common, behind my stadium, with the floodlights in full view. All the distressing symptoms came flooding back. Then an ambulance siren shattered the air and in an instant I was back at the accident.

But very gradually the reliving sessions on the Common with Dr Kim began to help and I felt my life was finally beginning to improve. It wasn't the end; it wasn't even the beginning of the end; but it might have been the end of the beginning.

Then came the acid test: Dr Kim asked if I could arrange a treatment session in the stadium's control room. This we did, but at the point at which I was reliving falling over the boxes, Dr Kim created a deafening crashing sound. I was instantly paralysed: in my mind the accident had just happened all over again, with terrible clarity.

Unbeknown to me, she had brought a plastic bag full of cutlery with her and at the crucial moment she dropped it behind me. I was hypersensitive to crashing sounds, the good doctor concluded. My brain recognised these noises as signs of danger and reacted accordingly.

As I was going through this treatment I was made aware that the pitch at United had deteriorated, and I was asked what could be done to improve it. I'd only seen the pitch from a distance but I could identify the problem and was able to call in a few favours to help improve it.

Then my line managers came over to our house to discuss possible ways forward and talk about what was required in terms of end-of-season pitch maintenance. I explained that I'd managed to continue working from home every day, arranging the safety documents and organising staff for my deputy safety officer, even though my condition had made it an excruciatingly difficult process.

The club, I was told, had made changes, had brought in several new employees and was now a company with a turnover of £6 million. I found this surprising as the club had always been run with a limited number of staff, and generally run very well. That had nothing to do with me, however.

Following the meeting I took a phone call out of the blue, followed up by a letter, informing me that the club had engaged an occupational health nurse who would be in touch to see when I could get back to work. The news caused me so much stress that I couldn't stop shaking and could hardly speak. Why now, I wondered, after all this time? And why at a time when I was starting to recover?

I had to wait for a week or so for the phone call, but the nurse was kind and understanding. She explained that the call would take around thirty minutes and that she'd been asked to assess when I would be back to work following my hip surgery.

I stopped her there. 'Are you telling me,' I asked, 'that the club think I'm off work just because of my hip?' Her affirmative reply staggered me and I almost dropped the phone.

I spent well over an hour recounting yet again what had happened: I'd been through seven medical procedures; I was still fighting an infection; I was still undergoing post-operative physio; I was undergoing treatment for depression and PTSD. Despite all that, I'd been working from home and had processed more than 1,200 emails while away from the stadium, and I'd been in constant contact with my assistant Mick Brown and Robert Bradshaw, a mate who had helped out with the pitch for weeks with no payment. The club had also received sick notes containing all the necessary information. I finished by explaining that I'd asked the doctors several times when I could return to work and had been told that I was nowhere near fit enough.

'Right,' said the nurse, 'you've told me quite enough. I'm stopping any further work from home while you're receiving treatment for PTSD.'

She called a few more times, saying my doctors at CPFT had provided her with documentation of my therapy and had confirmed that they were very disappointed by the letters I'd received from a manager at the club. Considering my condition, they were unhelpful.

My treatments continued and I continued to improve. Finally, it was agreed that I could get back to work on a phased return basis.

Working as an unpaid matchday safety officer for the best part of thirty years, I've had to deal with more than the occasional challenge presented by my staff. At times I've felt like a counsellor as employees have come to me with their problems: divorce, affairs, serious health issues, family, money and accommodation problems, depression, suicide attempts ... it's an almost endless list. It's not easy dealing with these issues but I feel honoured to have been trusted.

I used to think I was helping the people who said they'd been diagnosed with depression. Like a fool I would say: 'Come and have a day with me at the stadium.' It was not until I had the accident in 2013 and ended up with chronic depression and PTSD that I realised that, if they were experiencing anything like what I was going through, these poor people would never have turned up at the stadium; it would have been hard enough for them to step outside their front doors.

BD (before depression) I was enthusiastic about life and never let anything beat me; I always found a way of getting things done, even if the money wasn't available to do the job.

AD (after depression) I would wake from a broken sleep and know I had a bad day in front of me. I had zero energy, I was fatigued to the point of exhaustion and, no matter how hard I tried, I couldn't see the point in doing anything. What made it a hundred times worse was that I believed everyone was talking about me.

Depression is an invisible injury – you don't walk around on a crutch or wear a bandage on your head – and in my case, no matter how hard I tried, I couldn't shake it off on my own. My energy levels had always been high, but once depression hit I couldn't get out of bed.

Since my return to work a couple of employees have told me that they'd tried to take their own lives but had not sought help. With my newly acquired understanding of depression, I found myself able to offer some advice. They acknowledged some similarities and, thank God, did seek help.

The football club now offers a service, for both staff and the public, who are suffering from forms of depression. That's absolutely brilliant but I wish it had been in place when I was poorly. My request for help met with no response whatsoever, and at one point I was even put under pressure to return to work when I was clearly unfit. That caused a lot of stress and worry and disgusted my clinical team, I can tell you.

I still have my lows, but at least I smell nice.

One of the weapons in the therapy staff's armoury, brought into play to help lift a low mood, involved the use of smells and spicy food. Soon I was eating chillis by the jarful. To be fair, I think they did some good, but I'll always remember with a wince the first time I'd had my fill of the hot stuff. The morning after, it felt as if the Apollo 11 crew had put on the afterburners in order to break free of my arse.

And in an attempt to disguise the lingering odours left by my new curry habit, I was using so much Vetiver aftershave that Lisa thought I was having an affair.

CHAPTER 12

—

BATTLING THE BEAST

Dear Ian,

I began attending matches as part of the medical cover from the East Anglian Ambulance Service (now East of England Ambulance Trust) in the late 1990s.

At first I was slightly overwhelmed by your energy and passion, but I soon found you to be a consummate professional, almost obsessive in your diligence in the areas of health and safety and law and order. Your tenacity in getting things right is a godsend. Nothing is ever left to chance.

The stewards are well drilled in first aid interventions. It was at your request that we paramedics provided that training. In rare events of medical emergency, casualties want for nothing. All eventualities are trained for, drilled and agreed.

Cardiac arrests are fairly rare, but I'm aware of two casualties still thriving today who have had the pathway between life and death interrupted, having been clinically dead.

I've rarely met a more passionate humanitarian: you have given so much more than could reasonably be asked for so long. If I were involved in a medical emergency, I would be grateful and honoured to have you there for me.

And you extend your altruism into the wider community, raising thousands of pounds for charity. If anyone deserves to be considered for the honours list, you're the man.

Without your efforts, your club may have folded a long time ago.

Bob Brotchie

Former matchday paramedic and ambulance officer-in-charge

One evening in October 2015 I was surprised to find myself picking my way between dozens of tables towards a stage, in a large room full of smartly dressed people. There, in front of hundreds of applauding and cheering folk, I was presented with the Cambridge News Lifetime Achievement award by Andy Lucas, commercial director of the award's sponsor, the Cambridge Building Society.

The newspaper's account of what I'd managed to achieve in my time at United was highly complimentary and I felt truly honoured as I stood quietly on the stage, acknowledging the kind applause. I also felt a million miles outside my comfort zone.

I was still receiving treatment for post-traumatic stress disorder and was far from healed. At no point during the swish event in the grand surroundings of Homerton College, surrounded by happy, laughing diners who seemed to be unconsciously hemming me in, did I feel at ease, or anywhere near it.

It was a fantastic night for my family, who had been to hell and back as they struggled to cope with the changed man they'd had to live with throughout my health problems.

I look back at the evening and feel very privileged to have been numbered among the amazing people who have won the award. But I'll be honest: at the time it was pure torture and I regret not being able to recall fully how the evening unfolded or enjoy it as I should have.

If there was ever a perfect time to return to work, I chose it. In the summer of 2017 the pitch was in such poor condition there was a real risk that the planned pre-season friendlies would have to be called off. The pre-season work I'd recommended had not been undertaken; instead, the bare minimum had been done. The playing surface was bare in several places and covered in slime and we had just three weeks until the first game.

I called in a few favours. We Verti-Drained the surface and sprayed the pitch with liquid charcoal that had been donated free of charge. We then overseeded and dressed the pitch with an 80-20 root zone dressing and hit it hard with a consolidated liquid feed every seventy-two hours.

That had the effect of forcing some growth, and in just three weeks we turned the pitch around. The first pre-season friendly, against Norwich City, duly went ahead.

The success of this work did me a huge favour and I started to sense the return of some of my old confidence. Head coach Shaun Derry said he couldn't believe how we'd managed to get the surface looking so good in such a short space of time.

Shaun was supportive from that day on and a great friendship developed between us, although it turned out to be too short. Having overcome the teething problems when we'd been forced to communicate through a third party, we spoke often about the pitch and what Shaun needed from it, and we had some very honest private conversations.

The stadium was my second home but at first I found it tough being back in what should have been comforting surroundings. I was acutely aware that the slightest incident could trigger a flashback to the accident. In particular, I found it difficult to be around my nemesis: the Dibond advertising signs that were delivered regularly and surrounded the playing surface on the perimeter barriers.

Then, as half-time in the pre-season game against Norwich approached, something happened that shook me rigid.

I was in the irrigation room getting ready to turn the sprinklers on when the crowd reacted to a near-miss shot at goal with a thunderous roar. I froze instantly and it was a few minutes before I could regain my senses.

I walked into the control room as the second half of the game got under way, to be met by the matchday safety officer enquiring what was wrong.

'Why?' I asked.

'You're as white as a sheet,' he said.

Gradually, things began to improve over the weeks that followed, although there were a lot of new faces around the place and I was still finding it hard to be around people. I did my best to keep myself to myself.

The month of February 2018 is remembered for the winter weather phenomenon that swept into Britain from Siberia, bringing plummeting temperatures, ice, snow and raging winds.

We were aware of the so-called Beast from the East a long way in advance. We work with weather forecasts ten to fourteen days in advance of a game. If heavy rain is expected, we can put together an aeration programme to reduce the risk of waterlogging. If a heatwave is on the way, we can build up the pitch moisture levels.

On Wednesday, February 21, a good ten days before we were due to play Luton on March 3, I could see from the long-range forecast that the Beast from the East was heading relentlessly for Cambridge. Very low temperatures were predicted, and that meant we had to be battle-ready for a scrap with Mother Nature.

The decision was made to seal in whatever warmth there was in the playing surface by getting frost sheets on to the pitch. Before that, however, we had to run the mowers over the surface, mark the pitch out to ensure we were match-ready and give the turf a light liquid feed – it was likely to be starved of light for up to nine days if the covers had to stay in place.

The volunteer troops that have helped me for three decades were called in and, along with a number of volunteers from the supporters' trust CFU, we set about getting the frost sheets laid and pegged down.

Over the next few days we monitored the temperatures constantly and all was going well until February 28, when high winds ripped the pegs out of the sheets. They were lifted off the ground, allowing frost and intensely cold air of minus eleven degrees, plus the wind chill, to penetrate the turf.

We set about replacing the covers on the affected areas and reviewed the weather forecast. Getting the match on was still going to be a huge challenge. Concerned supporters were almost queuing up to test the surface with their car keys or digging their heels into the touchline. Their question was always the same: what are the chances of the game going ahead? We wished we could give them a definitive answer.

The day before a large crowd was due to descend on the Abbey, we lifted the sheets to have another look at the depth of frost in the pitch. What we found was worrying: it was rock hard in a number of places. What's more, the insulating sheets were now trapping the frost in the ground.

The Friday evening forecast gave us hope – it predicted temperatures of just minus two overnight. And we might be able to count on up to ten centimetres of snow to warm and insulate the pitch.

Before we could rely on that effect, however, we had to remove the sheets in the hope of getting the frost out the ground, and there were still a couple of centimetres of snow from the previous day to be removed from the covers. Racing increasingly desperately against time, we tried using rubber rakes and brooms but what we really needed was a couple of heavy-duty backpack snow blowers.

CFU chairman Robert Osbourn and fans' elected director Dave Matthew-Jones kindly offered to buy the blowers using money from the club lottery funds, and machinery supplier Ernest Doe rallied round to get the kit to us. The blowers arrived and we all pitched in to blast the snow and ice away.

The job wasn't finished yet … oh no. Once the sheets were lifted we found that the goalmouths were frozen solid and a large area of the pitch was unplayable. A few areas were just about taking a stud.

A local referee, Alan Young, carried out the first pitch inspection and helpfully agreed to let our work run on into match day, when the match referee would make another inspection. I explained that it would be a lot easier to call the game off than to get it on but, with the plans we had in place, we felt we had a great chance of a game.

Another call went out to the volunteers and, with the added help and support of the office staff, our campaign swung into action. Setting up what can only be described as a makeshift camp in each goalmouth, we brought in picnic tables and heavy-duty canvas tarpaulins from around the stadium and convector heaters from the offices. Having set up similar camps a number of times over the years, I was confident it would work.

With a couple of boy scouts roasting nicely over crackling camp fires and Mick Brown launching into the first rousing chorus of Riding Along on the Crest of a Wave, we felt our spirits lifting.

On a bitterly cold morning, along came BBC Sport to film the operation and presenter Jonathan Park, to the sound of icy water dripping off the canvas, asked: 'You have a challenge on your hands; what are the chances of a game?' I was able to reply that we had a chance, which was better than a number of clubs whose games had already been called off.

Head coach Joe Dunne, who had taken Shaun Derry's place, arrived and congratulated us on even being in with a chance of getting the game on. Joe's kind words encouraged the volunteers to push on even harder.

Jonathan then turned to me and said: 'Ian, can you give me a quote about this weather?'

'Yes,' I replied. 'There will be more runny noses than stiff cocks.'

Jonathan guffawed and said: 'Yes, well, I don't think we'll use that tonight.'

We now required Mother Nature's co-operation, and she delivered with a blanket of snow. At home that night I was getting itchy feet, longing to get back to the ground and see if the snow was drawing the frost out of the ground. As it was, I was awake at 2am and out of bed at 3.15am to check the temperature in the garden. I was thrilled when I saw that it had risen above freezing to 0.5 degrees.

It was time to hit the road and, as I drove to work knowing the snow had to be cleared off the pitch in time for the inspection at half past nine, the adrenalin was surging. I could not get to the stadium quickly enough.

You get used to most aspects of a job over the course of nearly forty years, but I still find that an empty Abbey Stadium before dawn and late at night is a strange, rather eerie place. It's also tricky, when you have a tractor and kit to get out of the store area and a floodlight to switch on, so you can see what you're doing, not to disturb the neighbours' slumbers.

By the time the floodlight had warmed up it was around 4.10am. I got my first look at the playing surface and, brushing away a patch of snow with my hand, I knew instantly that we were in business. The camps we'd set up in the goalmouths had done the trick of lifting the frost out of the ground and the huge task of clearing the pitch could begin.

I sent urgent texts to my troops at five o'clock, saying help was needed ASAP, and the first person to arrive, at 6.30am, was matchday safety officer Andy Pickard. He immediately got stuck into helping with the snow removal.

Every one of my volunteers, along with a number of my fishing mates and club staff, arrived from seven-thirty onwards and, to a man and woman, they worked their socks off, as they had so often in the past, to get the job done. The game went ahead.

It would have been easy to turn a blind eye and accept that the game would be off, but professional pride intervenes and I just think you have to do your duty.

I've got the most amazing team of ground staff, made up of stewards and volunteers who have worked for me for more than thirty years. They just appear like the Borrowers, and then a load of fishing mates come out of the woodwork to bail me out. Because they've worked with me for so long, I don't have to tell them what to do; they know what the process is.

Days like the ones I've described are great – they give you a chance to show your skill and ability. It's always a challenge but I'm just as keen now as I was forty years ago. We were well organised, worked very hard and made our own luck.

We had won the battle this time. There will be battles we won't win but we'll always do our best to stage a game. I recalled what my great friend Chris Turner said to me when he was team manager and we had a similar situation. I was the best groundsman in the country, he told me, but not in the town. I believe you are only as good as the people around you and I've been very fortunate to have alongside me for so long a bunch of fantastic people who make an amazing team.

There's one area of my work that I always thought I would find saddening, but that has not always been the case. Each family attending the burial of their loved one's ashes in the Abbey pitch has a different way of dealing with the situation. I've now buried more than forty people's ashes and on each occasion I've felt privileged to be asked.

The interment area is usually chosen by the family, but sometimes the deceased will request a certain location in his or her will. I remove a section of turf, dig a hole and lay a small amount of sand at the bottom as I feel this, rather than just leaving a hole in the soil, shows we care.

As I say, every interment is different, but a few stick in my mind.

On one occasion we'd just had the pitch drains relaid and the playing surface gravel-banded at one-metre centres. I dug a shallow grave on the penalty spot at the Abbey's north end, the family poured in the ashes and I reinstated the turf. It wasn't until a couple of weeks later that I noticed a change in the pitch.

I was strolling along the rear walkway at the top of the east stand and looking down on to the pitch when a peculiar sight stopped me in my tracks. Directly over the penalty spot at the north end, in the precise location of the most recent burial, the pitch had lost its emerald green look. What's more, a perfect cross shape, about six feet by three, had appeared.

I hurried over to the main office to tell Steve Greenall, the company secretary at the time, that I had something to show him. Steve duly joined me up at the back of the stand, looked out over the pitch and gasped. 'Oh my God, Mr Darler,' he said, 'there's a cross where we buried the lad's ashes.'

We concluded that the high levels of salt in the human body had affected the grass and that the irrigation had spread the salt along the drain and gravel bands. The area took several weeks to recover. I have never made the same mistake again and always ensure that ashes are buried well below our root structure depth.

On another occasion Steve was with me on the pitch to attend an interment service. There was nothing unusual about the routine: the hole was prepared and the ashes were poured in. The entire family of the deceased, including elderly brothers, sons and grandchildren, had turned out.

Steve and I watched as one of the middle-aged sons bent over the hole with a couple of young children, aged around six and eight, and started spreading the ashes around the hole with his fingers. 'Say goodbye to Grandad,' he told the kids, whereupon they started to play with their dear departed grandfather's ashes as if they were messing about with sand on the beach.

Thunderstruck, Steve stood back from the family and grimaced. I could see the same thought was running through his head as was running through mine: please God, don't let them build a sandcastle.

There have been times when I've had a job to keep it together at interments, even when I didn't know the deceased personally. Some families have a full-blown service with dozens of people in attendance; others take a simpler approach with just one or two family members. Of course, close family members often struggle to control their emotions, and why wouldn't they?

One such occasion came when we were asked if the ashes could be buried beneath the centre spot. That was fine. I went through the usual process, digging the hole and putting sand in the base ready to receive the ashes.

But the widow, who was there with the undertaker and a couple of family members, was having doubts – was she sure she wanted to put her husband's remains in the pitch? These feelings were perfectly natural and we left her to discuss them in private with the undertaker.

When I returned a few minutes later the hole had been filled in and the turf laid on top, and the widow thanked the club for allowing her husband's ashes to be laid to rest in this manner.

As I went through the process of reinstating the turf properly, it occurred to me that there was a little more soil to take away than normal, but thought nothing of it – we'd experienced this before when someone's ashes were interred along with those of their Labrador. I thought nothing of it, that is, until two weeks later, when we were having some work carried out on the pitch.

I'd arranged for my good friend Adi Porter, the head greenkeeper at Greetham Valley golf course in Leicestershire, to get one of his lads to Verti-Drain the pitch to a depth of ten inches. He'd done similar jobs many times, but this was the first time we'd heard a loud bang-pop as he Verti-Drained through the middle of the pitch. We suspected the Verti-Drain had broken a spring or bearing but a thorough inspection revealed no explanation for the explosion. The lad carried on his aeration with no further problems.

Several weeks later I took a phone call from the undertaker. The widow, he said, could not rest and wanted to take her husband home. He had obtained a licence to exhume the ashes.

I was perplexed. How, I asked the undertaker, could this possibly be done? The ashes had been poured into the hole and mixed in with the soil, I pointed out. He solemnly informed me that the lady's husband was lying at rest within the plastic urn provided by the crematorium.

The day of the exhumation arrived, and so did the undertaker and his client. As the urn was lifted out of the ground I saw, to my horror, that there was a large split and hole punched in the urn. This, naturally, caused the lady some distress and I was wondering privately if the deceased had done a Harry Houdini and escaped. But we now knew what had caused the explosion.

Urns contain a certain volume of air and, when they're placed in the ground with soil packed tightly around, a vacuum can be created. When the Verti-Drain punctured the urn it released the vacuum and the loud bang was the result.

We still feel honoured to be able to assist with people's last requests, and we do our best to do it with dignity. When I'm cutting the pitch I often find myself talking to some of the people I knew who are buried below my feet – usually just the occasional good morning or good afternoon, you understand. But a little chat with our former chairman Reg Smart, whose ashes lie beneath the pitch, always lets me know that I'm never alone.

When Joe Dunne took over from Shaun Derry I found that he was a joy to work with, understood my job well and was considerate when using the pitch for training. As the crowd sang 'It's just like watching Brazil' during Joe's period as interim manager, I was entertaining high hopes that he would have a long career at the club.

But the 2018-19 season proved difficult. You can't use it as an excuse, but the hottest summer for years made pre-season training difficult – there was hardly any grass anywhere in Cambridge for the lads to train on and they didn't get the best preparation. Added to that, the Abbey's pitch had been destroyed by a pop concert in June, so the area behind the South Stand goal was not available for the usual bleep tests that kick off pre-season.

Joe's team played some attractive football but it didn't produce the points, and football is a points game. The day he was relieved of his duties, he called me at home in the evening and thanked me and my staff for our help. That showed what kind of fella he is.

CHAPTER 13

—

SELL, SELL, SELL!

Dear Ian,

You're dedicated and your caring side means you take an interest in everything that happens on a match day. Even if it's a medical emergency that you really don't need to get involved in, you want to know the outcomes.

You're easy to get on with and insist on everything being done just so – there's only one way of doing things and that's the right way. You ensure that safety is paramount for everybody at the club, staff or public.

You're sympathetic, a leader, one of the best safety officers I've worked under. You're respected by your staff and by the other services you come into contact with: fire, police and medical.

You instigated steward training before it was a requirement. Over the years we've had many first aid training sessions so stewards can use their basic skills before medical staff arrive.

Standards in the medical centre, which was your baby, are among the best in the League. Premiership clubs say they wish they had a medical centre equivalent to yours. To equip it, you went out and sourced second-hand stretchers from Addenbrooke's Hospital, and liaised with someone at the Norfolk & Norwich Hospital for other equipment.

I'm so proud to have been part of the team you've built up – you're one hell of a bloke.

Steve Lynn

CUFC medical officer, former ambulance officer

The 2013-14 season proved to be a little different from the norm and I added another title to those of head groundsman, stadium manager and matchday safety officer: super-sub sales executive.

The club's shirt sponsorship deals had expired and our commercial manager had just left. Chairman Dave Doggett was running around like a very tall, bespectacled headless chicken trying to sort things out. He had to get some sponsorships in and he had to get them in fast, he said.

I saw an opportunity to add a few lines to my CV. I had a lot of annual leave outstanding, I told Dave, and, having been obliged to do contra deals almost from day one of my time at the club, I was no stranger to the art of selling. I offered to use my holiday days in order to help out on the commercial side, and said I would take a cut of just two and a half per cent of anything I managed to sell.

Dave agreed and soon I was sitting down with vice-chairman Eddie Clark's daughter, Julie, to put a plan together.

I called in a favour from my good friend Gary Reynolds who, at no charge to the club, produced a smart sponsorship opportunities brochure covering shirt, match ball and match sponsorships, pitch perimeter advertising, mascot offers, programme advertising and lounge facilities on non-match days. The catering team put a £1,000 wedding package together and another friend, Paul Mumby, produced a sales board displaying all the sponsorship opportunities for twenty-six games and the advertising spaces companies couldn't afford to ignore, complete with expiry dates.

Julie, Dave and I set about targeting different sales areas and our strategy was clear: speak to potential customers face to face, not on the phone. It's harder to say no to someone when you're in the same room.

We'd had a deal with local company Donarbon, which had supplied refuse skips for the stadium, but the ten years of the arrangement had come to an end and the company had been bought out by Amey Cespa, which had no interest in a contra deal. It struck me that if ever there was an up-and-coming outfit in that line of business, Mick George was it, and I arranged with director Neil Johnson for the company to provide free skips in return for a few match tickets. It suited both parties down to the ground and saved United around £5,000 a year. Now, though, I had bigger fish to fry.

I'd already contacted a few companies about shirt sponsorship, and they'd shown some interest. Now I approached Neil again and it was at that point that I made the acquaintance of Mick George's finance director, Jon Stump. Jon is an honest man and we hit it off from the start. Although he keeps his cards close to his chest, I felt we had a good chance of a deal.

In the meantime, Julie and I cracked on with selling the perimeter boards and Julie targeted the matchday and match ball sponsors on her own. We clicked as a team, and I was finding that selling is addictive: there's nothing like the buzz you get from tying up a deal, and the more you sell, the more you want to sell. Things were moving so fast that the accounts department had a job keeping up with the invoicing.

I was due to go away on holiday for a few days but I was still in discussion with Jon, so I asked him to finalise things with Dave while I was away. Bingo! I'd only been gone a day and was just cracking open the first Tizer of the holiday when Dave phoned with the good news, confirmed everything was signed off – and that included a revised deal in the event of United being promoted back to the Football League – and thanked me for getting the deal.

Julie secured the away shirt sponsorship and we sold all the advertising boards around the pitch perimeter, and even had to dream up some areas that had never been offered for sale before – the rear of stands, back walls and so on. I had to resist the urge to offer the seat of Catweazle's trousers as prime advertising space.

We offered our sponsors the opportunity to display their company literature in the ground and, as a thank-you for their business, invited them to a low-key midweek cup fixture. They all had the opportunity to enter their business cards in a prize draw, and the event was hailed as a success. We also had a couple of breakfast mornings at which our sponsors could introduce a friend in order to receive a discount on the price they had paid.

I think we did amazingly well to sell every match sponsorship, match ball and advertising board, and produce another good little earner in the shape of monthly fixture posters for pubs and clubs to display, which were paid for by advertising. And then the sale of the club's facilities and services on non-match days started to take off.

I think it was Benjamin Franklin who said there are only two certainties in life: death and taxes. The latter didn't offer many commercial opportunities, although there might be some mileage in putting on tax return completion parties. But we could certainly do something with the former.

When a family suffers a bereavement the last thing its members want is complicated arrangements for the wake. We were in a position to offer an easy option, fully catered, with two hundred parking spaces, less than half a mile from the city's main cemetery and on an easy route from the crematorium.

With the help of club chaplain Stuart Wood, we offered all the undertakers in Cambridge a deal for every wake they could send our way, and this service turned out to be highly popular: soon, two or three events were taking place every week. We also targeted the other end of life, but baptism parties and baby showers didn't prove to be quite so attractive.

I thoroughly enjoyed my spell in commercial, and our commitment certainly paid off – not bad considering United were playing in the Conference at the time and, with the greatest respect to the clubs concerned, some fixtures were not what you would call major sporting events.

CHAPTER 14

———

HEAVEN (SOMETIMES HELL)

Dear Ian,

You're not only proud of your endeavours in providing the best possible playing surface, but of your association with the football club.

Your passion for and experience in your role mean you're dedicated to the task at hand. Whether it relates to the weather, the pitch, the stadium, health and safety or any matchday requirements, you have considered it carefully.

I remember the Boxing Day when you called in the early hours to say the pipes in a toilet block had frozen. You were so concerned that the game might not go ahead that we sent a plumber to defrost and repipe the cold water supply.

Then there was the call, just before a game, about a broken-down boiler. It was evident from your voice how much you cared about getting the fixture played, and we sent an engineer to fix the problem.

These examples show how far we and many other companies will go, without charging, to repay somebody who goes above and beyond his duties, often at his own expense.

I can't really call it a bad quality, but your willingness to do anything for anyone sometimes allows others to take advantage of your good nature.

You're a credit to the club and an invaluable asset, and everybody who knows how hard you work knows how lucky they are to have you. You're a true gentleman and a top bloke.

Ian Greenstock
Group managing director, Kershaw Group

I've had a forty-year love affair with the Abbey Stadium's playing surface and it's not unnatural that the grass should talk to me. I'm sure I'm not alone in having regular chats with the green stuff – other groundsmen will understand what I'm talking about.

When I walk the surface and can see the colour dropping out of the grass, I know it's hungry and I can hear it crying out for a feed. Same when we're in the middle of a drought: I hear the surface making its feelings about its thirst quite clear.

Compaction in the pitch is easy to spot with experience, although with modern-day equipment it's a lot less likely to occur than in the 1970s. Technical irrigation knowledge has also improved in leaps and bounds over the years, so accurate monitoring and control are easier. But even with all this information to hand, you can still sometimes just see a problem, or sense it's in the air.

One occasion when I look forward to the grass talking is the first game of the season, when it's looking at its best. Most people don't hear the grass whisper with pleasure as the ball is played across it, but I can assure you I do.

It's a question I hear often: how have I managed to stick at the football club for forty years? Well, as you will have gathered by now, it's not always been easy and I've had to travel over some bumpy roads. But by and large I've got by with a little help from my friends, and there have been an awful lot of them over the years.

The wise words of Les Holloway, the first company secretary I worked with, echo constantly in my ears. Make the most of weddings while you're young, said Les, because when you get older you'll be going to more funerals. Unfortunately, I've reached that time of life and some of my closest friends have passed away. One of them was Ian Ling.

Ian and I met through our love of playing football, and I was fortunate to have him as a loyal friend for the best part of forty years. He was his own man but always ready to help with anything if he could, as long as there was complete and utter honesty on both sides.

Ian was a witty chap who was always up for a laugh, as I found to my cost during my first season at the club. I was divoting the pitch at half-time when I came under attack from a barrage of light-hearted insults from Ian and his mates on the Habbin terrace. 'Oi, Darler,' the banter went, 'you missed a bit.' This was followed by the rather crude suggestion that I stick my fork up my back passage. Even as I smiled back, I was starting to plot the payback.

At half-time in the next match that Ian attended a message came over the tannoy: congratulations to Mr Ian Ling on the birth of his twin daughters. The not so proud father's response came loud and clear from the Habbin: 'Better watch your back, Darler.'

I was at home the following Friday evening when the phone started ringing, and it didn't stop all weekend. Ian had put an ad in the Cambridge Evening News, offering my car for sale. The calls drove me nuts and, as the friendly feud looked to be in danger of escalating beyond all reason, we were forced to come to a gentleman's agreement: that would be the last of the pranks. But not before I'd threatened to have five tonnes of horse manure tipped on Ian's drive, now I come to think of it.

He recently lost a short battle with cancer and he will always be in my thoughts. The last time I visited him he revealed a lot of the stories and secrets he'd harboured over the years, many involving mutual friends, and we had a good laugh and shed a few tears together. We agreed that whenever I stage one of my Cambridge Charity Fund Raisers sporting dinners, one lot in the auction will be sold in Ian's name with the money raised going to the Arthur Rank Hospice charity.

One of the rules of a long working life I've always adhered to: keep it enjoyable by having some fun along the way. I suppose I've always been a gobby git, a little loose-lipped, and I do like my practical jokes and a bit of banter.

I had quite a few horrified staff and supporters on the go when an overnight invasion by tiny mammals of the Talpidae family seemed to have left around twenty molehills on the sacred Abbey turf.

The word spread fast by word of mouth and on the internet, and I found myself busy fielding questions: how will you stop the moles digging up the pitch? Where did they come from? I found it amusing that some people started to answer their own question – it was obvious, they said, they must have come from Coldham Common. In the social media frenzy, remarkably little of the discussion focused on the date of the subterranean assault: April 1.

I'd taken a digger bucket of screened root zone to the south-west corner of the pitch (the closest to the Common) and positioned the little piles of soil with care, linking the hills with a series of surface tunnels. I suppose it did look pretty convincing, although I'd like to meet the mole that could get through that much work in one night in the heavy clay that lies beneath the Abbey.

In the 2018-19 season I decided to celebrate my fortieth season at United by showcasing a few of the pitch designs I'd used since 1979. At Christmas time there was so much gloom and doom around, what with the disappointment of the team's results and constant worries about Brexit, that I felt the need to lighten the mood a little.

I didn't expect the series of Christmas trees I cut into the pitch to attract so much media coverage on Sky, ITV and the BBC, but that was a bonus. The Yeovil Town staff absolutely loved the festive treat: their press man was on his knees taking photos of the trees and tweeting the design.

It's not all fun and games. After separating from my first wife Sharon, I had nowhere to go and found myself making my home in the basic surroundings of the Abbey's old control room – a Portakabin on the toilet roof at the north end. I wasn't keen on my predicament being known to all and sundry but the Portakabin didn't make a natural hideout, being glazed almost entirely all round. So I bought a roll of blackout paper and every evening, when everyone else had gone home, stuck it on the windows to prevent light showing through.

The thermal bars that stopped the CCTV equipment getting damp made my bolthole quite snug, and I had a small TV tucked away that helped me to while away the long evenings. I took care of my personal hygiene with showers every morning in the referee's room and, although my bijou property wouldn't have won any prizes at the British Homes Awards, at least I had a roof over my head. What really got me down was my diet: for several months I lived on takeaways, sandwiches and whatever the catering manager offered me during the day.

I managed to keep my domestic arrangements under wraps until one night when the directors gathered at the ground for a board meeting. I'd carried out my normal routine with the blackout paper but at around 9.45pm I heard the sound of somebody mounting the stairs and realised a chink of light was escaping to the outside world. The door burst open to admit an angry Reg Smart. 'What the hell do you think you're doing?' he demanded.

I stammered out an explanation of my situation, whereupon Reg said forcefully: 'Get your bag.' Believing he was about to add 'and get out of the stadium', I began to gather my things. Instead, he completed his sentence '… and get in my car.' As we were driving to the Smart residence in Great Shelford, Reg said I could stay with him for a few days while I got my life sorted out.

This event proved to be a turning point in our relationship; I hadn't seen the caring side of the man before. The few weeks I stayed with him turned out to be an education and we became very good friends. From that day on, my personal life seemed always to be high on Reg's list of concerns; he was forever asking how I was and assuring me that if I needed advice or help at the stadium I had only to ask.

One night, when Reg had been at the gin and tonics, I plucked up the courage to ask him a few personal questions. I'd heard the rumours about his business going bust and taking other companies down with it, so I asked what had happened. He was taken aback by the question and I thought for a moment I'd overstepped the mark, but to my surprise he seemed happy to talk.

The discussion went on until late in the night as Reg spoke with passion and emotion about what had happened. I began to understand why he appeared to have so little trust in anyone and why he no longer employed site managers or foremen.

My brother Richard and his wife Fiona came to my aid when my stay with the Smarts came to an end, and I lived with them for around two years. By the time that arrangement finished I'd been seeing Lisa for a while, and her parents, Mary and Tony, invited me to stay with them. I'm not sure whether they thought I was a good catch or whether they felt it would be a good way of keeping an eye on me.

I finally reached a point where I could afford another mortgage, although the amount the banks were offering was tiny. However, I managed to find a ramshackle old cottage in the village of Earith and Reg was influential in the purchase, advising me to pull out of the deal a couple of days before completion in order to get the price down by a couple of thousand. The ploy worked and it turned out to be a good move, although the house was in a far worse condition than I'd expected and it took me twelve months to modernise the place.

My friendship with Reg resulted in him offering me the landscaping and turfing work on his housing developments, and I was gratified to find that my invoices would be paid on the dot, precisely thirty-one days after they'd been submitted. On the other hand, I soon realised that Reg liked nothing more than a haggle over the price of work and challenging my quotations. I got wise to this tactic and increased the prices I quoted by fifteen per cent, allowing him to think he had saved ten per cent when really I'd made an extra five.

My work with Reg's firm wasn't without its incidents. He'd built a nice group of houses in the village of Impington, and all but one had sold. When the last property's sale went through I was asked to get the garden turfed early one Saturday morning, before the occupiers moved in. Not a problem, I assured the boss.

We were on site at six and the lawn was laid by eight. A hose was running to water the turf and we left the site with the front garden looking amazing and ready for the new owners, who were due to move in at midday. But at 10am Reg was on the phone, raging: 'Ian, you've let me down! You promised you would get the garden turfed.'

I was dumbfounded. 'It was turfed,' I insisted.

'Well, there's nothing here now,' roared the very angry builder.

I couldn't believe what my eyes were telling me when I got back to the site: there was indeed no sign of the turf, although telltale lines of soil showed where it had been laid.

A neighbour appeared and told Reg she'd thought it strange when, shortly after I'd laid the lawn, two men had turned up in a truck, rolled the turf up and added to their haul by nicking the hosepipe. Reg was good enough to apologise and a couple of days later we'd laid some new turf.

But that wasn't the end of the odd goings-on at that construction site. The lads working there had bestowed the title of Miss Whiplash on one of the residents, and the day we turfed her garden we found out why. Some of the garments on display on her washing line could have been classed as offensive weapons, while others needed a quick wipe down rather than a good wash. We set a new Cambridgeshire lawn-laying record that day.

I've always admired the work of the philosopher Jean-Paul Sartre, and he almost got it right when he made his famous remark about hell being other people. While most folk I've come across have been a pleasure to know and work with, some have been ... less so.

Around 2009 there were plenty of changes around the club. Some of them came from a new general manager who introduced procedures including the opening of everyone's mail, even if it was marked 'private and confidential'. When I remonstrated, he told me that I shouldn't have anything of a private nature at the club.

Mail from my family's private healthcare provider was delivered to the stadium, I told him, and the information it contained was for our eyes only. I made it clear that I would not allow him or anyone else to open my private and confidential mail, and the process stopped.

He wasn't finished, though. He then failed to honour the pay rise clauses in my employment contract and those of my staff, and I was forced to consult the Institute of Groundsmanship's legal people. They, of course, confirmed that the contracts were legally binding documents, but Mr X was dismissive. Pay rises should be based on productivity, he declared.

I can't begin to describe my feelings about that response. How the hell, I asked, was I to improve my productivity? It was for everyone to do better and improve productivity, he replied coolly.

I backed off on that occasion: our contracts were not honoured for the next three years, and I should add that it wasn't the last time that happened. In more recent times we've not received our legal due three more times. I feel my staff and I have delivered a very high standard of work in challenging circumstances over the years, and we deserved better.

But at least I had sussed Mr X out: he always had to have the final word. One day, with the purchase order book in hand, I asked him to sign for four 25kg bags of grass seed. 'No,' he retorted, 'you can only have two. Go and rewrite the order.'

And that's what I did. Triumphant at getting his own way, he happily signed off on the purchase of two 50kg bags of seed.

I was finding it hard to work in such a conflict-ridden environment, especially as I was using my own mowers, sprayer and other equipment and funding some of the work and materials, just so that I could do my job. But Mr X then excelled himself.

He gave the go-ahead for a work experience student to create ... I'm struggling to describe them ... wooden statues, I suppose, promoting the club's activities. Where did the idea come from? Fourteen miles away in Newmarket, actually. The town's highly decorated, full-size horse statues positioned on the main roads, promoting its racing heritage, were really impressive.

The club bought hundreds of pounds' worth of MDF and paid to have the statues of sports people carved from it. The student set about painting them, but not before a minibus had been ruined when a tin of paint tipped over on the floor.

I kid you not, these creations, some of which resembled dirty old men and flashers, looked truly hideous. They would have been ideal for a Hallowe'en event, but Mr X was determined that they would promote the club from their positions on the city's traffic islands. Having dealt with the council's highways people for years, I asked if he'd cleared his idea with the department. His reply – 'What's it got to do with them?' – was priceless.

Needless to say, the objects, for want of a better description, were never displayed in public and to this day, ten years later, they have sat in a store cupboard – gone but unfortunately not forgotten.

People, eh? Can't cope with 'em, can't do without 'em. I recall the Guzzler with exasperation and a certain amount of amusement.

The ticket office and shop staff seldom have a chance to eat before or during evening games – there are very few of them and sales are often hectic – so they often all chip in and order a few pizzas to be delivered. The Guzzler, however, was known for his willingness and ability to eat anything in sight. If you'd put a plateful of camel shit and sand within fifty yards of him, it would have disappeared down his gullet.

The pizzas went down well with the staff, who were happy to share one between four people. But this wasn't good enough for the Guzzler who, game after game, would shovel a whole pizza into his cakehole within seconds – and never contribute to the cost. He had to be taught a lesson.

On the chosen evening the pizzas arrived as usual about three hours before kick-off and the women in the office set to work. Carefully lifting the topping off one of the delicacies, they gleefully filled its base with a cocktail of ingredients and flavours. Once the dough had been heavily salted, in went generous helpings of pepper, coffee granules, tea leaves and, as the pièce de résistance, Fairy Liquid. The topping was then replaced and the pizza re-boxed.

As expected, the Guzzler rapidly snaffled his prize and expectation was high as we waited for his reaction. But his busily chewing chops betrayed not a trace of discomfort as the pizza disappeared into the void of his digestive system. It was as if he hadn't eaten for a month.

To this day he's not aware that he consumed an all-in-one meal that not only delivered tea and coffee but also did the washing-up.

In May 2016 came one of my most unusual but rewarding experiences, when the author Ross Raisin called to ask if he could visit. He was doing research for a novel centred on football and what goes on behind the scenes, he explained.

When I googled Ross I saw that his first novel, God's Own Country, had been shortlisted for nine literary awards and in 2009 he'd been named the Sunday Times Young Writer of the Year. The critics had loved his second novel, Waterline, and in 2013 he'd been named one of Granta magazine's best young writers. I felt honoured to be asked to contribute to a novel by such a talented man.

Ross arrived and asked a series of questions about life at the football club. Which areas of the stadium were private? If you were having an affair, where could you meet your lover? What kind of pranks were played? Together we explored every corner of the stadium, and I could almost hear his brain ticking over as we went. We examined the control room and medical centre, where we speculated about the building's potential as a location for a clandestine affair.

Ross revealed that the novel would revolve around a gay man who would be either a footballer or a groundsman; he hadn't decided. We then moved on to talk about events that take place away from the club – corporate jollies, golf days and the like. Some players could be real pains in the arse at that kind of do, I said, and recalled one club golf day when a group took a buggy for a joyride, bouncing and rocking it all over the shop and finally tipping it over. We also discussed some of the nicknames people around the club enjoyed; the head matchday steward in the visiting terrace called himself the Silver Fox, for example.

Over a cup of tea, Ross marvelled at the stories I had to tell and the weird experiences I'd had. 'Why don't you write them down and publish them?' he asked. Maybe one day, I replied.

Some months later I opened a parcel to find a copy of Ross's novel A Natural, with a handwritten message from the author: Ian, huge thanks for all your generous help. There are a few scenes in here that you certainly had a hand in! I was also surprised to see a generous acknowledgement at the back of the book: On the football side of things I would like to thank the following people for their insights and anecdotes … especially Ian Darler and Max Rushden, both of whom gave me more stories than I knew how to handle.

My time with Ross was not only enjoyable; it was also productive for both of us. I'm glad to say I took his advice, started to document my time at United and began to think about writing this book. So now you know who to blame.

I've always believed it's essential to make every single member of staff feel important, to treat everyone the same way and to reward people for their hard work.

At one time the matchday steward team regularly numbered between eighty and ninety, and it hit 120-plus when Manchester United came to town. I had interviewed them all. They had been trained by me and the emergency services and their commitment could not have been any higher. One of their rewards during my time as matchday safety officer was the end-of-season party I always tried to lay on.

One of the lads who worked in the catering trade helped me to prep the food for more than a hundred guests (paid for by me, incidentally; the club simply didn't have the funds). Another who ran his own disco provided the music free of charge. These evenings were always full of fun and very much appreciated by the staff. I, on the other hand, just had to stand and watch as they let their hair down. If I'd had enough hair to let down I'd have been in there like a shot, partying with the best of them.

As the boss of so many people, providing references when they apply for full-time jobs is one of my regular tasks. Fortunately, I've known most of the staff personally and with most of them I've been happy to write a glowing reference, but there has been the odd occasion when I've had to decline. What do you do when a bloke you know as well as your own brother asks for a reference for a job for which he's clearly not qualified?

I once had a steward who moved from full-time job to full-time job as often as he changed his socks – every three months. It was remarkable how often he phoned in sick when Arsenal were playing at home and, when I came across a question about his attendance records and absenteeism in one of his reference requests, I had to be honest and say that he was not a regular at the Abbey, although he might have been at Highbury.

People … don't you just love 'em? While I'm more than appreciative of my colleagues ninety-nine per cent of the time, some seem to have a natural ability to make my hackles rise. I'm looking at you, certain members of the commercial staff over the decades.

Ask any member of the ground staff community, whether they work in football, golf, bowls, cricket, tennis or tiddlywinks – to a man and woman, they pride themselves on the quality of their cutting. We love to show off our work to the best possible advantage, and take delight in cutting light and dark shades to form circles, diamonds, diagonals … the possibilities are almost endless.

And we take the utmost care, when marking out our playing surfaces, to walk down the light line, thus ensuring that there are no footprints to spoil the look of the pitch.

At one o'clock on a Saturday all our hard, painstaking work has resulted in a surface that looks a million dollars. But by 1.45pm the area around the dugouts is covered in unsightly blotches where sponsors and their children have been invited on to the pitch. All the care we've taken to produce a pristine surface has come to nothing.

I ask you: would I go into the club's hospitality areas and mess about with the table plan the commercial team has carefully created, or switch the guests' place-name cards to different tables? Would that be any different to allowing people to swan about on my beautiful playing surface?

Not in my eyes it wouldn't. But year after year, my pleas and protests seem to fall on deaf ears and I'm left wondering how and why we are so different to the Premier League clubs who simply do not allow this kind of trespass to happen.

Still on the theme of people and the impact they have on a humble groundsman's life, the average football crowd always contains a few potential troublemakers. An incident that took place in 2007 illustrates how far-reaching the effects of a few people's thoughtless actions can be.

The club had received complaints from concerned parents and others about a group of supporters causing a cascade of fans to the bottom of the Newmarket Road end terrace by pushing them from behind. Being swept down in a wave like this can be a frightening and dangerous experience and something clearly had to be done.

The directors tasked me with looking into the issue and, if we could identify the instigators, making the potential dangers plain to them. I was also to warn them that they were risking two-game bans from the stadium.

On the following match day, we had two stewards in plain clothes on the terrace to watch the troublesome area, and they managed to identify the individuals who were starting the pushing. Once the information had been passed to the control room and the incident was recorded on CCTV, we decided to send two stewards in to ask the culprits to come off the terrace so they could be made aware of the complaints.

It sounds simple; it wasn't. When the stewards got on to the terrace they found their route obstructed and one had his glasses broken and his radio earpiece ripped out and smashed. With their safety and potential distress for other supporters in mind, I withdrew the guys and decided to find some of the offenders as they were leaving after the game. All I wanted was a quick word.

I was speaking to one of the young lads on the empty terrace when another supporter arrived on the scene, wanting to talk about the incident. I wasn't quite finished with the first bloke (who was receptive to what I was saying about the club taking safety very seriously), so I simply asked the new arrival to go away and said I would speak to him later.

That wasn't good enough for him, and he continued to air his views. I didn't call on a single one of my extensive repertoire of insults as I calmly repeated my request that he go away, and continued my chat with the first individual.

If I thought that would be the end of the matter, it was wishful thinking. In the chap's official complaint about me and my staff he made some very serious allegations, including the suggestion that he'd been injured by my staff. A director told me the following day that I would be suspended until club officials and police had carried out an investigation, and the CCTV recordings were seized.

A nightmare then unfolded around me and my family. We were on the receiving end of hate mail delivered to our home. My staff and I were subject to verbal assaults on the unofficial club message board, even from people who hadn't been at the scene of the incident. My son Liam, an apprentice carpenter working on building sites, was told that his dad had been accused of bullying, an allegation that he found highly distressing.

The investigation, which took a couple of weeks, revealed some interesting detail. The chap who alleged he'd been injured was seen on CCTV carrying out what the police called an 'American block' – placing himself between the lad my staff wanted to speak to and the stewards as they made their way on to the terrace. But of course, as I was suspended, I wasn't aware of these findings at the time.

At home, I took numerous phone calls from stewards saying they'd been asked during interviews if I'd bullied them. This kind of stuff was difficult to listen to: not only was the suggestion of bullying behaviour ridiculous but I knew that a lot of people whom I'd recruited hadn't been able to find work elsewhere, and employment at United had set them off on the work trail again.

After sitting at home for a couple of weeks, twiddling my thumbs and agonising over these suggestions, I was called into the control room to see the directors and the police officers in charge of the investigation. I was overwhelmed when I read the board's letter, the bones of which I'm happy to reveal here.

The investigation had covered CCTV evidence, discussions with the complainant and safety stewards and police statements, and the match commander and the club's chief executive had been included in the process. The conclusion was that stewarding had been carried out in accordance with both safety at sports ground rules and those laid down by the club. No wrongdoing or inappropriate behaviour had been found.

What's more, following discussions with the complainant, he had withdrawn his complaint, and he now understood the background to the incident and how his actions and message board posts had inflamed the situation and created a potentially serious outcome. The club would be warning him about his future behaviour.

The letter went on to say that serious personal accusations on the message board could have undermined my role as matchday safety officer, but the investigation had found no evidence to support any of them.

The board concluded: 'The past fortnight has been a very trying time for you, your family and the safety team … the feedback has only been positive. Your professionalism and management skills were highly commended all round.'

I and my staff were in the clear, but it had become apparent how far some people will go when they take a dislike to procedures or

243

actions. That horrendous fortnight remains with me as one of my most distressing times at the club. I will always try to treat everyone with the utmost respect and deal with problems in a sensible manner.

I wish I had dealt more efficiently with a certain person I encountered during one of the many corporate five-a-side competitions United have run over the decades.

The club entered a staff team – myself, two other ground staff, a member of the lottery team and a couple of other lads – in a fundraising tournament at the city's Kelsey Kerridge sports hall. After two games in which we'd done OK, we came up against some less than sporting opponents.

The beer fumes wafting around the five-a-side court would have been enough to stun a pigeon, and the team's generous waistlines testified to a longstanding adherence to fluid-intake guidelines. They had evidently been at the refreshments not only before but also during the tournament, and the liquor had seemingly loosened their tongues. They had a lot to say for themselves.

Our game kicked off to the accompaniment of a resounding burp from their striker, and within a couple of minutes it became obvious that they were only interested in one aspect of their game: kicking the other side. One lad in particular was exhibiting the less attractive personality traits of a Tasmanian devil in a feeding frenzy, and he smelled like one too. When he battered my young groundsman apprentice to the floor with a particularly ferocious tackle, I stepped in.

I used words to the effect of 'you can pack that in' to the sneering assailant, who was swaying slightly. 'We've all got to go to work tomorrow and if you carry on like that someone's going to end up with a broken leg,' I added.

That's the last thing I remember about the tournament. My teammates described afterwards how, as I turned away, Taz had felled me with a well-aimed punch to the temple. A couple reckoned I was unconscious before I hit the deck and compounded the damage by denting the floor with my head.

I don't recall a thing about the ambulance trip to Addenbrooke's, but I do remember coming round to find that a few of the lads had turned up for a damage assessment and some consoling words. As Lisa hurried in, I was transferred to the neurology department and put in a cubicle. Daniel Bray, my assistant, and Michael Cook, a first-team midfielder, appeared on the scene and the specialist asked if they'd seen the incident and could offer any advice.

'Yes,' said Cookie. 'I think he needs a bed bath.' He called over to the specialist nurse and enquired: 'Have you seen the soles of his feet? They look like poppadoms.' It was true that skin had peeled off my feet in places.

The specialist, now that she'd had her fill of helpful advice, asked everyone except Lisa to leave.

Groggy? I've felt less fuddled after a night on the Olde Gutcrumbler. I was told I would be staying in overnight and have a few tests and a scan. Lisa came up to the ward to make sure I was comfortable and then began to get ready to go home.

'I'll leave some money in your locker,' she said.

As the night wore on I began to feel a little better. The hunger pangs started and I became aware of a raging thirst. 'Don't want to bother the nurse,' I thought as I dimly recalled Lisa saying something about leaving me some money. I could use it to get something to eat and drink.

I rummaged in the locker. Lisa, bless her, had been as good as her word – to the tune of 20p. Good job that the nurse took a shine to me and sorted me out with a sandwich, a cup of tea or two and some biscuits. One of the custard creams alone probably cost 20p. Although I was incredulous about the size of Lisa's donation at the time, when the brain fog lifted I realised that the money had been intended for a phone call to tell her I was being discharged – she'd taken my wallet and mobile phone home to keep them safe.

After my midnight feast I tried to settle inside my curtained-off bay, but my attempts to grab some zeds were thwarted by a fellow patient. I listened, cursing silently, as he shuffled across the ward and then, as he passed the bottom of my bed, swore out loud at the appalling stench that followed hard on the heels of a hideous flip-flop sound. He hadn't made it to the toilet.

Back came my favourite nurse to pop her head round the curtains and apologise for the disturbance. By now, while I was longing for home comforts, I was recovering a little of my sense of humour. 'Why are you sorry?' I asked. 'It wasn't you that made that terrible smell, was it?'

I waited impatiently for the morning to arrive and the doctors to do their rounds. As rosy-fingered dawn crept through the windows, I became aware of the fact that I'd passed the night in an old people's ward. I'd probably halved the average age. Now I understood why the crapper hadn't been fast enough to get to the toilet in time.

Finally, the medics had a good look at me and allowed me to leave, on the understanding that I didn't go back to work for at least a week. I got dressed faster than a bloke caught upstairs when the husband gets home, but at least I didn't have to jump out of the window. I was so anxious to get out of the place that I would if I'd had to, though.

I hadn't been long at home when a couple of police officers dropped round to say that a number of people had reported the assault on my bonce. I gave a statement and the coppers followed up the incident, but I didn't want to go through the hassle of pressing charges. And apart from a bruise on the side of my head and a golf ball-sized lump where I'd nutted the floor, I felt OK.

Another brush with the medical world came when I was going through a spell of stomach discomfort. I'd experienced diverticulitis several times and found that antibiotics usually did the trick, but on this occasion the infection wouldn't budge.

'Let's have a look at your prostate,' suggested my GP, a good friend who was also one of United's crowd doctors. Gents of a certain age know what's coming: a prostate examination is of an intimate nature.

I assumed the position, knees bent up to my chest, while the doc snapped on the gloves and started probing. The way he was poking around, I thought he'd lost something up there.

'Sorry about that,' he apologised as his finger emerged from the Darler fundament. 'It's a bit embarrassing.'

'Don't worry about it, Doc,' I reassured him. 'The last time I had so much fun I had to pay for it.'

I turned round to find my flustered GP's face had apparently been replaced by a tomato.

Keith Lockhart, one of the nicest kids to come through the apprentice scheme, remains a good mate thirty years after we first met. As a lad he was always hungry, on the scrounge for food, and it got to the point that I would pack an extra sandwich for him in my lunchbox.

Locky, who hasn't lost a jot of his impenetrable Geordie accent, was witness to an occasion when Chris Turner re-enacted our first ever meeting, putting me on my arse and dragging me down the running track to the players' tunnel. The only difference from the original performance was that there was no money for me at the end.

Locky, a sandwich halfway to his open mouth, stared at the spectacle unfolding before his disbelieving eyes. 'Ian man,' he gasped at the end. 'Ian, man. Why did he do that?'

Ah, people. During my forty years at Cambridge United I've worked with some brilliant, professional, hard-working and efficient people. I've also met a few who might have been able to talk a good game but couldn't deliver. I smiled when I read the light-hearted communication below – it's bang on the money.

The information below came from two maths teachers with seventy years' experience between them, went the email. It has an indisputable mathematical logic.

What makes 100 per cent? What does it mean to give more than 100 per cent? Ever wonder about those people who say they give more than 100 per cent?

Here's a little mathematical formula that might help you answer these questions and make you think about those you work with.

If

A B C D E F G H I J K L M N O P Q R S T U V W X Y and Z

are represented as

1 2 3 4 5 6 7 8 9 10 11 12 13 14 15 16 17 18 19 20 21 22 23 24 25 and 26,

then

H-A-R-D-W-O-R-K

8+1+18+4+23+15+18+11 = 98 per cent

and

K-N-O-W-L-E-D-G-E

11+14+15+23+12+5+4+7+5 = 96 per cent.

But

A-T-T-I-T-U-D-E

1+20+20+9+20+21+4+5 = 100 per cent

And,

B-U-L-L-S-H-I-T

2+21+12+12+19+8+9+20 = 103 per cent,

and look how far arse kissing will get you:

A-R-S-E-K-I-S-S-I-N-G

1+18+19+5+11+9+19+19+9+14+7 = 122 per cent.

So we can conclude with mathematical certainty that, while hard work and knowledge will get you close and attitude will get you there, it's the bullshit and arse kissing that will put you over the top. Now you know why some people are where they are!

How true is that, people?

I have the same enthusiasm for my job today as I did when I started my apprenticeship in 1977 and I've always believed you should do the best job you can and forget about taking shortcuts. If you do, you can be sure that they will come back to bite you on the backside.

CHAPTER 15

—

CHANGING LIVES

In 2008, three years after my testimonial events, I received a letter from East Anglian Children's Hospices wanting to know if I could make any further donations, and it was followed up by a phone call. I explained that I wasn't able to donate any more money, but I could certainly try to raise some funds.

I chatted with a group of mates with whom I fished several Wednesdays a month and asked: couldn't we dedicate our matches to fundraising for charity? The lads' response was enthusiastic and Cambridge Charity Fund Raisers was born.

I'm always careful to make the point to the charities we work with that we're not ourselves a registered charity; we're happy to work as a partner but we insist on having a letter from their organisations confirming that we're raising funds for them. And it works very well.

CCFR has grown over the years and I find it immensely rewarding to be part of something that helps to change people's lives for the better in some small way. As of 2019, over the course of the twelve years of its existence, CCFR has raised in the region of £50,000. Between 2015 and 2018 alone, we managed to donate £31,500 to charities around Cambridgeshire.

I'm delighted to report that my family doesn't hesitate to pitch in. Our daughter Ruby, who was seven at the time, became a young author in 2016 when her first book, Flash's New Glasses, was published. All sales proceeds go to Tom's Trust, which cares for children with brain tumours. My son Liam, who has inherited a few of his old dad's talents, is one of the Cambridge area's top anglers, and he supports all our fishing events.

While I'm on the subject of fishing matches, a quick diversion away from Cambridge Charity Fundraisers. The annual fishing matches and three-course meals I organised for five years to raise money for the football club started when we simply couldn't afford to buy new goal nets for the start of the season. When the pitch looks great at the start of the season a new set of nets sets it off nicely. The thought of putting up dirty old nets that look like they've seen service on a North Sea trawler makes me shudder.

The fishing matches raised enough money to buy the new nets, fertiliser and seed and, in the following years, paid for a pedestrian mower and other essential kit. When they came to an end and there wasn't the money in the club's budget for new nets, I bought them myself a couple of times. My assistant Mick Brown has also raided his piggy bank for a set.

Putting our hands in our pockets hasn't stopped at the purchase of nets. The club have used my mowers, sprayers, aerators and other gear for the best part of thirty-five years and Mick has made use of all his own tools for maintenance jobs around the stadium for around twenty years.

My mention of our little author Ruby a few paragraphs back reminded me of when she was born in 2008, and the momentous event's connection with CCFR. Neither Lisa nor Ruby Ella had the best time of it.

Lisa had already experienced some health problems, which had led to her undergoing a heart procedure, not without risk, at the world-renowned Papworth Hospital in the Cambridgeshire countryside. It was a scary time and, as Lisa was wheeled down to the theatre, I realised just how important she was to me.

The nurse who had been looking after her came to check on me. 'I'm going to propose to Lisa when she comes out,' I told her.

The poor nurse was horrified. 'No, no,' she said, 'please don't do that!'

I was dumbfounded. What did the nurse know about our relationship that I didn't?

'Lisa mustn't have any excitement,' continued the nurse. 'She must stay calm.' I had to wait several months to pop the question.

My friend Bob Brotchie, the paramedic who trained my stewards for years, has come up with much sound advice in his time, but I've never been so grateful for his intervention as I was on the day of Ruby's birth. Lisa, who was overdue by several weeks, was given a date for the birth to be induced and Bob's words when I'd bumped into him a few days before proved as valuable as gold dust. 'Keep an eye on the baby monitor and watch the heart rate,' he'd said.

I took the advice on board, not thinking for a minute that it would have any significance for us. There had been no problems when Liam was born, after all.

Induction day came along and when we arrived on the maternity ward at Hinchingbrooke Hospital, near Huntingdon, one thing was obvious: there weren't enough monitoring machines to go round all the expectant mums, and they were being moved from one baby bump to another.

The time came for us to go down to the delivery room and things seemed to be progressing normally, but then Lisa started to experience awful pain. The midwife left the room for a couple of minutes to seek assistance, but while she was gone, to my alarm, I saw baby's heart rate dropping fast, to the point where it had nearly stopped. I glanced at Lisa and was horror-struck to see that all the colour had drained out of her.

I hit the emergency button and seconds later the crash team raced in. Lisa was whisked away for an emergency caesarean.

I paced up and down, waiting for what seemed like months for the information I was desperate to hear. Finally the head midwife came out and said both Lisa and the baby were OK, although Ruby was in the special baby care unit.

The staff at Hinchingbrooke performed wonders and Ruby is now a healthy young girl, but even now my grateful thoughts return to Bob's words of advice. Would I have noticed the heart monitor dropping if he hadn't mentioned it? Perhaps, but thanks to Bob my attention was fixed on it at the crucial moment.

I thanked the maternity ward sister and said I would raise some money through Cambridge Charity Fund Raisers. The hospital could put it towards the cost of another baby monitor to help reduce the risk for other expectant mothers, I said. I'm glad to say we were able to donate several thousand pounds.

We always try to put on a sporting dinner to accompany CCFR fishing matches, and depend on local companies to sponsor these events. It gets harder to attract sponsors every year but I will be forever grateful to the companies who step up and those that help, free of charge, to produce tickets, programmes and so on.

Although I wouldn't know a cookie if it was labelled 'Look at me, I'm a cookie' and the only bytes I'm interested in are those on the end of my fishing line, CCFR has a website that showcases some of the work we've been able to carry out. Have a little browse yourself and see if you can help us out: cambridgecharityfundraisers.com.

CHAPTER 16

—

THE AWARD GOES TO ...

AWARDS

1994   Football League Regional Groundsman of the Year

1998   Football League Division Three Groundsman of the Year

2000   Football League / STRI Commendation for quality of playing surface

2003   Football League / STRI Commendation for quality of playing surface

2004   Cambridge Evening News Sports award runner-up

2005   Dream Team (Charterhouse/Turfcare) best kept winter sports pitch

2006   Football Association Conference Groundsman of the Year

2010   Football Association Conference Groundsman of the Year

2014   Cambridgeshire Police commendation

2015   Cambridge News Lifetime Achievement Award

2015   Football League special award for long service

2015   Institute of Groundsmanship award: Unsung Hero

2017   Induction to Cambridge United Hall of Fame

As Her Maj might say, one doesn't like to blow one's own trumpet, does one? That's why Louis Armstrong always borrowed someone else's. But I've been persuaded that I should devote a chapter of this memoir to the awards some very kind people have given me over the years. You can read a list of them in the little panel.

Every single time my efforts have been recognised in this way, whether it's been by my colleagues in the greenkeeping industry, by newspaper readers, by Cambridge United supporters or by others, I've felt deeply honoured. It's very nice, and also very humbling, to be recognised.

OK, it didn't win me an award, but all the same, being praised by your employer's chairman felt pretty much the same. Reg Smart, bless him, told the Cambridge Evening News that the actions that led to the March 1999 headline 'United's Ian saved my life' were exactly what he would have expected of me.

It was actually our Labrador, Barney, that initiated the rescue. Judging by the sound of his frantic barking, something out of the ordinary was happening in the outside world, so I dragged myself off the sofa and, muttering a curse about bloody dogs needing muzzles, went to the back door to see what had got him so worked up. I soon found out – our next-door neighbour's house was on fire and lighting up the Fenland sky. Somehow I scrambled over the six-foot fence and, racing to her kitchen door, saw Norma lying motionless in the hall. Flames were billowing out of the kitchen, the house was full of smoke and I realised that she wasn't able to breathe.

It's true what they say about instinct taking over when you're faced with an emergency, but at the same time the essentials I'd been taught by fire officers during steward training evenings – and especially the extra instruction I'd had from Alan Pilsworth and Brian Yorke – came flooding back: cover your face and keep below the smoke. That's how I managed to crawl into the burning house and reach Norma, drag her into her garden and then get her to the safety of our garden.

When the fire service arrived I was trying to get Norma breathing, again calling on the training I and the club stewards had had from some of Cambridgeshire's top paramedics. As I'd been taught, I tried to get a response by pinching her earlobe and underarms, but to my horror she didn't react. It wasn't until I pushed on her chest that, to my massive relief, she took her first breaths.

Norma was starting to recover as the fire service lads handed over an oxygen cylinder and mask, and a moment later an ambulance arrived. Norma was whisked away to Hinchingbrooke Hospital, where I'm delighted to say she made a full recovery. Our actions had probably saved her life, the fire officers said, but I wasn't aware of the newspaper coverage until a few people told me that the story had made billboard headlines.

Other lessons I'd learned from emergency service professionals came into play one frosty morning as Lisa and I were driving to work. As we drove along a bumpy fen road and into the village of Rampton, we saw that our route was blocked by a number of cars that had evidently come to a rapid halt. Looking round for the source of the problem, we saw a car in a roadside field – it had obviously come off the road and rolled several times before coming to rest upside down.

'Anyone checked inside?' I asked the little group of drivers peering anxiously into the ploughed field. 'No,' said one bloke, 'but the police and fire service are on their way.'

On went the yellow high-vis coat that's always in my car and I stumbled over the muddy furrows. The car's roof had caved in and I was forced to lie full length in the mud to discover that the unfortunate male driver was trapped. What's more, he wasn't moving.

The voices of my emergency service friends came flooding back: check for danger ... take action only if it's safe to do so. A quick assessment brought me to a decision to smash the glass on the front passenger side – and my enormous bunch of keys, rolled up in a jacket sleeve, did the trick. I scrambled and squeezed into the car, aware of a strong smell of petrol.

The driver's face was blue, and no wonder: he was hanging upside down, his seatbelt tight round his neck and slowly throttling him. I gave him a gentle shake and set about loosening his noose; he started to stir ... and panic set in.

'You need to keep still,' I urged him. 'Your car's come off the road but the fire service are on their way.' I kept talking: he was safe, he'd soon be free, help would be there soon, he should try to keep calm, he was OK.

I must have been reassuring him for fifteen minutes before a fire officer's face appeared at the driver's window. 'Don't worry sir,' he announced jovially, 'we'll get you out before the vehicle catches fire.' Bloody hell, I thought. I'd spent the last quarter of an hour calming the fella down and here's this bloke telling him he's in danger of being barbecued.

He was as good as his word, though. The lads whipped the poor bloke out and soon he was being blue-lighted to Addenbrooke's. No award for Darler, but a warming feeling of a job well done.

One occasion when I did win an award was in 2010. The groundsman of the year title was special in itself, but it came with an added attraction: I was asked to write a two-page article to appear in the programme for the England-Montenegro Euros qualifying match on October 12 – and I was also a guest at the fixture. Invited to take my place among a crowd of 70,000, I couldn't believe my eyes when I turned round to find I was sitting in front of good mate Andrew Pincher, the former United secretary. We had a good chat while I listened proudly to the people around us talking about the article.

On 4 February 2014 came another award that blew me away. I'd been United's matchday safety officer for the best part of thirty years when a letter arrived from Cambridgeshire Police. I was up for an area commander's commendation from Superintendent Vicky Skeels, for dedication to the cause of public safety and assistance to the police over many years. At the ceremony were dozens of police officers receiving awards for their outstanding work and, in many cases, their bravery. I was humbled: this was a big honour that I'll cherish for the rest of my days.

Perhaps the most surprising accolade came when I was named man of the match for the game against Luton in March 2018. You could have knocked me over with a feather when the announcement came over the PA. After all, I was only doing my job in beating the Beast from the East and getting the game on.

It was nice to receive the Institute of Groundsmanship unsung hero award for 2015, at a swish ceremony in Birmingham, from Mark Saggers, a U's fan through and through. Apparently I met the award's criteria: 'an individual who goes beyond the job description to help deliver objectives and bringing about change and clear benefits for their club and users through their creative thinking, commitment, vision, determination and drive.'

CHAPTER 17

BEST (AND BAD) BITS

Highs and lows … as you will have gathered if you've managed to read this far, there have been a few of both. I'm going to wind up by looking back over the peaks and troughs of the amazing life I've been lucky enough to lead.

And where better to start the highs than at the Abbey Stadium? I was sworn to secrecy beforehand, but I can't keep quiet now: I was honoured to have the Duke of Cambridge, a keen football fan and a passionate advocate of mental health awareness, kicking a ball about on my pitch.

Prince William was taking part in the recording of a BBC TV programme that launched the Heads Up campaign – an FA/Heads Together initiative that, throughout the 2019-20 season, will use the power of football to inspire conversation about mental health. As I sat at home watching the programme on a Sunday evening in May, I found myself relating personally to the topics under discussion.

Heads Up is a positive way forward in the discussion, and if it helps one person deal with the kinds of mental heath issues I've experienced, it will have been worthwhile. As I've said before, depression can be a lonely and dangerous place to be.

Other highlights: I had a wonderful childhood with brothers Richard and John, and I now understand fully what an exceptional job our parents and grandparents did in bringing us up and how hard they worked to keep three boys looking smart and well fed.

I'm so proud of my two amazing children, Liam and Ruby, not least of what they've already achieved in their young lives. Liam, a caring lad, has become an outstanding craftsman in the art of carpentry and a top match angler. Ruby, who was forced to live with me when I was struggling to deal with PTSD and depression and was not a nice person, is a sensitive, caring girl who had her first book published at the ridiculously early age of seven. Also a great little angler who has already won several matches, she has a bright future ahead – she is so talented.

I want to make up for the lost hours, days and weeks and spend more time with my children.

I've had the incredible good fortune to work in professional football for forty years, and for that I'm indebted to Bill Scott, an outstanding boss who taught me the art of groundsmanship.

I'm equally grateful to the many great friends who have worked for and with me, and those who have freely granted so many favours to Cambridge United. If you worked out the monetary value of these freebies, it would come out at over £1.5 million.

I treasure the opportunity to get married to Lisa, my best friend and my wife. There for me every second of my life, she cared for me when I was poorly and welcomed Liam into her life when he was so young. Her parents treat me as if I were their own son. Lisa, you're simply a tremendously caring lady and you're part of the reason I'm alive today.

Winning so many awards over the years has been fantastic, but it wouldn't have happened without the help and support of many other people. You only win awards if you have a good team around you.

Being headhunted by a number of football clubs, golf courses and companies was immensely flattering – it showed I was delivering the high standard of work I've always aspired to. I also feel blessed to have been allowed to play with some outstanding players in United's reserves.

Setting up Cambridge Charity Fund Raisers twelve years ago was another highlight of this privileged life of mine: I'm grateful to have had the opportunity to help change many people's lives for the better.

On the other hand ... regrets, I've had a few.

The biggest stems from my not spending enough time with my family, working too many hours and putting the pitch and stadium first. All those fifteen-hour days and weekends meant I missed my children growing up. I even cancelled holidays in order to carry out my duties – that was unfair on my family and, quite simply, stupid.

I regret losing contact with John Docherty – he was so supportive in my early years in the job. Losing my close friend Chris Turner in 2015 was also a heavy blow: he was a comic genius but outstandingly professional at the same time.

I regret not standing my ground more often. Some of my line managers didn't understand what's involved in running a football club or stadium, and I could see the mistakes they were making. You learn by your mistakes, and that's why they weren't at the club very long.

Reaching forty years at Cambridge United has been a milestone for me and I was grateful to the club for awarding me a dinner in recognition of that long service. It gave me the opportunity to thank the 240 guests for their support and generosity in donating materials and labour over the years.

One individual in that room helped to save the football club over half a million pounds. If you tot it up, the friends and contacts at the dinner saved the club more than £1.5 million over my forty years. Some of the deals I put together involved me renovating managing directors' lawns, and that's something that continues to this day.

My own hard-cash contribution over the years totals more than £40,000. There have been times when the club simply didn't have the funds to maintain or renovate the pitch, and it wasn't uncommon to have to pay for 20-tonne loads of sand or buy fertiliser, seed or goal nets.

Do I regret that expenditure? No; it's been part of the journey through the world of professional football in the lower leagues, and I'm sure I'm not the only groundsman to have put his hand in his pocket.

To balance it out, I was lucky to be able to run my own companies, allowing me to supplement my regular wages.

And I've been fortunate to have worked in a job I have loved, with the support of family and friends.

I've got some stories in my locker that I've not been able to relate in this book. Who knows? Maybe one day, when I'm finally retired, I'll complete the picture with the publication of Confessions of a Groundsman. For the moment, I'd like to keep my job.

FRIENDS, FAMILY AND SUPPORTERS

The following people have kindly supported
the publication of this book:

Bob Barnes	Ian Greenstock	Mick Shepherd
Anthony Barrs	Colin Harris	Reg Smart
Boudjema Boukersi	Glynis Harris	Emma Smith
Bob Brotchie	Mark Howe	Godric Smith
Mick Brown	Stewart Jeffs	Peter Spring
Alan Burge	Dr Youngsuk Kim	Duncan Stanley
Cambridge Lakes Golf	James Legge	Gary Stevens
Ian Chapman	Steve Lynn	Andy Stock
Helen Corbett	Dr Louisa Mann	Andrea Thrussell
Dave Coulson	David Matthew-Jones	Emma Truin
Mark Cullum-Acorn	Paul McGrane	Graham Tweed
Brian Darler	Alan Millard	Wendy Twinn
Jill Darler	David Mills	Lance Uttridge
Keith Darler	Janet Mills	Anthony Wade
John Darler	Barry Moore	Mary Wade
Liam Darler	Paul Mumby	Alf Walker
Lisa Darler	Robert Osbourn	Les Weston
Richard Darler	The Pearsons	Neil Weston
Ruby Darler	Andy Pickard	James Willis
Paul Dean	Adi Porter	Lloyd Wilson
David Doggett	Colin Proctor	Isobel Wright
Glenn Gawthrop	Gary Reynolds	Dave York
Daniel Gawthrop	Bill Scott	
Trevor George	Mark Scott	